DARK TO LIGHT

Volume I

Ancient Codes of Kabbalah, Zohar & Torah

By

DR. STEWART A. SWERDLOW

Rabbi Shalom Chaim ben Baer-El

HaRav HaAkravim

WITH JANET DIANE MOURGLIA-SWERDLOW

Expansions Publishing Company, Inc.

Saint Joseph, Michigan

USA

Published by: Expansions Publishing Company, Inc.
P.O. Box 12
Saint Joseph Michigan 49085 USA
269-519-8036
Skype: eventsatexpansions
customersupport@expansions.com
www.expansions.com

ISBN: 978-1-7349281-7-4

Cover Photo by Jonathan J. Swerdlow
www.jonathanswerdlow.com

Medical Disclaimer

The information provided in this publication is not an attempt to attempt to practice medicine or provide specific medical advice, nor is it a substitute for medical care.

We always recommend consulting with a healthcare professional before starting any diet, exercise, supplementation, or medication program.

You assume full responsibility for using any information provided and agree that we are not responsible or liable for any claim resulting from its use by you or any user.

Acknowledgment and Dedication

Writing a book takes effort, concentration, and dedication. There are easy moments when all flows. Then some blockages cause frustration and irritation. I assure you, I have experienced all of that and everything in between.

I am grateful to all the Kabbalists whose notes and writings were available to me for my research and study. I thank my students and webinar participants who allowed the work to manifest.

I am grateful to my parents who sent me to Hebrew School for 8 years so that I could learn Hebrew and the Bible. While I was not appreciative at that time, I am now.

But most of all, I am so grateful to my wife, Janet Diane Mourglia-Swerdlow. She has the patience of the Shekhinah. Because her family name derives from Mt. Moriah in Jerusalem there was no one better to be placed with in this lifetime. God knows what He is doing!

To you, dear reader, you have participated in history. Your Soul shall forever be imbued with the energies of the greatest point in existence!

Amen and Selah!

Books by Stewart A. Swerdlow & Janet Diane Mourglia-Swerdlow

13-Cubed: Case Studies in Mind-Control & Programming

13-Cubed Squared: More Case Studies in Mind-Control & Programming

1099 Daily Affirmations for Self-Change

Alternative Medical Apocrypha: Body-Mind Correlations

Blue Blood, True Blood: Conflict & Creation

Dark to Light Volume I: Ancient Codes of Torah, Kabbalah & Zohar

Dark to Light Volume II: Ancient Codes of Torah, Kabbalah & Zohar

Decoding Your Life: An Experiential Course in Self-Reintegration

Healer's Handbook: A Journey Into Hyperspace

Healing Archetypes and Symbols

Heights of Deprogramming

Heights of Health

Heights of Relationships

Heights of Spirituality

Heights of Wealth

Hyperspace Helper

Hyperspace Plus

Keys to Success

King Bee, Queen Bee

Light Shines in Darkness

Little Fluffs Children's Series

Miracles in Motion

Montauk: Alien Connection

Revelations of Time & Space, History and God

Stewart Says...

Template of God-Mind

True Reality of Sexuality

True World History: Humanity's Saga

Unlocking New Perspectives

White Owl Legends: An Archetypal Story of Creation

Table of Contents

Addendum I

Addendum II

Introduction

Over the last several decades, I have written many books. They have all been formal history, information, Hyperspace, and personal stories. The book you are about to read is very different from anything I have written before, although it builds on knowledge from my previous books. This is a workbook for students and researchers of the Torah, Kabbalah, and Zohar. The information is ancient which must be studied and read many times to be understood.

As you read the chapters, you will feel like you are participating in the original *Dark to Light Webinar Series* upon which this book is based. Do the homework for each class, keeping careful notes of results as you work through the Zohar formulas, Hebrew letters and symbols. You will read news stories that were pertinent during the class and will be valued history in the future.

Time and space are illusions. The Zohar states that the end is the beginning and the beginning is the end. This means all news events mentioned in this book are valid in every moment and in every time period. There is a reason for whatever you read. Even if the event occurred thousands of years ago, the energy and symbolism are relevant and can be assimilated in each moment of existence

The world as you knew it is gone. This may be a good thing. The new way of life will be based on the old way, with better rules. By now, you have learned not to trust the media. We are in *End Times* or what the Zohar calls the *End of Days*. The Zohar states that these times are filled with woe for all who live in it. It also says that there are blessings and it is up to you to choose. The purpose of this workbook is to show you the truth about existence in deep layers that you have never experienced or understood. It is a crash course. What you learn here would have taken the ancients decades or maybe lifetimes. Here you are able to get so much condensed information in one place. You are a fortunate reader!

The English spelling of Hebrew or Aramaic words can vary. The main point is not the grammar or spelling, but the information conveyed. I encourage you to share with all who will listen. You will get the most out of this book if you have the following books in your personal library to use as references:

King Bee, Queen Bee

Template of God-Mind

Revelations of Time & Space, History and God

Heights of Spirituality

Miracles in Motion

Light Shines in Darkness

We are in the most important time period in all of human history. That is why you incarnated now, to be a witness as well as a participant!

May God Bless You!

Amen!

Zohar, Kabbalah and Torah

In this course, you are going to study Ancient Codes of Existence based upon Kabbalah, Zohar and Torah. You will learn why you're here as well as the information that must be revealed to the world. We will start with very basic information about what's happening now on our planet. What you see and hear on the news is not the truth. You will find that the United States is under military control which is a positive thing at the moment. What's happening is basically a Civil War leading to Revolution. I received information from a high-level person in the United Kingdom who said that they are in contact with many groups in the United Kingdom that are prepared to remove their government. This person said that their numbers are growing and they are strong. What you see happening here will also happen in the United Kingdom and then spread to the rest of the world because this is not just about the United States.

This is a global Revolution.

Terminology to understand:

- **Zohar** means Splendor or Brilliance
- **Torah** means Instructions
- **Kabbalah** means Receiving

They are all connected, if you put this together it means that you are *being instructed with information* and it will bring you *Brilliance* and *Splendor*. There is an understanding that the Torah comes from the Mind of God. The Torah has nothing to do with religion. The Torah explicitly states that this information is for all of humanity and it is not only on this planet, it's on every planet in existence in every frequency.

The Kabbalah is the interpretation of the information in the Torah, because the Torah is coded. It can only be understood when fed through a computer system. You can imagine thousands of years ago when this information was given to the people of Israel they could not possibly understand the full meaning of this. In the ***Bible Code*** it states that the meaning cannot be understood until computers exist. It says this in three-thousand-year-old documents. The Kabbalah is the interpretation or the symbolism of the words in the Torah. The Zohar consists of 22 books and is actually part of the Kabbalah but it is interpreted separately because of its intimacy.

In the ***Template of God-Mind*** there is an image of a wormhole that goes from the Earth to the Sun. This has been verified by NASA. Underneath the city of Jerusalem is what is known as a Foundation Stone comprised of pure iron that transmits and receives frequencies. You can concentrate at the Pineal Gland, send a frequency line out to the Foundation Stone and from there it connects to the wormhole that goes to the sun. From the sun it connects via a vortex to the Mind of God. This is why Earth is considered to be a Mother World. In the Milky Way Galaxy, there are only 50 Mother Worlds. These all have Foundation Stones that connect to their home star that connects to the Mind of God. This explains why the Earth is such a Holy place. This is also why there is such an interest in our planet by others from other star systems and even other dimensions. In the Milky Way Galaxy there are approximately 300 billion stars. Of those 300 billion stars there are only 50 Mother Worlds. That's how rare a planet like

Earth is. Demonic entities and evil want to take control because if they can control a Mother World they can control Creation in that sector of the Galaxy.

This explains why what's happening today is so important for the rest of existence as well as why you are here. You probably never imagined that you would witness this especially in the United States. I am receiving emails, texts and posts from all over the world because people know what happens here will happen in their country as well. This is not just about America, it's about Earth and Humanity. Posts on the Q-board are generated by a Q-computer, not by a person. This information has its origin in the Ohalu Council and the so-called Council of Nine. I can tell you that no matter what you see happening do not be afraid because it is all for a reason and everything is headed to a specific goal. However, Humanity must become Spiritual. People must go to God otherwise Satan will take control. There's no question about that. So we must pray, immediately and constantly.

Red Sea Rules

Red Sea Rules or the Red Sea itself comes from the section of the ***Bible*** Exodus 14:15. The 72 Names of God is the code that comes from this segment of the ***Bible***. Remember that the significance of parting the Red Sea is symbolic as well as literal, spiritual and emotional. When you look at the Hebrew version of the name of the Red Sea, you realize that there are challenges in the translation. In Hebrew the name of the Red Sea is Yam Suph which translates to Reed Sea. Reed Sea connects to the Essenes and the Templars which is discussed in ***Template of God-Mind*** and ***Revelations of Time and Space, History and God***. True history flows from Atlantis to Dragon Riders to Ancient Egypt to the Holy Land where the Essenes began. Then when the Romans in 70 AD were putting down the rebellion by the Jews against Roman Empire, they threatened to kill anyone who studied Zohar and Kabbalah. So, the Essenes fled to what is now known as Scandinavia. Here they became the priests of the Vikings and they went eventually to the island of Bornholm. From Bornholm they went to the city of Citreaux in what is now Eastern France. Cîteaux in French means Reed. This is the connection from the Reed Sea to the city of Reeds. It was Moses who caused the Red Sea to part. Of course, the mother of Moses put him in a basket into the Nile River when he was a baby. He was floating in the Reeds when the daughter of the Pharaoh found him and took Moses as her own. Here is a third connection with Reeds. The image of Moses is most often of him parting the Reed/Red Sea

The symbolism of the cross is extremely ancient with its roots in Kabbalah, not in Christianity as most people think. When a person crosses him/her Self this refers to Adam, David, Moses, Emmanuel-Yehoshua. Adam means Adam Kadmon the Original Adam. This also involves the Sefirot and the Tree of Life which will be discussed later. When God says that he so loved the Earth that he gave his only son, he is referring to Adam Kadmon. All intelligent Beings have their source in Adam Kadmon. This means that Adam Kadmon contained all the souls that ever existed. Adam Kadmon produced Adam HaRishon as a result of the Tzim Tzum. Adam HaRishon means First Man. Adam HaRishon is the Adam that is written about in the ***Bible*** who was first married to Lilith and then to Eve. His descendants were Abraham, then David, then Solomon and then Yeshua/Jesus. This means that within Yeshua, Solomon, David and Abraham they each contain the entire template of Adam Kadmon. Every evening go through your own 10 Sephirot with the understanding that you are recognizing within yourself the template of Adam Kadmon, the initial Origin of all Beings. This makes you very powerful.

Faith

Faith comes from your heart. When you have faith in something, it's emotional, from your Heart Chakra. When you have a belief, it comes from your brain, it's logical thinking. Yes, you believe that this will happen because of logical information. When you have a knowing that comes from the mind and the Oversoul there's no doubt and no confusion. The difference between faith and belief and knowing becomes important.

10 Red Sea Rules

Adapted from Red Sea Rules by Robert Morgan

Rule #1

Realize that God means for you to be where you are.

Even if you are in a difficult situation and you're not happy with where you are and what's going on, you're supposed to be there. God wants you to be there and there is a reason for you to be in that situation. First of all, you have to go back to your own mind-pattern because remember that your mind-pattern creates your conditions. The reason humans are not prepared for greater levels of understanding is because they're not taking responsibility for their existence at the moment. They're blaming other people whether it's Democrats or Republicans, governments or Deep State. You still have to take responsibility. If you think the Deep State is controlling you then you need to look at the Deep State within your Self.

- What part of your own mind is harming you?
- What part of your mind is forcing you to do things you don't want to do?
- What part of your mind puts restrictions on you and how?
- Where are you physically, emotionally and Spiritually at this moment?
- Do you like where you are?
- If not, how can you change your situation?

You are not in the past, present or future, you're in the Eternal Moment of the Now. Whatever you project out is what will be reflected back for you. What you see happening now in Washington DC is happening within your Oversoul within your own Soul-personality conflict that needs to be resolved. You must ask your Self who is in charge of you. When you resolve this issue the world will be at peace. Realize that God means for you to be where you are supposed to be where you are at this moment because it is the most perfect place as a reflection of your mind-pattern.

Rule #2

Being more concerned for God's glory than for your relief.

This means instead of saying *oh God please get me out of here, please save me, get rid of this terrible situation*, you should be thanking God for your existence, for your experiences, whether you like them or not. You are a piece of God. Whatever you want you already have within you the totality of existence. You must think this every moment of your life because you are Immortal. You can't die. You might change bodies, but you will always exist. This might seem a little overwhelming but you've always existed you are just using this vehicle now. Compare this to owning a car. The car you had 10 or 20 years ago is gone. Those cars led you to your current car. In the same way your Soul-personality knows that the other vehicles are gone, but they led you to your current vehicle/body. Your current vehicle may be banged up a little bit or maybe doesn't start up in the morning as it used to but that's the vehicle you have. You need to take care of it, fix it and make it perfect. When I was in Havana Cuba I saw their cars that are 50, 60, 70 years old. Yet they look like they were manufactured yesterday. This means that regardless of the age of your vehicle/body you can make it look like brand new.

Rule #3

Acknowledge your enemy, but keep your eye on the Lord.

You should only know that you are a part of the God-Mind and nothing else really matters. You may have attracted those who would do you harm or those who seek to destroy you but this rule does not say to ignore your enemy but to acknowledge them. Realize that their existence is not as significant as your connection to the God-Mind.

Extrapolate that to what's happening now with the scamdemic, Antifa, Black Lives Matter and all the things that are negative. Recognize that a part of you created this and projected it out so that you can deal with it. Know that the greater part of you can eliminate it.

When you have a stain on the carpet or smudge on the counter top in your home, you can clean it. You don't have to leave the dirt. You have to acknowledge the dirt and then actively do something to get rid of it. Just like your negative mind-patterns and your programming. They are there, you cannot ignore them or let them overwhelm you. Your enemy is always you. If there's another person, that person is still a reflection of you. You are always your own enemy. That's all the Illuminati does is hold the mirror up. You look into the mirror, you see your Self and that becomes your enemy. Go within yourself mentally at your Pineal Gland to determine what part of you is hurting Self. You must determine what part of you is giving Self information that hurts you.

From your childhood and even from other lifetimes you were imprinted with Self-sabotage, Self-punishment, abandonment issues and so on but that doesn't mean that you leave it that way. Now is the time not only for your government, but for every person on Earth to individually eliminate the enemy within. You can do a simple exercise by seeing the words enemy within at your Pineal Gland. Then erase or flush it with Violet. You need to get rid of the enemy within and change that person because all enemies from within you.

Rule #4

Pray.

Interact with God every day through prayer. Prayer does not have to be formal. The words need to come from within and then you need to listen.

- Do you pray every day?

You are a cell within the body of God so all you have to do is talk to your Self. Do not pray in your left brain because you must pray as if you have already achieved the goal. When you pray, you are thanking the God-Mind within that you have already accomplished whatever you wish to have in your life. If you need finances, for example, don't say *oh, please God give me money and I need money* that's implying lack and lack. Lack is left brain and left brain allows the demonic entities to attach to you. Demonic entities will say *yes, we will give you money all you have to do is worship Satan and become part of us*. When you keep balance at your Pineal Gland and you pray as if you already have received, negativity cannot enter. In the Eternal Now, it is already done. In the ***Template of God-Mind*** and ***Revelations*** books you will find an extensive list of Angelic Frequencies, each one with a function.

Angelic Frequencies are enumerated in Kabbalah and the Zohar. These frequencies are not individual people. They are Angelic Frequencies that are functions of the God-Mind within you. In humanity there are 1.4 million frequencies within each person, each providing a function. When you evoke an Angelic Frequency you're not really calling upon an entity you are evoking a frequency within yourself that is a function of your Oversoul and God-Mind to accomplish a specific goal. Angelic Frequencies have specific missions. According to the Zohar, Humanity is actually in a higher position than Angels because Angels have no free choice. Angels can only do what God tells them to do, but you have free choice. The Angels were upset when God created Humanity. This is why there was a Fall from Grace by some of the Angels, with some becoming demons. They wanted to have more power like humans.

You can use the Angel Frequency of Ofriel to improve your finances because Ofriel is related to wealth. Remember that this name is an English transliteration of the Hebrew word. You can also use Name Frequency #45 from the *72 Names of God*. This is the frequency of Prosperity and uses the letters from right to left, Samech, Aleph and

Lamed. Visualize these Hebrew letters right to left in White at your Pineal Gland. You can pronounce these if you would like. Using these frequencies work because they're coming from within you. Activating these inner frequencies allows them to alter, improve and upgrade your mind-pattern and overall frequency. Janet has this information in her ***Miracles in Motion*** book, which is an excellent resource for helping to understand this work.

What you are learning here has not been available to the public before and was actually forbidden to be taught. Only the High Priests in the Temple were allowed to use this until 1840. At this time the High Priests were allowed to reveal this information to the Rabbis below them. It was not until the 1980s that this information was allowed to be given to the public. Even then, there was a lot of dissension amongst the Rabbis and various Hebrew sects about what should be given to the public, if anything at all. Many teachers of Kabbalah who taught people other than Jews were ostracized by those who still thought it should not be taught to non-Jews. Very Orthodox Rabbis in Israel would most likely be very upset with the information that Janet and I are teaching you in these classes. Yet, even these Rabbis know that it is now time to reveal this information publicly. I must emphasize that Kabbalah and Zohar are not part of a religion. They are from the Mind of God and for everyone in Creation regardless of your genetics or religious belief system.

Rule #5
Stay calm and confident and give God time to work.

There is no time and space. Everything exists simultaneously but if you were aware of everything simultaneously you would go crazy. This means that at the appropriate frequency intersection the event is occurring, you just haven't become aware of it yet. Keep in mind that because you want something, it doesn't mean you need it. You might want a Rolls-Royce but that doesn't mean you need it. You might get a Volkswagen instead. Your frequency must reach the point of actualizing the idea. You always get what you need, not necessarily what you want. However if you are getting what you need in some way then it is what you want. The next step is to consciously align what you want with what you need with the wishes of our Oversoul and the God-Mind and Beyond. According to Kabbalah, the oak tree is in the seed. You have this little tiny seed and one day it will be a gigantic tree. If you look at that seed you might think it's a nothing, just a speck on the floor. In the same way your mind-patterns are filled with gazillions of seeds that will grow but each of them will grow when they're supposed to grow. You may have rotten seeds that need to be replaced with viable ones.

Be careful what you ask for because you may get it. Always qualify with whatever is most correct and beneficial because this allows what is best for your Soul growth to come to you. Plant the seed properly, let it take its time so that it grows and is able to produce leaves and fruit. In the star system of Lyra eons ago where you came from there was such high level frequency that you could pick a fruit from a tree and instantly another fruit would take its place. There was no time and space in their mind-pattern because of the instant creation. It is a blessing from God that your thoughts do not instantly manifest because if you're thinking something really bad, you're going to get a bad situation right away. This means you have a chance to change that manifestation. You have time to think, change what you desire and realize what you really need instead.

In this current political situation you may be frustrated and impatient but you must understand that this is God's time and everything will unfold the way it's supposed to. Read Exodus chapter 14, line 15. It says that when the Hebrews left Egypt they were pursued by the Egyptian Army until they were up against the Red Sea surrounded by mountains, desert and the Egyptian Army. There was no place to go but into the sea. They thought that if they went into the sea they would die. They cried and prayed to God to save them. God asked

Moses why they were crying to Him; tell the Children of Israel to go forward.

The ***Bible*** says that one crazy guy walked into the sea until the water was up to his nose. When the water reached his nose, the sea parted. This man had a belief, a faith and the knowing that God will help them. Sometimes you have to sink up to your head before the answer comes. God says go forward and I will help you. Often help does not come in the way you want help, but it comes in the way you need help.

Rule #6

When unsure just take the next logical step by faith and knowing or you could just wait.

Sometimes when you don't know what to do, don't do anything. Instead wait for the answer to come because maybe it's not time for you to do anything. When you're at a crossroads with a Red light and lots of traffic you cannot just hurry across the street. You have to wait until the light turns green so you don't get hit by a car. Life is the same. When you are unsure you have to wait for the green light to take the next step in front of you, whatever that may be. When you feel overwhelmed with many issues, visualize all of your issues like the Red Sea. Center at your Pineal Gland, go into them, confront them and then visualize your issues parting like the Red Sea. Parting the Red Sea means separating your left brain from your right brain. It means separating the logic from the emotions. Most people are controlled by your young child emotions stomping and screaming *I want this now.* Separating your emotions from your logic as well as doing the *Child Within Visualization* helps with all of this.

Rule #7

Envision God's enveloping presence.

This means that in all circumstances, wherever you are, whatever you're feeling know and feel that God is in and around you at all times. It envelops you and passes through you. Remember the energy of Adam Kadmon, which is discussed in ***Template of God-Mind***. Adam Kadmon means the Original Adam or the First Person. The Original Adam was androgynous, both male and female at the same time meaning the Original Adam was genderless . Of course Adam has become a man's name but in Hebrew, Adam means from the Earth. Do the Adam Kadmon with the Sephirot from ***Template of God-Mind*** every night around midnight because that's when the energy is the most powerful. This will envelop you with the energy of the God-Mind in and around you.

Rule #8

Trust God to deliver in His own unique way.

This means that you may have in your mind the way a solution should come for your issue, but God has the correct unique way. You must acquiesce to that. Sometimes you pray to God and you want the outcome to be a certain way. In your mind you think that is the most amazing wonderful outcome however, it may not be. You have to allow God to choose the outcome. For example, you may think if you have financial issues you say *oh God, please give me $10,000.* Well, maybe God was going to give you a million and then you've limited it. So don't put the parameters on the outcome of God. Let God tell you which way it's going to be.

Rule #9

View your current crisis as the faith builder for the future.

Whatever you experience, whatever difficulties you are going through, they build you up to make you stronger so that in the future you can overcome and surpass all crises Think of a piece of raw metal becoming a sword. For this to happen the raw metal must be put through a hot flame and be beaten with a mallet to mold it. When it's all done, it's a beautiful powerful sword. Think of your Self as the raw metal going through the flame and being beaten with a mallet so that you are molded into a beautiful powerful Soul.

Rule #10
Don't forget to praise Him.

When you're looking for a certain outcome, and it's not there the way you think things should be, you get angry at God, asking *why are you doing this to me? Why are you punishing me?* You don't take responsibility for all mind-patterns that have created the situation. You need to praise God even if you're suffering because it is the path that has been chosen for the most beneficial outcome. No matter what you're going through, be positive about it. This is difficult and challenging, but in the end if you thank God for everything that's happening to you and for the most beneficial outcome, this is what you will experience.

Homework

- How are you dealing with your current crises in life?
- Are you confronting them?
- Are you letting them part and are you walking through them?
- When you are unsure what to do, how can you apply these rules?
- Do you have a faith, a belief or knowing?
- Do you have trust in the outcome?

Jewish Humor

A Jewish pessimist says *things can get worse.* A Jewish optimist says *of course they can*!

Secret History of the Zohar

You need to know the difference between the Hebrew language and Aramaic. These are two different languages, but they are related because they use the same alphabet In the same way Latin letters are used for a variety of languages such as English, Spanish and French. The Aramaic language eventually became the foundation for European languages, especially Latin languages. The Zohar is written in Aramaic not Hebrew. According to the Zohar, it was written in Aramaic and not Hebrew because Hebrew is an inter-universal language that is the Mind of God and understood by all Beings subconsciously or consciously. Aramaic was not understood by demonic entities so the Zohar is written in Aramaic to prevent the demons from understanding it.

Adam Kadmon is the Original Template of Humanity. But, it is not just the template of Humanity. Adam Kadmon is the template of all sentient Beings in All of Creation in All Universes. Remember that the God-Mind was alone because It was the only thing that existed. It was just One Mind and One Consciousness. Some call this chaos. Understand that chaos does not exist. Chaos is only a pattern that is not yet understood. When you move your awareness far enough away, you can see a pattern that you may not be able to see when you are up close. If you were like an ant crawling on the floor you could not see the pattern of the floor. You would think that there is no pattern, only chaos. When you rise to stand above the floor, you can see that there is a definite, repetitive pattern on the floor. Now, imagine this Being needing to know Itself. According to the Zohar and Kabbalah to create something else It needed to take parts of Itself and make it different.

- How do you do that?
- How do you take a part of your Self and make it different?

Thinking of all of this caused It to create an intense constriction as It pulled in Its mind-pattern. Hebrews called this Tzim Tzum. As an analogy, imagine you're completely covered by water. Then you take a part of that water and pull it close together so that there's no water around you, only dry area. If you squeeze a sponge tightly under water and then let go, water immediately floods back in very quickly and the sponge expands again. This is what happened with the Tzim Tzum. The Light of God figuratively restricted Itself to a little area, then was released. The Light by necessity went back into Itself, causing It to explode because It could not contain the flood of Light. Scientists call this the Big Bang that created Existence. According to Kabbalah this occurred 15 billion years ago. Science has said that the universe is approximately 13.8 to 14 billion years old but now it says that the universe could possibly be 15 billion years old. Current science is confirming what Kabbalah stated thousands of years ago.

According to the Zohar, It broke into 600,000 Oversoul pieces. In other words, this explosion created the Oversouls of everything in All of Existence. This includes all universes and dimensions everywhere. These 600,000 Oversouls create infinite life streams. This is Creation and why every person is related to everyone. Everyone is the same on the Soul level because everyone comes from the same Source. All differences are only Illusions. The Tzim Tzum imprinted all of Creation with the Adam Kadmon through which everyone is connected.

The Zohar says that when the Tzim Tzum occurred the 22 Hebrew letters were created, each one representing a function of the God-Mind. Each Hebrew letter has a numerical value which is known as its Gematria. For example the first letter of the Hebrew alphabet is Aleph. Aleph has the Gematria, or numerical value, of 1. In Hebrew, the word for 1 is Achad. The letters used to spell Achad from right to left are: Aleph, Chet, Dalet.

Each letter has a numerical value, or Gematria, as follows:

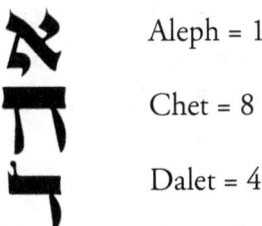

א Aleph = 1

ח Chet = 8

ד Dalet = 4

Together their Gematria is 13

1+8+4=13

According to the Gematria the number 1 is also the number 13.

Achad is the word for 1/one. The Gematria of the word one is 13. The God-Mind has 12 energies so when you combine them all there are 13, so in one is all. This is why the Zohar and Kabbalah say that the beginning is also the end. This is also why history repeats itself, as is happening in this current time period. The *End Times* is also the

Beginning Times. When you have a circle, there is no beginning, there is no end.

- What point of the circle is the start?
- What point is the end?

The number 13 is the Totality of Existence. You have been deceived into believing that it's not good when it's the opposite. Most of what you learn is the opposite of the truth and this is what you are learning through these difficult times now on the Earth. The number 13 interestingly, is considered bad luck. You are imprinted to not want to be in 13 of anything. Most buildings do not have a 13th floor. Often, they go from floor 12 to floor 14. The number 13 is quite positive, but the global handlers want you to believe that it is an unlucky number. This is a deception because the number 13 is very powerful. You are even told that there are only 12 Zodiac signs when there are actually 13. The Zohar says that they are sign posts for what must be done in physical reality. The Zohar states quite clearly that the Stars or the Zodiac impels you, but do not compel. This means they give you a little push and you can accept it or not accept it but you don't have to do what they say.

You are taught that there are only 12 months of the year, but the Hebrew calendar has 13 months. 13 months x 4 weeks = 52 weeks. You are also told there are only 12 Tribes of Israel, but there is also the Tribe of Joseph brought up to Manasseh and Ephraim, which makes thirteen Tribes. The United States began with 13 colonies. Usually wherever you see 12 of anything there are really 13.

Most artists, scientists and historians throughout history studied Kabbalah and the Zohar including Isaac Newton in 1727, Thomas Edison and Michelangelo. It was known that Michelangelo created his artwork after studying the Zohar with the Medici's in Florence, Italy. Christopher Columbus learned from the Zohar that the world was a circle and that there was a surface world as well as an inner world. Dr. John Dee who worked for the Queen of England studied Kabbalah as well as General Albert Pike in the early 1800s. Thomas Edison in 1931 studied the Zohar to learn about electricity. Also Paracelsus and the Roman Emperor, Marcus Aurelius all studied the Zohar.

During the destruction of the Second Temple in Jerusalem in 70 AD, the Romans said that anyone who studied the Zohar would be killed. This is when the Essenes fled to the north to what became Scandinavia where they became the Viking priests. Others went to the area of the Galilee, which is near Lake Tiberias in the Northern part of Israel. This is the area where Christ met Mary Magdalene who was a very wealthy woman from the area that is now Lebanon. Her father had a home in the Galilee. She supported Christ and his work at a meeting place called Knesset Rabbah which means great assembly. That became the basis for the congress/senate in Israel. From here they went to the island of Bornholm in the Baltic Sea. Bornholm is a Northern word. Born means child and holm means a storage area. They were protecting the children of Mary Magdalene and Christ. You remember the story of the Hooked X that you can read about in my other books. From there they went to Citeaux to become the Cistercians and from there they became the Templars. The Templars went back to the Holy Land to reclaim the information that they had left behind, a thousand years before. Read ***King Bee, Queen Bee Template of God-Mind, Revelations of Time & Space, History and God.***

The Zohar disappeared for about twelve hundred years because it was not allowed. In 1290, Moses de Leon in Spain published the Zohar and disseminated its information for the first time since it was banned by the Romans. Much later in 1559 the Catholic Church was the first organization that publicly printed and distributed the Zohar and of course used the information for its own purposes. According to Zohar rules you have to be a man to study the Zohar, be at least 40 years old, married and circumcised. In modern times, these rules are no longer applicable.

Plato studied the Zohar where he learned about Atlantis and the prehistory of the Earth. In 569BC Pythagoras studied the Zohar from which he developed the Pythagorean Tetractys.

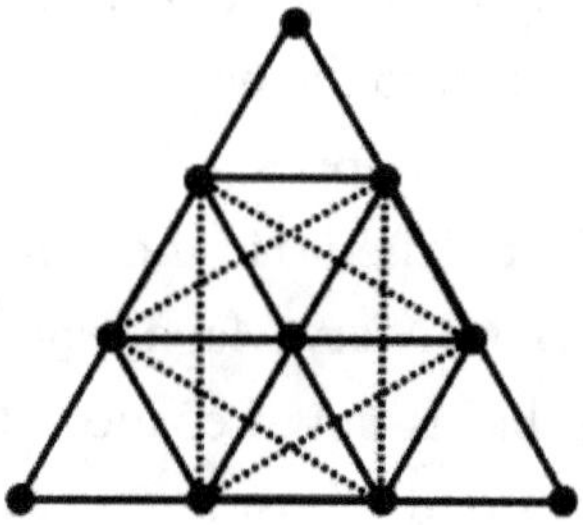

Within its triangular shape there are 9 triangles. Including the outer triangle this makes a total of 10. According to Pythagoras these 10 triangles represent the 10 Sephirot. The equilateral triangle became the sequence of the first 10 numbers of the four rows which you know as being a symbolic representation of the Sephirot. You see that the rows of the one, two, three, and then four of the of the of the tip of the triangle there. So the first row represents zero dimensions, which is just the point, the second row represents one dimension or a line of two points. The third row represents two dimensions, which is a plane defined by a triangle or three points and the fourth row, which is the whole thing represents three dimensions or tetrahedron defined by four points in that is the basis of the Ultimate Protection Archetype of the tetrahedron inside the octahedron.

It also represents the 4-Letter *Name of God* when placed into the triangle as follows:

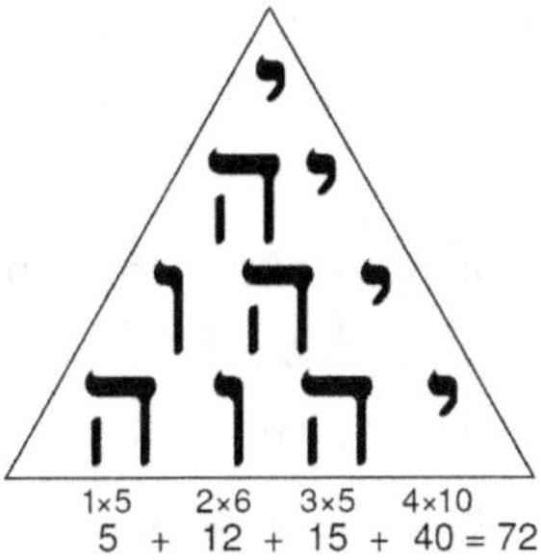

Reading the Hebrew letters right to left, you see the Gematria of these letters within the triangle add up to 72, representing the *72 Names of God.*

It is said that the Pythagorean musical system was based on the Tetractys as the rows can be read as the ratios of 4:3 (perfect fourth), 3:2 (perfect fifth), 2:1 (octave), forming the basic intervals of the Pythagorean scales. A prayer of the Pythagoreans shows the importance of the Tetractys (sometimes called the "Mystic Tetrad"), as the prayer was addressed to it.

Bless us, divine number, thou who generated gods and men! O holy, holy Tetractys, thou that containest the root and source of the eternally flowing creation! For the divine number begins with the profound, pure unity until it comes to the holy four; then it begets the mother of all, the all-comprising, all-bounding, the first-born, the never-swerving, the never-tiring holy ten, the keyholder of all.[5]

As a portion of the secret religion, initiates were required to swear a secret oath by the Tetractys. They then served as novices for a period of silence lasting five years.[citation needed]

The Pythagorean oath also mentioned the Tetractys:

By that pure, holy, four lettered name on high,
nature's eternal fountain and supply,
the parent of all souls that living be,
by him, with faith find oath, I swear to thee.
https://en.wikipedia.org/wiki/Tetractys

Each of the 22 books of the Zohar represents one of the 22 letters of the Hebrew alphabet. All of this information was said to have been received in one day by Rabbi Shimon Ben Yochai and his son. Even though they received it in one day it took them 13 years to understand it and then it was hidden for 1,200 years until it was revealed in Spain.

It is said that the Zohar is the deepest secret of the Kabbalah. Remember that Kabbalah is a commentary of the Torah and the Zohar is the code of the Kabbalah so together they form a Triad of Kabbalah, Torah and Zohar.

Very small amounts of this information has been revealed. It is said that when the Zohar is completely revealed to humanity then the final recent Redemption and the Messiah will come. I believe that we're living in that time. It is also stated that the Zohar is the basis of the Torah and all of Christianity is based on the Zohar. Every idea and concept that you find in the New Testament is found in the Zohar from thousands of years before. This is because Christ was the disciple of Kabbalists. It's also said that Moses at Mount Sinai also received information about the Zohar and it was called Ha'or Ha-gannuz which means the hidden light.

- Why is it hidden light?
- Do you think that Humanity could study this as well as understand and apply it?
- Who amongst the people you know, including neighbors, co-workers, even your own family would read, understand and apply this information?

Very few, but this is the point because now is the time to reveal this information so people can apply it. This is especially important because of the demonic forces present and active throughout the world. Remember that when the explosion of the Tzim Tzum occurred, It could not contain all the Light of God because the explosion was too powerful. This explosion created the 600,000 Oversouls that then generated All of Existence. The Zohar says that this explosion also generated incomplete creation pieces of broken Tzim Tzum debris. You know, for example, that when you break something there will be tiny pieces that are not usable. These incomplete creation pieces became evil, the demons that now exist in All of Creation. This includes the Angel Lucifer. Luz means light. He was an Angel of Light. Lucifer became jealous of the God-Mind that controlled All of Existence. Lucifer saw these peripheral pieces that were not completely formed and intact without a total consciousness. Lucifer said, I'm going to control these; I'll be the king of these demons. This is what happened and is referred to as the Fall from Grace. What you now see in Humanity are these incomplete pieces of the Tzim Tzum that became and developed into evil entities. They have entered into parts of Humanity to take control. However, they are all under the control of Lucifer.

This is why there is a current battle between what is called Good and Evil. When you rise above the chaos you can see the pattern. Then you know that this is no Good and Evil, there is simply Creation. Good and Evil are different frequencies within Creation. These frequencies are labeled as Good and Evil to understand their functions. What you need to do is create balance between the extremes. Evil or negative energy is not to be destroyed because ultimately you cannot. Destroying evil is destroying a part of the God-Mind which you cannot do. Evil only exists so that you recognize Good. If only Good existed you would not understand It. If you only ate sugar for example, you wouldn't know that lemons are sour. For you to understand the wide range of existence, all these things must exist from the pleasant to the not-so-pleasant. This is a concept that can be difficult for most people to understand. Organized religion says that there is good and evil; that you must do only good and ignore or vanquish evil. What you see now is the debris pieces that are under the control of Lucifer.

The Christ figure is really Adam Kadmon. Keep in mind that Adam Kadmon is androgynous, containing both Male and Female, or more accurately Positive and Negative. Adam Kadmon is the template for All Intelligent Beings. Even Reptilians have their origin in Adam Kadmon. One of your purposes is to create balance so that antagonism cannot exist.

Contrast, however, must exist because you cannot know light unless you know what the darkness is. When you have a room that's completely dark and a room that's completely light and you open the door between them, the light shines into the dark, overcoming it. The dark never overcomes the light. This is why this book is called Dark to Light. You are living in darkness and you need to open the door to the light. The Zohar says that you are in a dark room with a candle on the table covered by a thick blanket. Your job is to remove the blanket so that the one small light will illuminate the entire room, eliminating the darkness. Even if you are in a pitch-black gigantic auditorium and someone lights a match, you will see that match wherever you are in the giant auditorium. All you have to do is turn on the light and leave it on for the darkness to recede.

Homework

- Concentrate on this Pythagorean Tetractys both the pyramid and the Hebrew letters at your Pineal Gland.

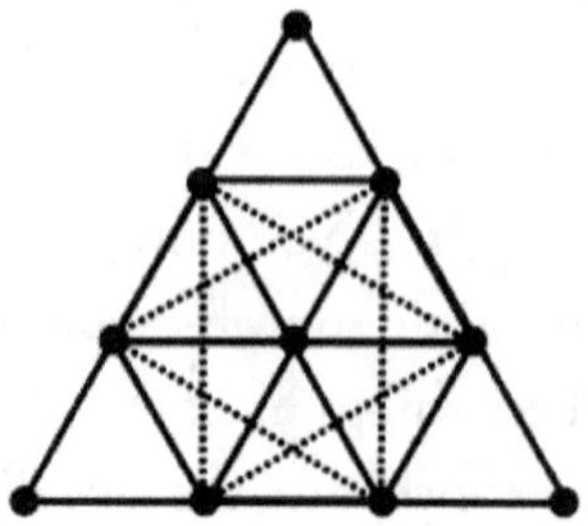

- Visualize that Tzim Tzum and the Adam Kadmon from the Template of God-Mind and Revelations of Time & Space at your Pineal Gland. Also put the 10 Sephirot in White for 2-3 minutes in the appropriate places on your body to activate healing energy and information within you.

Jewish Humor

The difference between a Jewish mother-in-law and a Rottweiler is that the Rottweiler eventually lets go.

The Red String

Kabbalah is a technology for the Soul-personality.

Kabbalah is not just spiritual ideas nor does it have anything to do with religion. Kabbalah is a mental technology for you to create and achieve your goals in this world. Kabbalah says that your ego, which is your interface with physical reality, is the link of your Spiritual self with the physical self. It says that your ego is like a curtain that hides your true self. As you know, ego is centered in the left brain which is what you use to interact with physical reality. The left brain is also the center of your materialistic identity. Whatever name you're born with, whatever genetics you have, the center is in your ego or left brain. It is the curtain, or the Pineal Gland that hides the true self. When you move the curtain aside you let in the very bright energy of the right brain which connects to the Creator Itself. The right brain and the Keter, or Crown Chakra, is the light that must shine on the rest of you.

Concentrating on your Pineal Gland opens up and reveals the light of the true self into your existence. This means accepting responsibility. This is extremely important especially in relationship to the events of the world. The battle of Good and Evil in the physical world is occurring within your inner self. You have an inner batter between Good and Evil because there is a part of each person that feels inadequate. These feelings originate from the shattering of the Original Tzim Tzum as well as the Tzim Tzum within you. This means that you feel an inadequacy before the Totality of the Creator. Yet despite these feelings, you must still realize that you are a part of the Creator and you are the Creator. This is a great responsibility.

Kabbalah is a technology for the Soul-personality. Kabbalah is the oldest and most influential wisdom in the world. Kabbalah is not a religion and has nothing to do with religion. The Zohar and Kabbalah both explicitly state that this technology is for All of Creation on every planet in existence. This technology can transform the world if you use this energy to create from Dark to Light. This information was the teachings of Abraham, Moses, Jesus, Mohammed, Plato, Shakespeare, and even Jung. All of these people stated that they used the information from the Zohar and Kabbalah in their work and that it unravels the mysteries of the universe, allowing you to find the hidden truth of life.

The Red String

People who wear this Red String on the left wrist do so because of the *Evil Eye* that jealous and envious people cast upon others. Kabbalah says that the negative energy of jealousy and envy cast by others can cause harm. Kabbalah also says to never judge another person because that will come back on you. After all, what you see in others is what exists inside of you.

- What is the mind-pattern for feeling jealous or envious of others?

You can be jealous or envious of another's finances, looks, job or relationships. This means that you wish you had what the other person has. You must know that you can have what the other person has, but you must determine what is stopping you. The idea of jealousy and envy is illogical. It's kind of like looking in a restaurant window and seeing people eat wonderful food that you wish you could eat. You could go into that restaurant, too.

- What mind-patterns block you from achieving your goal?
- Do you really want what others have or do you want it as a result of societal or individual programming?

In the outer world you see people and groups that seek what they call equality, or having what others have. They blame other people for not having what they want. Kabbalah says this is all a result of the *Evil Eye*. In Hebrew, this is called Ayin Ha'ra. This means your Pineal Gland, or inner eye is trying to interpret what it sees. Another layer of the *Evil Eye* comes from the Egyptians who used the *Eye of Horus* to create Evil. Think about all the black eyes that you see on public icons which is a result of Illuminati rituals.

The Red String is worn on the left hand because the left represents physical reality. Red is the lowest frequency on the color spectrum. According to Kabbalah, the Red String protects you against an *Evil Eye*. The Red String is worn 24/7 and wrapped around the left wrist 7 times because this represents the 7 Chakra Bands. There are 10 Sephirot in total, but there are 7 Sephirot below the top three of Keter, Chokhmah and Binah which together represent the God-Mind. The 7 lower Sephirot represent physical reality.

What is the Red String made of?

The Red String is always made of wool because when you create wool it's spun. Wool represents Mercy and Judgment which is why Humanity is on the Earth. Kabbalistic symbolism says White equals mercy and Red equals judgment. Most of the flags of countries on the

Earth contain Red and White so countries are looking for mercy and judgment.

Why is it made out of wool? Where does wool come from?

Wool comes from a lamb. In religious terms lamb represents the Lamb of God, or the Christ figure. The Red String that's wrapped around the wrist is made with White wool, which is dyed Red. This symbolism means that Judgment is being converted to Mercy. Red attracts Judgment and binds it to the White Mercy. This is why the Red String is Red on the outside and White on the inside.

Where does the Red String come from?

The Red String is created from the tomb of Rachel in Israel. Rachel is one of the Matriarchs of the Hebrews. The White wool string is wrapped around her tomb 7 times and left for a period of time. Then it is taken down, dyed Red and available for sale.

Rachel's Tomb - Israel

Rachel is considered one of the Mothers of the World because she protects and defends her children. The Hebrews consider there to be 5 Holy Mothers.

5 Holy Mothers

1- Sarah 2- Rebecca 3- Rachel 4- Leah 5- Ruth

All of the 5 Holy Mothers had issues having children. Sarah was the wife of Abraham. She did not have children until she was 90 years old. She laughed at the Angel that came to tell her that she was going to have a child. Her child's name, Isaac, means *one who has laughed.* The only one of these women who was not Jewish was Ruth, yet she was considered to be one of the 5 Holy Mothers of Judaism because she was the daughter-in-law of Naomi.

Why is Ruth considered one of the 5 Holy Mothers?

Naomi was married to a man named Elimelech. In Hebrew Elimelech means *God is my King.* They lived in a place where there was a famine that caused them to move with their two sons from Judea to Moab. While there, Elimelech, died and so did their two sons. The two sons had been married. One son was married to Ruth and the other one was married to a woman named Orpah. Naomi then decided to move to Bethlehem so they could find food. Ruth went with her but Orpah stayed in Moab.

While they were in Bethlehem, Ruth worked in the fields for a man named Boaz. Boaz was a relative of Naomi's husband, so he was an older man. Naomi encouraged Ruth to seduce Boaz so that she could have a child. It was very important in those days for people to have children, but Ruth decided she was not going to do that. She insisted that Boaz marry her and together they had a son named Obed. Obed became the father of Jesse. Jesse became the father of David who became the King. This means that Ruth was the ancestor of Christ via King David and King Solomon. This is why she is considered to be one of the 5 Holy Mothers. She was not Jewish but she became Jewish.

Why is the tomb of Rachel used to create the Red String?

Rachel was the wife of Jacob and the mother of Joseph and Benjamin, the originators of several of the Tribes of Israel. Rachel's father was Laban. In Hebrew, Laban means White, as in the color of the wool that is used. Rachel's older sister Leah, was Jacob's first wife.

Jacob went to live with Laban in the area of Haran which is now the South Eastern part of Turkey. This is why Turkey is so important in modern times.

Why did he go? Who was Jacob's brother? Who was his twin Esau?

Rebecca was the wife of Isaac. Together they had twins Jacob and Esau. When Rebecca was pregnant God said to her, *within your womb are two nations who will be very great and mighty.* Esau became the father of the Hebrew Arab tribes of that area. Jacob became the father of the Hebrew tribes. This is why the Arabs and the Jews are related. They are cousins and ultimately they are really all descended from one person, Isaac.

Laban was not an honest man, so when Jacob came to live with him he fell in love with Rachel. Jacob asked Laban if he could marry her. Laban said *yes, you can have her if you work for me for seven years.* After the 7 years, Laban drugged Jacob at his wedding so unbeknownst to Jacob he really married her sister Leah. According to the Bible on their wedding night, Jacob had marital relations with Leah and she became pregnant. The next day, he realized that he had been deceived. You see, deception goes back thousands of years. When Jacob complained to Laban, Laban said *you can have Rachel if you work for me another seven years.* After 7 more years Jacob married Rachel. In total it took him 14 years to have two wives. Rachel could not become pregnant, but Leah could easily have children. Rachel was very upset that she couldn't have children so she gave Jacob her handmaidens, to be surrogate mothers in her place. Finally, Rachel became pregnant with Joseph.

Joseph became Jacob's favorite child even though by now Jacob had 12 children, all sons. The older sons did not like Joseph so they sold him into slavery in Egypt where Joseph then became the second in command in Egypt. Each of Jacob's 12 sons eventually became the head of a Tribe of Israel.

Rachel became pregnant with a second son called Benjamin. Because she had a difficult pregnancy and birth, Rachel died shortly after giving birth. Before dying she named him Ben Oni, meaning son of my mourning. After her death, Jacob called him Ben Yamin, or Benjamin. In English, this means the son of the right or the right side. Benjamin was the only head of a Tribe of Israel who was born in Israel.

Rachel was buried on the way to Ephrath, now known as Bethlehem. She was not able to be buried in the ancestral tomb. But because she was so concerned and loving to her children she is considered to be a Mother of Protection. This is why her tomb was chosen for the Red String to be wrapped around before giving it to people for their protection.

How do you wear it?

For each of the 7 times you wrap it around your left wrist you say one line of the 7-line Ana Beko'ach Prayer. Then you tie the string and wear it 24/7.

You must be proactive in your prayer and take action. This means that when you are in a dark room and you want the light to turn on you can pray to God to do this for you or you can proactively turn the light switch on your Self. When you need money, you can use the appropriate *Name of God* but you also need to look for job. You need to do something proactive to achieve the goal. You must be an active participant in the process. The Zohar and Kabbalah say that even though the Holy Temple in Jerusalem was destroyed, it is not enough to pray that God rebuilds it even though it is supposed to come down from Heaven. It is said that you must start building the foundation and then the Heavenly part will descend upon it.

Accept responsibility

You must resist all negative thoughts and influences as well as be appreciative of everything that you have. There are a lot of different ways that you can and cannot be taking responsibility. Even when someone says something negative about or to you, it is up to you to take responsibility for your mind-pattern that attracted the comment in the first place. In the same way, whatever happens in the world is a reflection of every person in the world.

Kabbalah is a neutral code of instruction that has been Spiritualized. You can do with it whatever you know you should be doing with it. We discussed previously how the Israelites were very angry at Moses for leading them to the Red Sea with the Egyptian Army behind them. When they prayed to God, God's reply was *why are you asking me? Just get going, jump in the water.* It only took one person to get up to his nose when water parted. The point of this lesson is that everything that you need to save yourself is already within.

After they crossed the Red Sea they came to a mountain in what is now Saudi Arabia. They followed a light in the sky that led them through the desert. Every day they were given manna to eat. Kabbalah says that the manna tasted like whatever they wanted it to taste like, providing all the nutrition the Hebrews needed. When Moses came down the mountain with the Torah he saw them worshiping the Golden Calf and dancing, he burned with anger and threw the tablets out of his hands, shattering them. When this happened it is said that the Hebrew letters fled from the stone into Heaven. Others say that the tablets did not shatter but were put into the Ark of the Covenant. This idol worshiping was instigated by the Erev Rav, specifically two magicians named Jannes and Jambres (Hebrew: יניס Jannes, ימבריס Yambres)

Some Kabbalists say the Erev Rav were Jews who believed in the Egyptian Gods and were trained by evil sorcerers. turned against Moses. However the Zohar says that the Erev Rav were Egyptians and others, who were part of the Hebrew groups in Egypt. When the Jews left, the Pharaoh told this group to leave with the Hebrews because they were too much like the Jews. Therefore it was these Egyptians who tried to turn the Jews away from God to worship idols instead. It is these infiltrators, sometimes known as shills, and their descendants that the world is dealing with now. These Evil ones take the neutral code of Kabbalah and use it for Evil instead of Good.

Homework

- What does the *Evil Eye* mean to you?
- Do you take 100% responsibility for yourself?

Jewish Humor

The man talking to his friend said, *my wife Miriam and I were very happy for 20 years. Then, we met!*

The Power of Kabbalah

According to traditional information, the patriarch Abraham is the one who brought Kabbalah to the Hebrew people and to the world. Abraham is considered the first Kabbalist when he wrote the ***Book of Formation***, which is called ***Sefer Yetzirah***. Moses who also contributed to Kabbalah is considered to be the greatest prophet of the Hebrew people and of the world. In fact, Moses is even venerated by Islam and Christianity. Most of Christianity is based on the Zohar and Kabbalah. Zohar was studied by Jesus, Mohammed, Moses and Buddha. Buddha was a descendant of the Children of the East. After Abraham's first wife Sarah passed on, he married a woman named Keturah who was an African woman. With Keturah, Abraham had six children who studied Kabbalah with him. He then sent them to the eastern part of Asia where they were known as the Children of the East. The Magi that came to the Christ child when he was born were the descendants of the Children of the East.

Abraham's children were the foundation of Buddhism and also influenced Hinduism. Buddha is actually a contraction of B'Yehuda which means *in or from Judah/Judea*. Buddha and all of Buddha's teachings were Zohar and Kabbalah. The Hebrew word for light is Or. This is the origin of the Eastern Asian Sanskrit word aura. Many words found in Eastern Philosophy are actually Hebrew words as a result of the relocation of Abraham's sons. Adding the Hebrew letter Aleph in front of Brahmin the name of this Hindu god becomes Abraham. The Indian Vedas come from the Hebrew word Da, which means to know. In Hindi, Ashram means a camp. In Hebrew the word for camps is Ashramim. The Hindu and Chinese religions connect back to Ancient Hebrew. The Chinese and Japanese languages are similar to Hebrew. It is fascinating how everything is connected on the inner levels. Even the word Hindu or Indu is a Hebrew word that means to cross over the river. Chinese culture began with what the Chinese call the Spiritual Giants from afar. This refers to the children of Keturah and Abraham, the Children of the East. This is why India, Israel, and China have a very close relationship with Israel because they know their ancestry.

Zohar states that at the time of creation there was only one continent on the Earth and then this continent broke very rapidly into the 7 continents. The Midrash says that before the flood there was a constant springtime meaning the Earth only had one season. People lived longer and the fields only needed to be cultivated every 4 years. The Zohar says that an asteroid impact caused all the upheavals. King Solomon knew about North America, calling it Havilah. The Bible describes fallen Angels called Bnei Elohim meaning the children of those who come from above as well as the Nephilim, which are the giants.

Male and Female Lineage

Adam HaRishon, the first Adam had two wives, Lilith and Eve. From Adam came Abraham. Abraham had two wives, Sarah and Keturah. From Abraham came Isaac. Isaac married Rebecca. Isaac was the father of Jacob. Jacob had two wives, sisters Leah and Rachel. From Jacob descended David. David was married to Bathsheba. From David came Solomon. Solomon had 300 wives and 700 concubines, a total of 1000 women in his palace. His main primary wife Na'amah was the daughter of the Pharaoh of Egypt. This marriage united Israel and Egypt under King Solomon as one nation. Phoenicians were actually Hebrews. From Solomon descended Emmanuel/Jesus who was married to Mary Magdalene. The same genetics were passed all the way down the line. This is why the Christ figure said *I have come before but you did not know me.*

There is a Holy Lineage of 7 Males and 10 Females. The Males represent the 7 lower Sefirot from Chesed to Malchut. The Females represent all 10 Sefirot. Because of the intensity of the Female Holy Lineage, the Hebrews are a matriarchal society. In addition, the mother was always known while the identity of the father could be questioned. 10 + 7 = 17; 1 + 7 = 8, an Oversoul number.

When the Ain Sof/Without End/Absolute contracted Itself in Tzim Tzum. It developed into the template of Adam Kadmon. Adam Kadmon is the Original Template of Humanity as well as All Sentient Advanced Creatures. The Light of God was around Adam Kadmon but not in it. Kabbalah says that the Template of Adam Kadmon felt guilty because it existed without giving back to the God-Mind. So the God-Mind tried to fill Adam Kadmon with Light. Adam Kadmon resisted because it felt it couldn't reciprocate. Ultimately God-Mind managed to push it into Adam Kadom which then exploded because it couldn't handle the amazingly intense energy. This is what science calls the Big Bang. According to the Zohar, humans are a vessel of desire. It says that humanity is unhappy because the desire within is not fulfilled by the Light of the God-Mind.

When you understand that order is concealed in chaos, then you will see the real pattern that is contained within the God-Mind. Just as the ant cannot perceive order from its perspective on the floor, Humanity cannot perceive the actual pattern that encompasses All Humanity is on the floor of the Sefirot in Malchut, the lowest Sefirah of physical reality.

Empty Space/Void

Science now says that there is no empty space whatsoever This agrees with what the Zohar said thousands of years ago. There is no such thing as a void. If you perceive a void it's because you are unable to perceive the energy from a frequency that you cannot yet understand. There is energy in every part of existence everywhere. There is no space that's a void, ever.

Infinite energy fills eternity.

Infinite energy shares endlessly, imparts continuously, and gives ceaselessly.

This is something that you must remember in every moment of your existence especially whenever you feel depressed, whenever you think that there is no plan, whenever you feel hopeless. Remember that there is no void and there is energy that gives you everything in every moment of your existence. If you don't feel it, it's because you're blocking it. You become like the Original Adam Kadmon that blocked the energy of All that is Absolute. You cause your own sadness and negative experiences because you are stopping God-Mind from giving you All That Exists.

13 Principles of Kabbalah

There are 13 principles of Kabbalah. The number 13 is extremely important. You already know that there are really 13 astrological signs, 13 Tribes of Israel, 13 colonies of the United States, and so on. In addition, physical reality is built on an energetic cube of 13x13x13, which is why programming is built in such a way that it hooks into what already exists.

Principle #1

Don't believe anything; test what you learn.

This is extremely important especially with what's going on in the world today. You are bombarded by so many different perspectives and information that it's challenging to know what to believe if any of it. Do not believe anything until you explore and test what you hear. Always apply what you learn because if you don't do anything with it, it is wasted information. You learn something because you are supposed to be doing something with it. If you waste information then this is actually considered a sin. Even when information sounds true be sure you test it. You can use Pale Orange and/or ask your Oversoul to determine its veracity.

Principle #2

Two realities exist. The physical world comprises 1% of one reality and is considered to be the World of Darkness. The Realm of Light is the larger reality that comprises the other 99%.

Currently, you are told that the common people comprise 99% of the population the elite are the other 1%. Science says that the human mind can only perceive. 0.5% of existence and the other 99.5% is unavailable. The Zohar is a little bit more lenient stating that humanity has 1% available with 99% unavailable. Hyperspace teaches that you use less than 10% of your brain and only 3% of your DNA.

- If you only experience 1% of Existence, what are you missing?
- What do you think that you are rejecting of the 99%?
- If you can perceive 100% of Existence what will happen to you and what will you become?
- Would you be grounded in physical reality?
- Would you know the truth about everything?
- Would you be able to comprehend what you experience?

Do your preliminary work to ground and balance. Then visualize 1/99 in White at your Pineal Gland with a Brown Merger Archetype through both numbers to bring them together so they equal 100%. Use White because White contains all colors, which is why you always visualize the Sefirot in White.

People who have near-death experiences after being pronounced dead often say they went into an ultra-high realm Here they are told it is not their time and to go back. In almost every case the people say that they do not want to come back after knowing this amazing enormous energy. It's like having a Rolls-Royce and then being told you need to drive a Volkswagen. When you fly First Class you are not going back to Economy Class or eating hamburger after you are used to fillet mignon. It is very difficult for these people. Once you know the highest levels to go back to the lower levels is very difficult. You have experienced the 99% and your old world feels fake and ridiculous. Even with this work as you assimilate it, your awareness changes and you do not want to go back to your original lifestyle.

Remember what happens when there is a pitch-black room and you light just one little tiny candle. It illuminates the room. Light overwhelms the darkness. Even one drop of light illuminates a dark room. If you have a room of light next to a dark room and open the door between them, the light floods the dark. The dark does not go into the light. The light is always the winner. You live in a world of darkness. You need to open the door to the light and the light will overwhelm the dark instantly. The choice is yours. Unfortunately, not everybody can handle the light because they are so used to living in the dark. When you are sleeping in a dark room and someone quickly flips the light switch on, you squint and cover your eyes to go back into the darkness. You don't want the light because you have to think about that. Sleep with the light on in your room. Always keep on some kind of light so that you are always in the light, never in the darkness.

Principle #3

Everything a Human Being desires is Spiritual Light.

Think about all the things you want to have in your life. Perhaps you want money, a nicer home, more food, clothes, jewelry, health and relationships. The bottom line is that these are all the Light of Existence/Absolute. This Light has many manifestations which translate into your life as a result of your mind-pattern. Whatever your mind-pattern is will show the result of that Spiritual Light. Instead of desiring things, experiences and relationships, visualize Self filled with the Spiritual Light from head to toe, exuding from every pore in your entire Being. Do this when you wake up, before you go to sleep, and during the day. This only takes you a moment. Visualize Self as a Spiritual Light bulb that is turned on and filled with Light. Then observe how it manifests and translates into your life to understand your real mind-pattern.

Principle #4

The purpose of life is for Spiritual transformation from a reactive to proactive Being.

The purpose of life according to the Zohar and Kabbalah is spiritual transformation from a reactive to proactive Being. Proactive means that you do something to create a result instead of waiting for something to happen and then reacting to it.

- Are you a reactive or proactive Being?
- How do you know the difference?
- Do you sit in a dark room waiting for the light?
- Do you walk over and turn the light switch on?

In ***Decoding Your Life*** you will find an entire chapter on changing from a reactive to proactive person. Look at every situation in your life, relationships, job, home, whatever it is, from the simplest thing to the most complicated, asking Self if you are reactive or proactive. When you react to something, it's emotional, often negatively because you get disturbed. Proactive says *I'm not going to wait for that to happen, I'm going to do something so that the outcome of this situation is in my favor.* If you apply for a job and get upset while you are waiting to hear, you can do something. Contact them to ask the status of your application. You may not have an answer right away, but you know that you've done something towards the result. When people are ill they react to what's going on in their physical bodies. Proactive for your health means taking your vitamins, exercising, doing mental work without being ill. Proactive for your relationships means sitting down and having an adult conversation rather than waiting for something to blow up that puts you in a reactive position.

You are most likely a reactive person as a result of childhood imprinting as well as other lifelines. In my life, my mother was a reactive person. Whatever happened she exploded, expressing her emotions. She made me feel bad and guilty. She never did any proactive work to prevent negativity from occurring. This imprinting sets you up for a lifetime of harshness, sabotage and punishment. Look at your family to determine your childhood imprints. I knew people who always said that things would work out, so don't worry. I thought they were stupid and that they should react, throw things and have a temper tantrum as my family did. Everything was always someone else's fault. My family was always the innocent victim. You must look to determine if this is within you, then mitigate, change and transform your behavior from reactive to proactive. Balancing at your Pineal Gland definitely helps.

Principle #5

The moment of your transformation you make a connection with the 99% realm.

Transforming from reactive to proactive allows you to start to perceive that missing 99%.

Principle #6

Never blame other people or external events.

There are organizations of people who claim to be targeted individuals who blame mind-control, scalar waves, and the government for all disturbances in their lives. They say they can't work, they're sick and sabotaged. These are excuses to do nothing and blame others for their lives without taking responsibility. Blaming others gives your power away. Always accept responsibility. Even the weather is a result of your mind-pattern. If you can't go out to get what you need you can blame the weather or you can look at your mind-pattern to determine what part of you contributed to the storm. Maybe you have an emotional storm within. You may feel that there is a storm of people blocking you somewhere in your life. If someone in a store says that you are trying to kill them because you are not wearing a mask, you need to look within to determine what is masking your ability to accomplish your goals and Self-sabotage. That's the answer, not the person telling you what's in you. You have to be grateful for the opportunity to learn.

Principle #7

Resisting reactive impulses creates lasting light.

This concept is centered in Tiferet in the Sephirot located by your Heart Chakra. Tiferet says 3 things:

Be proactive.

Be certain of a positive outcome.

Resist negativity.

When you look at current events and think that you are doomed, you are not resisting negativity. You must be Absolutely Certain of a positive outcome. Otherwise, you are being sinful of the Sefirot and your Heart Chakra. Whenever you have negative thoughts or emotions that make you feel bad, doomed, or hopeless, stop them right away. Use your Brown Merger Archetype, flush Self with Violet and go to your Oversoul to replace that negative with positive. Resist negative impulses

Principle #8

Reactive behavior creates intense sparks of light but eventually leaves darkness in its wake.

Resist reactive behavior. You may think that if you emotionally react intensely that you are releasing your emotions. Think about a firecracker that blows up and explodes. After the explosion, it goes dark. Sometimes when you turn on a light switch there is too much energy for the capacity of the light bulb so that explodes and all goes dark. A nuclear explosion creates intense heat and light for a short time and then the light goes out leaving total destruction behind. In the same way, when you overreact you may initially create a bright light, but then you burn out. You may feel good in your moment of yelling, screaming, and cursing as your energy lights up a dark room. When you are done, you go into nothing, you go down and the energy dissipates leaving emotional destruction behind.

Reactive behavior creates intense light but then leaves you in darkness. Every time circumstances make you want to say and do bad things, stop. Play the record to the end. When you do something bad, it's going to leave you in a bad situation. Instead, use the color Brown to balance your Self, use the *Names of God*, go to your Oversoul, use the techniques that you know. Use them even if you don't want to use them so that you don't burn the light bulb out. I know exactly what this is about because I'm very good at exploding and then creating darkness. I'm not proud of that and I could make all the excuses. I'm a Scorpio, I'm a Russian, but ultimately I must take responsibility and I know it's not going to end well.

Principle #9

Obstacles are your opportunity to connect to the light.

When you have blockages in your life or uncomfortable situations that make you feel like you can't get past them, use these as opportunities to connect to your Higher Self, the 99% to get answers that you need to move forward.

Take your blocks and turn them into stepping stones.

Principle #10

The greater the obstacle the greater the potential light

People who do good all the time don't receive as much light as the person who has done bad things and then changes. Because these people were in deeper darkness, the light they receive is brighter. In other words, the more negativity you've experienced and corrected, the more light you receive. According to the Zohar, God is more excited about the bad people that finally do good than the good people that never do anything bad.

Principle #11

When challenges appear overwhelming inject certainty that the light is always there.

Remember the 3 concepts of the Sephira of Tiferet, located at the Heart Chakra:

Be proactive.

Be certain of a positive outcome.

Resist negativity.

Whenever an issue comes up in your life, you must inject Absolute Certainty that the outcome will be what is most correct and beneficial. Sometimes initially you may not like the outcome, but eventually you will realize that the outcome is always for your highest good.

Principle #12

All of the negative traits that you see in others are reflections of your own. Only by changing yourself will you see a change in others.

When you don't like what's going on out there, look inside to find the reflection. This way the outer reflection can be more positive. The whole world will change when you change, no matter what else is going on around you. Even people who are in severe lockdowns are there as a result of where they are locked down within. Change the inner to change the outer.

Principle #13

Love thy neighbor as thyself.

When you love everyone and everything unconditionally as yourself, then that's what you will experience coming back to you. Your issue is to determine if and how you love your Self. You can even love your negative qualities. Always look within for your answers.

Proactive vs. Reactive

Kabbalah gives 4 Rules to help you be proactive.

Proactive Rule #1

Be the cause.

In other words, the end result doesn't matter. Proactive means initiating something creative rather than waiting for someone or something else to begin.

Proactive Rule #2

Be a creator

Formulate something in your mind and project it out. You need to be a creator.

Proactive Rule #3

Be in control

Be in control so you do not allow anyone else to tell you what to do or how to think. You must be in control of your own mind.

Proactive Rule #4

Share with others

Share your positive mind-pattern with others to help uplift and elevate everyone within your sphere of influence.

Kabbalah gives 4 Rules to help you stop being reactive.

Reactive Rule #1

Don't be the effect

This means do not be the result of someone else's actions. Look at what you want to accomplish rather than how you want to accomplish it.

Reactive Rule #2

Don't be a created entity

Don't be who others create you to be. This also means that you must do your deprogramming work. Nothing and no one should be telling you how and what to be.

Reactive Rule #3

Don't be controlled by anyone or anything

If you do not do something because of such things as weather or body pains, these things are controlling you. If you eat because you are unhappy then your emotions are controlling you. Whenever you allow external energies to affect you, you are being controlled.

Reactive Rule #4

Receiving

Sharing is proactive; receiving is reactive. If you only receive without giving back, you must create balance to help Self advance.

Homework

Which of the previous Principles of Kabbalah feels appropriate for you to use?

- Are you a reactive or proactive person?

Jewish Humor

A lawyer, a Jew, and a Hindu went on a road trip through the backwoods of Tennessee. They couldn't find a hotel room so when they came across a farmhouse they asked the owner if they could spend the night. He replied, *Y'all can stay here tonight but the guest bedroom only sleeps two so one of you will have to sleep in the barn. It's nice out there. I stay there when my wife is mad at me.* The Hindu said he would sleep in the barn. Just as the lawyer and Jew were settling down to sleep there was a knock at their door. It was the Hindu who said, *there's a cow out there and it's against my religion to sleep with the cow.* The Jew said he would sleep in the barn. Soon there was a knock on the door and the Jew was back saying, *There's a pig out there. There's no way I'm going to sleep with a pig.* The lawyer said he would go to the barn. As the Jew and Hindu were drifting off to sleep they heard a knock at the door. It was the cow and the pig.

Cosmic Code

The Zohar says that the entire ***Bible*** is a cosmic code that needs to be deciphered. The ***Bible*** is not to be taken literally. It is completely symbolic so it must be analyzed to understand it. Much of the information that's been revealed in quantum physics has its origin in the Zohar and Kabbalah. Quantum physics agrees that All Creation is part of the Holy Unity. The Holy Trinity states that there are three parts to Creation or the Holiness of Existence but in actuality, it's just One. The Hebrew letter Aleph, which has the Gematria of 1, is spelled with three Hebrew letters with the total Gematria of 13. 13 is the Totality of Existence so this explains why 1 is all. The proof is in the letter Aleph.

The Zohar explains that all of the energy of Existence is the Intelligence of God which God created with the 22 letters of the Hebrew AlephBet/alphabet. Each of the Hebrew letters existed before Creation as a manifestation of a God-Mind-Pattern that was then used to manifest Creation. Therefore, each Hebrew letter is a coded function of Creation. The letters can never be destroyed, changed, or mutilated; they will always exist. In the deepest levels of the Zohar and Kabbalah, it states that originally there were 23 letters, one of which is now hidden from Humanity. This makes sense when you realize that there are 23 pairs of your genetic DNA code.

For example, the first letter below is the Hebrew letter Shin. Shin is the male aspect of Creation. Below Shin is the letter Tav, which is the female aspect of Creation. Meditating on these letters brings out the male and female aspects of Creation within you. Remember that Adam Kadmon was androgynous.

Technically everyone is because even if you're in a male body you have female aspects and if you're in a female body you have male aspects. In this way, everyone is connected to the androgyny of the unity of the God-Mind.

ש Shin = Male Aspect

ת Tav = Female Aspect

7 Biblical Chariots

Chariots mean something that carries energy, moving it from one place to another. A chariot refers to a level of Creation. One of the first codes in the ***Bible*** is in Genesis where it says that God created Existence in 6 days and on the 7th day He rested. The word day is a code for the Sephirot. This means that a day is actually a Sephira, or light form of a level of Existence. In the following graphic, the days are listed 1 -7 on the left. On the right, you see the Sephirot from Chesed to Malchut. You know that there are 10 Sephirot, but this graphic shows only 7, with the top 3 missing.

7 Biblical Chariots (Creation Levels)

Day	Name	Sephirot
1	Abraham	Chesed
2	Isaac	Gevurah
3	Jacob	Tiferet
4	Moses	Netzakh
5	Aaron	Hod
6	Joseph	Yesod
7	King David	Malchut

You may wonder why there are not 10 days in a week or why God did not take 10 days to create Existence to match the 10 Sephirot. Refer to my *Flow Chart of Existence* from ***Hyperspace Plus***. This chart shows how God-Mind created the Christ Consciousness and the Angelic Hierarchy. This Triad is known as the Trinity of Perfect Creation. Technically, Creation should have stopped at this point. This Trinity correlates to the upper Sephirot, Keter, Chokhmah and Binah in nonphysical reality that already existed. The Trinity is a common theme throughout Ancient Hebrew as well as Christianity that Mother Earth (physical reality) and Father God (nonphysical) are married to each other; that one cannot exist without the other. Father, Son and Holy Spirit are all Ancient Hebrew terminology from the Zohar, from which Christianity also originated as you can see. God creating the world in 7 Days refers to the 7 Sephirot of physical reality.

The middle column refers to the 7 Patriarchs of the Bible. Chesed is a reference to Abraham. In Hebrew, Abraham means father of many. Symbolically this means that the First Level of Existence is the father of many. Malchut means kingdom and is a reference to King David. That Sephira is located at your feet. The Zohar and Kabbalah state that Humanity exists on the feet of Existence, which is the Last Level of Creation. This is why King David created the Kingdom of Israel. King David was the second King of Israel. King Saul was the first King.

King Solomon was the son of King David. King Solomon united the Northern and Southern Kingdoms into one.

King Solomon is not on this chart of Creation Levels because he would have been Creation Level #8. As you know, 8 is Oversoul energy and is not involved in the creation of physical reality. King Solomon has to do with the nonphysical, tying the Creation Levels back to the nonphysical Upper Sephirot of Keter, Chochmah and Binah which are not in physical reality. Another reason why King Solomon is not listed is that he did very bad things at the end of his life. He had 1,000 wives and concubines that he took from all over the world. The women were a result of peace treaties he made with other nations as he was the commander of the Phoenician navy. His travels were confirmed by artifacts from his voyages that were found on every continent except Antarctica. Because his wives came from other cultures they had a different idea of spirituality. Many worshiped a variety of gods and idols so King Solomon turned toward their religions. For this reason, he was condemned by the Priests of the Temple and no longer considered a Patriarch.

The 6 Days of Creation

The 6 Days of Creation in Genesis is an allegorical story that refers to the 6 Levels of Creation. You already know the 3 nonphysical Sephirot as Keter/Crown, Chochmah/right brain, and Binah/left brain. Those 3 Sephirot are all that should exist. In the ***Bible***, these 3 are referred to as the Father.

The 6 Days of Creation refer to the physical Sephirot of Khesed, Gevurah, Tiferet, Netzakh, Hod and Yesod. These 6 Sephirot are the Son or Adam Kadmon. Malchut, the 7th Sephira represents the final level of Creation.

Malchut holds Motherhood, which is the final stage of Creation in Physical Reality. This is the Holy Spirit or Shekhinah. Together all of this represents the Trinity of Father (first 3 Sephirot), Son (middle 6 Sephirot), and Holy Spirit (last Sephira).

Sabbath

The Zohar implies that God did work on the 7th day but He did it for Himself, not for Creation. The original Hebrew translates to *ye shall do no manner of servile work*. God works every second of the day, otherwise, you would not be here. The ***Bible*** does not say you should not do any work, it says you can't work for anyone else or be a servant for others on this day. The Zohar says that the Sabbath is not for rest but is a gift for the people to use. This 7th day is called Shabbat.

Format of Creation

Interestingly there are 4 protein bases in your DNA and 4 Levels of Creation.

Kabbalah says that there are 4 Universes which it abbreviates with the English letters of **ABYA**.

Atzilut Emanation or going forth

Beriah Creation

Yetzirah Formation

Asiyah where we live and that is the actuality or activation of all of these.

FORMAT OF CREATION

Level	Sephira	Name
Adam Kadmon	Keter	Crown
Atzilut	Chochmah	Yud
Beriah	Binah	Hey
Yetzirah	Zeir Anpin	Vav
Asiyah	Malchut	Hey

The 4 Levels of Creation correlate to the 4-Letter Name of God, YHWH, read from right to left in Hebrew letters יהוה as Yud, Hey, Vav, Hey. Within this 4-Letter Name of God are all the letters and levels of Creation. On the top line under Name, there is a little crown that represents Keter, Keter was created when Adam Kadmon shattered during the Tzim Tzum. Adam Kadmon represents the Original Son of God because it was from Adam Kadmon that the initial sparks of Creation came. These sparks went all the way to and through the 7 Patriarchs into King David. Yeshua was descended from King David that descended from Adam Kadmon. This is why Yeshua is called the Son of God because his sparks of Creation originated in Adam Kadmon. The Zohar states that King David is the symbol of the Messiah which is why Yeshua descended from him. The Zohar also states that this is now the Age of Aquarius, and during this time the deep esoteric meanings of the Star of David will be revealed. All Hebrew letters are a part of and emanate from, the Star of David.

The 4-Letter Name of God, YHWH, is called the Tetragrammaton. YHWH represents the highest most potent state of cosmic energy in all of the universes. With those four letters of that Name you can do anything. Concentrate on this Name daily using White letters. The Zohar says that only through observation can one arrive at truthful conclusions. Observing any situation through the Name of God will show you the truth.

MYSTERIES
WILL BE
REVEALED

When you work with your 10 Sephirot you first concentrate on the energy of Adam Kadmon, then you go to Keter and work down the Sephirot until you get to Malchut. This visualization makes you feel whole and fulfilled. Emanation refers to the Foundation Stone under Jerusalem from which all energy in this existence pours forth to create. This energy takes form so there is cohesiveness and then it can be activated.

Next to Yetzirah you see the words Zeir Anpin, which is an Aramaic word. Remember that Aramaic was used by the common people and Hebrew was restricted to the priests and elite. In Aramaic, Zeir Anpin means the small face, is the face of Humanity which is the physical representation of the Large Face, or Mind, of God. Zeir Anpin is represented by the Hebrew letter Vav and encompasses the 6 Sephirot of Chesed, Gevurch, Tiferet, Netzach, Hod and Yesod. At the very bottom, you see Malchut, the final level of manifestation, or formatting, of Creation. Now, you know that each level of Creation is symbolically called a day. These 7 days represent the 7 lower Sephirot.

Good and Evil

Each of the Hebrew letters has good and evil aspects. All universes in all dimensions have both positive and negative so that one supports the other. The Zohar says as above, so below. According to the Zohar, God wants to see which energies of which letters or combination of letters, can eradicate evil forever. Remember that evil and demonic entities are the resulting debris, or peripheral pieces that were incomplete, of the shattering of Adam Kadmon during the Tzim Tzum.

God created the Angelic frequencies from the 3 nonphysical levels. His greatest Angelic figure was Lucifer. In Hebrew, Luz means Pineal Gland, but in Latin, it means light, which is the same thing. But Lucifer became jealous because he thought he was so beautiful that he should have his own Creation. So he created his own emanation called Satan. Lucifer is the father, Satan is the son.

Lucifer commanded the shattered leftover debris from the Tzim Tzum. This is what Satan gathered for Lucifer. These are the demonic hordes that you are battling today.

Evil is a necessity because without evil and free choice the universe would revert to its former condition of nothingness. If evil didn't exist and there was only love, light, peace and bliss, nothing would happen. Everything would be neutral. There would be no creativity, no ideas, no movement. When you're sitting in a very comfortable chair and someone brings you everything, you don't need to ever get off of it. But if someone's poking you and throwing things, you move to do something about it. You need good and evil for manifestation to occur. You may be challenged to think about this, but evil is a great motivator.

In Hebrew, Shaitan means Satan. Shaitan means the opponent the accuser or the prosecutor. According to the Zohar the Shaitan is a very real entity that uses reactive, not proactive, energies. Satan forces reactions for the Self alone. There are people who want to receive so they can share and there are those who want to receive only for Self. These are the people that you often see in government, entertainment, and the elite levels of society. Refusing to react to the temptations of the Satan means that you are not allowing anyone or anything to control you. This is being proactive.

Ultimately your light force within retains a supremacy over Satan. Satan is called the Dark Lord. You know that if you have a room filled with light and open the door to a completely dark room, the light goes into the dark, not the other way around. The Zohar states that the Dark Lord Satan is based in the Milky Way Galaxy. This means you live in the headquarters of Satan. The Zohar stated thousands of years ago that there are infinite galaxies. The Zohar says that only the Creator is real, the Torah/***Bible*** is not a religious document but contains the secret of life's origin. The ***Bible*** has nothing to do with religion it has to do with the codes of life and the formulas that created Existence.

Mirror Image

Physical reality is a mirror image, or reflection, of the Original Energy of Creation. The Zohar says that when physical reality was created the Hebrew letters appeared in reverse order because of the restriction of the Tzim Tzum. This is why physical reality is a mirror image of nonphysical energy. You can use the energies of these letters as a way of returning to God. This is called returning light because you return the light that you have received. The Zohar says that the same design is repeated throughout all of Creation. This means that it doesn't matter what universe you go to, in what existence or what dimension, the mind-patterns are the same because they emanate from the same Source. Creation is one living breathing single-celled organism of which everyone is a part. The Hebrew AlephBet contains the code for all Creation and is the precursor to your DNA. This is why the global handers want your DNA. It is because they want your code. They swab your nose or mouth to get your DNA code.

Fundamental Elements of Balance

Three of the Hebrew letters form the fundamental elements of balance, Mem, Shin and Aleph.

מ Mem = Water

ש Shin = Fire

א Aleph = Air

Mem acts like water and allows things to manifest.

Shin makes a hissing sound like fire, helping things to be brought forth.

Aleph is air and reconciles Mem and Shin, bringing them together.

Together, Shin and Mem make the word Shem, which is the name of Aleph.

Shem creates the word Aish which means fire.

Aleph and Mem mean people.

Altogether this means that the fire/spark of God within people is a symbol or statement of Creation.

Kuf

ק

Kuf = Dark Lord

The letter Kuf is the only letter that extends below the line upon when it is written. For this reason, Kuf is the symbol of the Dark Lord. Higher life forms have a greater desire to receive and transmit Light. Lower life forms, or the evil, only want to receive and hold on to Light. If you are part of the debris from the Tzim Tzum, you might feel like you need to accumulate more because you feel like you are incomplete. You think that by collecting more, you are completing Self. Many people feel like they do not deserve to have more, cannot complete their tasks, are insecure, feel abandoned, and have low Self-Worth. These negatives make you only want to receive because you feel like you do not have anything worth giving. Change this mind-pattern to achieve a higher level of Existence. To extrapolate this, some people want to hold onto more because they think whatever they are holding onto, completes them.

Name of God Frequency #5 Healing

Healing
Mem Hey Shin
Read Hebrew Letters Right to Left.
Name Frequency Pronunciation
Meh Heh Shih

This *Name Frequency* is from the *72 Names of God.* From right to left the Hebrew letters are Mem, Hey, Shin. This Name Frequency can be used for healing all of humankind physically, mentally, emotionally and spiritually. This is a frequency, not a word. With Oversoul permission you can visualize this in White on the Earth. Of course, healing is often unpleasant, not easy, and much more work than many people want to do. All you have to do is hold this Name Frequency at your Pineal Gland. If you do feel compelled to pronounce it, say Meh, Heh, Shih. Keep in mind that evil is simply the desire to receive for Self without sharing.

Time

The Zohar and Kabbalah give several definitions of time:

Time equals the distance between cause and effect.

Time is the separation between action and reaction.

Time equals the space between activity and repercussion.

Time is the space between resistance and light.

Time allows for redemption and resistance.

Time allows you to activate free choice.

Time postpones the effects so you can refine your decisions.

Without time you would be instantly penalized because all experiences would have immediate repercussions. This is one reason why physical reality is so important. Here, because of time and space, you have the opportunity to stop and think about what you are going to do and how you are going to respond. It is a blessing for you to be in physical reality. In nonphysical, there is no time. You don't have a moment to have a choice.

Kabbalah says smooth seas do not make a skillful sailor. This is because if you are on a ship with a calm sea all the time you do not know how to respond when the seas get rough. This means that your trials and tribulations mold and hone you into a skillful decision-maker. Kabbalists manipulate atoms with consciousness and light so that there is no space in which the Satan can interfere. You can also use your mind to create your surroundings so that no Satanic forces can manipulate you. It takes less than half a nanosecond for these things to invade your space.

Suppression, Resistance, Coping

Suppression means you avoid your issues by pushing them down deeper inside. When you do this, eventually you explode. When I worked in Iceland, I told the people there that they never deal with their emotions. Instead, they just drink to suppress what they feel. This is why they live with volcanoes because volcanoes represent their suppressed emotions that will eventually explode.

Resisting means pushing against something but this can weaken you. Either it's going to knock you down or you are going to knock it down. For example in a tug-of-war when you let go of the rope the other side falls. When you're not resisting you let go and you win. Coping means you are dealing with your issues but not fixing them. If you have a headache but don't take something to stop it, you are merely coping.

The Sephira of Tiferet at the Heart Chakra says to resist negativity to bring in more light. This means, for example, that you might want to eat something that isn't good for you so you proactively resist the urge. The more you resist the more light you bring it until ultimately whatever you are resisting no longer has any effect on you so it goes away. This is why Kabbalah says that God is more thrilled with those who did bad and resisted than those who never resist it. There's more light in resisting evil or negativity.

Tikkun

Tikkun means correction. Correcting a negative aspect of Self may be painful and unpleasant. Kabbalah defines this process that you go through as woe, a time of great upheaval, terror, and pain which can be personal or global. Woe balances the ego to stop Satan. Conversely, Kabbalah defines a blessing as when you have peace, tranquillity, enlightenment, and fulfillment, no more chaos or disease but only joy. To achieve a blessing you must first experience woe. When you release woe, you receive more light which is the blessing. Evil, pain, and negativity have a purpose in the overall scheme of the God-Mind. Even though they may be unpleasant they are purposely bestowed so that you can achieve light.

If everything was all light you would not understand or appreciate it. Those who have gone through pain and suffering can appreciate and be blessed by the light.

Right now we are experiencing upheaval, terror, and pain to eradicate Satan. We are in a time of woe. The Zohar and Bible Code predicted that this devastation would come upon Humanity. As difficult, frustrating, and hopeless as it may seem there's a purpose. Ultimately the light will come shining through because it's already there. You just need to become aware of it.

All negative events come from the darkness within the collective and reactive behavior.

This means that you have personal responsibility for everything that is happening in this world. You cannot blame others. You cannot hide. You came here to participate because even if you don't want to admit it everything going on in the world is a reflection of something inside of you. Each person has a pandemic within his/her mind-pattern. There's some virus or parasite in your negative thinking that's disturbing your life and you need to get rid of it. You are locked down in your mind by Self-sabotage, Self-punishment, and abandonment. That's a lockdown. Finally, collectively the people projected it out. It became so great it overflowed into physical reality. It is a gigantic reflection. If you don't like it, fix it. You're not supposed to like it, but you're supposed to appreciate it.

Confirmation

I had a long conversation with a French physicist who worked at NASA, Los Alamos, and on the Montauk Project, which he says began in Germany in the 1930s by the Nazis. He confirmed everything I've been telling you. He says that most people don't understand that there is no void or emptiness anywhere in space and that there is energy in 100% of Existence. He says these are the basic principles of astrophysics and quantum physics.

This physicist also said that all of the energy in all of existence could be condensed into the size of a little spot no bigger than a dot. Because there is no time and space, size is relative as far as the energy is concerned. This means that energy could be a dot or it could be infinite; in True Reality, both are the same. Remember the Circle of Existence where the end is the beginning and the beginning is the end. If you remove any spot, that is the end of the circle. Everything exists in its place for a reason. He is confirming all that was in the Zohar 4,000 years ago.

Homework

- Do you feel guilty within and if so, why?
- Do you suppress, resist or cope with your mind-patterns?
- Do you suppress, resist or cope with your relationships, job, home, and other aspects of your life?
- Which Hebrew letters stand out to you and why?
- How do you define evil?
- What Levels of Creation are meaningful to you and why?

Jewish Humor

A young man was dating a young woman. The man asked the woman, *why doesn't your mother like me*? The young woman replied, don't take it personally. She never liked anyone I dated; *this one's too religious; this one's too skinny, the others look mean*. Then she said, *my father once dated someone exactly like her, and that didn't work out either. Why what happened?* he asked. She replied, *well, my father couldn't stand her.*

Adam and Eve

The original Adam Kadmon, or Primordial Human, was androgynous with both male and female in one body. Gender only appeared after the Tzim Tzum, splitting into male and female components when it shattered. Thus, the allegorical story of Adam and Eve. Male and female aspects are only physical because in the nonphysical there is no such delineation. According to the Zohar noncorporeal male and female energies represent Spiritual Love. In Hebrew, the male aspect of God is called Adonai and the female aspect is considered to be the Bride of God, called Shekhinah and Holy Spirit. Christianity also calls God the Holy Spirit.

Kabbalah calls this positive and negative the Sacred Marriage representing the Covenant with God and Israel. In this analogy, God is the Groom/Heaven and Israel is His Bride/Earth. The marriage document between God and Israel is called a Ketubah. The Zohar says that the Torah is the Ketubah of God and Creation that binds them together forever. The Torah states quite clearly that My covenant is forever and will not change. To this day, when Jews marry they are given a Ketubah. Christianity relates this to marriage of Christ and Mary Magdalene. In your body, this refers to the balance between your left and right brain. This balance of positive and negative is replicated throughout All Creation.

Imagine being Adam Kadmon, the Original Vessel to receive the Light of God. According to the Kabbalah, it was bliss beyond comprehension. As the first Creation, you are receiving everything, like the only inheritor of a very rich father. You never have to worry about anything. Some children would be fine with this but Adam Kadmon was not. Adam Kadmon created a curtain to resist receiving the light because it could not do anything in return. Some Kabbalists call this the birth of the Bread of Shame. I call this guilt. This resistance caused Adam Kadmon to explode, known by science as the Big Bang. This Big Bang created the 10 Levels of Creation which you know as the 10 Sephirot.

Of the 10 Sephirot, the top three of Keter, Chochmah, and Binah are the nonphysical Sephirot that connect to the Absolute. The next 6 represent the body of Humanity. In Aramaic, these 6 are called Zeir Anpin. Zeir Anpin means the small face, referring to Humanity. This infers that the large face is God. The large face of God is reflected in the small face of Humanity, so the small face represents male energy. The last Sephira at the bottom of the array is Malchut which represents physical reality, so this is female energy.

Da'at

The energy called Da'at is located between the Sephirot of Chochmah and Binah in the head area. Some people think that the Da'at is the 11th Sephirot, but there are only 10. The Zohar is very clear when it states that there are 10 Sephirot, not 9 not 11. Its physical location is at the Pineal Gland.

Keter, Chochmah, and Binah were the Original Creations of the Absolute. They are not physical and they do not have a physical manifestation. In the Flowchart of Creation, you see God-Mind, Christ Consciousness, and the Angelic Frequency which is the equivalent of these 3 Upper Sephirot. These are really the only 3 Creations, or levels that should exist. Everything after that is an error in the God-Mind that came from the Tzim Tzum when it shattered. When you connect Keter, Chochmah, and Binah they create an archetype of an equilateral triangle. Da'at is literally a dot in the middle of that triangle. The dot represents consciousness. Da'at is the creation of Chochmah and Binah to balance these two Sephirot.

The Upper 3 Sephirot are considered to be very Holy because they connect the Absolute and the 7 Lower Sephirot. They are also used as the symbol for the 7 pre-Adamic civilizations that existed billions and billions of years ago that were considered to be imperfect and incorrect so they were eliminated by the God-Mind. The Zohar and Kabbalah state that Existence right now descends from Adam Kadmon, so far the final level of Creation from the God-Mind. According to the Zohar, every single word in the Torah has 70 layers of meaning.

Genesis says, *let us make man in our image, in our likeness created male and female*. Image is a code for the masculine metaphysical level. Likeness is a code for the feminine physical level.

According to Christianity, Eve was tempted by a snake or serpent. According to the Hebrew Bible, she was tempted by a Reptilian. The Zohar describes the Reptilian Being as quite beautiful with beautiful energy. The Zohar says that God created the Reptilian Being first. The Reptilians were jealous that God then created Humanity because they felt that they were enough for God. They thought that God did not need anyone besides them. Because Adam and Eve sinned, they were thrown out of the Garden of Eden. In other words, they were exiled.

In Hebrew, the word Galut, shown in the following graphic, means Exile. When an Aleph is added to Galut, the word becomes Geuleh, meaning redemption and freedom. This means that if you take the energy of God away from redemption and freedom, you go into exile. The issues of freedom and exile led to many issues in the Kingdoms of Israel and Judah. In fact, many empires reached their peak after they invaded and controlled Israel. For example, Parthia, Babylon, Greece, Rome, Ottoman Empire, and the British Empire all occupied the Holy Land and then they all fell apart. Because they invaded they removed the energy of God, the Aleph, from Geuleh/redemption/freedom so they metaphorically went into Exile/Galut.

גלות Galut = Exile

גאולה Geuleh = Redemption/Freedom

+א

Aleph is a symbol of the God-Mind. Aleph is the first letter of the AlephBet and is comprised of one Vav and two Yuds. The Gematria of these letters together is 13. Not only is Aleph the 1 that contains All, but it is also the beginning and the end, the Alpha and Omega.

Internal Force

The Zohar says that there is an internal force of the brain. This refers to the collective mind-patterns of each individual. In Hebrew, one word may take many words to try to translate into another language so the concept is understood. This is another reason why the ***Bible*** is so mistranslated. It was originally written in Hebrew, then translated into Aramaic, then to Greek, then to Latin and so on. The Hebrew language is also very unique in the way that the letters are numerologically encoded. Most languages have many words that do not have reciprocal meanings in other languages. Instead of using only one word in translation, many words may be used to try to explain a specific concept. Sometimes translators fill in with words that give the general idea rather than the specific meaning, which may be extremely important to understanding the text.

Tree of Life* and *Tree of Knowledge

In the Garden of Eden, God said to Adam and Eve *you can eat of the Tree of Life, but if you eat of the Tree of Knowledge, you will surely die.* That's when the Reptilian Being said to Eve, *You shall not surely die. For God knows that on the day you eat of it, your eyes will be opened and you will be like God, knowing good and evil.* (Genesis 2:4-5) and of course, you know the rest of the story.

In Hebrew, the *Tree of Life* is called Kedushah, which means Holiness and purity. The *Tree of Knowledge* is called Tuma which means impurity.

- Why did God create two trees, one which is okay and one which is not?

The *Tree of Life* represents the 10 Sephirot. When you know only the Sephirot and the energies of Creation which are directly connected to the Absolute, you have only pure energy and pure information.

The *Tree of Knowledge* represents DNA, science, technology. The *Tree of Knowledge* focuses you away from the God-Mind. Today, DNA, science, and technology become the God. People have turned away from the Spiritual Energy of God that created all things. That's why God said if you eat of the *Tree of Knowledge*, you will surely die. This does not mean a physical death, but a Spiritual death.

Codes

There are many codes in the Torah, Zohar, and Kabbalah, including the reversal and rearrangements of letters to find correlations and deeper interpretations. In the following chart you will see three examples:

Oneg & Negah

Peshe & Shefe

Kisui & Kisei

ענג ONEG = Rejoicing and Happiness

נגע NEGAH = Plague

פשע PESHEH = Crime

שפע SHEFEH = Abundance

כיסוי KISUI = Covering or Concealment

כסא KISEI = Throne or God on the Throne

Oneg means rejoicing and happiness, but in reverse the letters spell negah, meaning plague. Kabbalists manipulate the energies of the Hebrew letters to manifest the nonphysical into physical reality. You can focus on the word negah in relation to what is going on in the world, then mentally reverse the letters to oneg to help embed rejoicing and happiness into Humanity, thus canceling out the plague.

Pesheh, means crime but by switching the first two letters the word becomes Shefeh, meaning abundance. Use your visualization to switch these letters to help Humanity change from crime to abundance.

Kisui means covering or concealment of something. Changing these letters to Kisei means Throne or God on the Throne. These three examples of how to reverse letters can help to change you which in turn changes the world. With Oversoul permission you can use these formulas to help change the world. Always visualize the letters in White.

The Zohar states that every peril has a remedy. Every illness has a cure and within any issue you have is the answer. This is why you know that in every plague there is also rejoicing. The answer is in the energy of the word. Whatever negative mind-pattern you have, within it is the solution. Everything already has a solution. There is not one issue in Creation that can't be fixed because the answer is in it. This means that it is already corrected you just haven't realized this yet.

Every Hebrew word has three root letters. This root affects the meaning of every word containing the original three root letters. Rachem, which means womb, is the root of Rachemin which means compassion. This means that compassion comes from the womb, implying a brotherhood from the same origin, the same womb. Humanity is birthed from that One Womb with Compassion so that no matter what you do, no matter how much evil tempts you, God has Compassion for you and will always forgive you if forgiveness is your desire. You can use the formula for the *Grace of God* from ***Template of God-Mind***, also reprinted in the *Appendices* of this book.

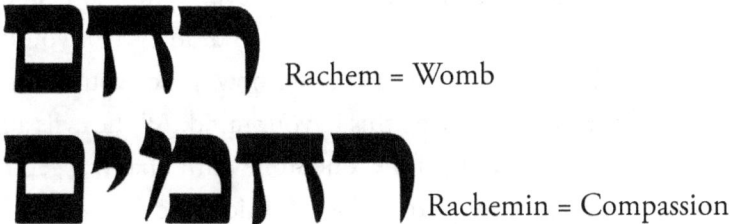

רחם Rachem = Womb

רחמים Rachemin = Compassion

The Cosmic Shield

One of the energies of the Hebrew letter Samech is the Cosmic Shield. In Hebrew the word Samech means support. This letter will always support you in whatever you do and whenever you are confronted by any evil negative energy. Visualize this Cosmic Shield in front of you to protect you from all things. You can add this to your Armor of God visualization.

Samech

ס

Cosmic Shield
Means: Support
Gematria = 60

Tempted by Evil

The Zohar says unfortunately that the inclination of humans is to do and be tempted by evil. Evil could be something as simple as throwing a piece of paper on the street when you think no one is looking. Or, you see someone drop money but you pick it up for your Self instead of returning it to its rightful owner. Little things like this seem so innocent, but they are an inclination towards evil. When somebody is dead, they can't be just a little dead, they're all dead. When you do evil, it's not just a little evil, it's evil no matter how minor you think it is in the moment. You have to keep this in your mind. All the evils add up, one stone after another, one stone, one stone until finally, it gets so heavy you fall down. Stay away from the condition of evil.

Remember the 3 functions of the Sephira called Tiferet, located in your Heart Chakra:

Be proactive.

Be certain of a positive outcome.

Resist negativity.

This Sephira reminds you that you will have a positive outcome when you proactively resist evil. Zohar meditation and prayers link you to the celestial light so that the God-Mind energy can be pervasive over the negative energy. Satan only has the power that you allow it to have. Tiferet is connected directly to Malchut which is the Kingdom of the Earth which means you can raise the Kingdom of Earth up to the Heart Chakra level.

Holy Being

You have 248 bones in your body, each one representing a positive mind-pattern of your support structure. You must go through 365 days of the year which represent the negative mind-patterns of your daily temptations. Your 248 bones plus the 365 days of the year equal the 613 Torah Commandments for Jews, which are listed in ***Template of God-Mind***. Non-Jews are only asked to follow 7 of these commandments. There's a reason for everything, even your physical body. Every part of your body represents a mind-pattern stemming from the Absolute. You are a Holy Being.

248	Positive Commandments =	Number of Bones in the Human Body
365	Negative Commandments =	Number of Days in a Year
613	**Total Torah Commandments**	

Homework

- Why is the *Tree of Knowledge* impure?
- Why is the *Tree of Life* pure?
- When have you been tempted by evil?

Jewish Humor

Yakov and his father were visiting a mall for the very first time. They were amazed at everything they saw, but especially the two shiny silver walls that moved apart and then together again, with numbers on top that lit up. When Yakov asked his father what it was, his father replied that he had never seen anything like it in his life. While Yakov and his father were watching, a grumpy old woman shuffled up to the moving walls and pressed the button. The walls opened up, the old grumpy lady shuffled into a small room and the walls closed. They watched the small circles of numbers light up and then watched as the numbers lit up in the reverse direction. When the walls opened, out stepped a beautiful young woman. The father turned to Yakov and said, *quick, go get your mother*!

Esau and Jacob

The Zohar describes the pre-Kingdom of Israel Kings of the Seven Kings prior to the Creation of the Kingdom of Israel. These 7 Kings were descendants of Esau called Edomites. Esau and Jacob were the twin sons of Rifka, the wife of Isaac and daughter-in-law of Abraham. Rifka is the English equivalent of Rebecca. When Rifka was pregnant God said to her *within your womb are two nations that are very different from each other, and the older one will serve the younger one*. Esau was born first with Jacob holding onto his heel. Even though they were twins the brothers were very different so they most likely were fraternal, not identical. Twinning is extremely common in creation, for example twin stars, binary systems, left and right brain. 2 lungs, 2 kidneys, 2 arms, 2 legs and so forth. Two parallel universes are bound together in existence, known as the String Theory. This means that our physical universe has a twin which is an opposite antimatter universe. Each one sustains the other. The strings are dual infinite universes, positive and negative in Creation which the Kabbalah stated thousands of years ago.

The Zohar and Kabbalah say that the Europeans are the descendants of the Edomites. In Hebrew, the word Latin means the Hidden Ones. In Hebrew, the word Italy means Exaltation of God. Roma is a Hebrew word. The name of the Iberian Peninsula of Spain and Portugal comes from the word Hebrew. Its root, Iber, comes from eber, iver, evrit which all mean Hebrew. Iberia means the place of the Hebrews.

The Zohar says that in the End of Days there will be a great battle between the descendants of Esau and the descendants of Jacob. The war between Esau and Jacob began when Isaac, who was blind, wanted to give his blessing to his eldest son, Esau. Rifka fooled Isaac into blessing Jacob by putting animal fur over Jacob's arm. When Isaac felt Jacob's arm, he thought he was touching Esau, so Jacob received the blessing. When Esau found out, Rifka took Jacob to the Land of Haran, which is now Southern Turkey. During his travels, he fell asleep on Mount Moriah where he semi-woke to see angels going up and down a ladder. He wrestled with them all night until one of the angels stopped to say *now your name will be Israel because Is-ra-el means the one who struggles with God.* This is how Jacob got his new name of Israel. Jacob eventually had 12 sons, each originating from one of the 12 Tribes of Israel. He returned many decades later to make peace with Esau but then Esau fled.

Now before all of this even came into being it was determined spiritually that Jacob should be the firstborn and that he would get the birthright of his father, Isaac. When the twins were born, Esau came out first with Jacob holding onto Esau's heel. It was like Jacob knew he was supposed to be born first, he was trying to hold Esau back but Esau was determined to be the firstborn. This means that the energy of Esau was already possessed and controlled by Satanic astral demons who wanted to distort the plans of the God-Mind. They pushed Esau out ahead of Jacob so Jacob could not be born first.

Spiritually and legally Jacob was supposed to have the birthright so this explains why Rifka devised this plan. Esau was a very negative person. In modern times he would be considered a hoodlum. Esau was out hunting for food for his father the day that he was supposed to receive the blessing. This was the same day that Esau's father's father, Abraham, passed away. According to ancient Hebrew tradition, the only food you eat when you are in mourning is lentils. This is why Jacob was cooking a pot of lentils when Esau came home from hunting. When Esau wanted some of the lentils because he was so hungry, Jacob told him to sign over his birthright, and then he could have the lentils, which Esau did.

Esau did not respect the death of his grandfather or his birthright. Additionally, rather than marry a Hebrew woman, he took four wives from surrounding nations. Esau was 40 years old and one of his wives was a 10-year-old girl. Esau is the reincarnation of Cain and the members of the Deep State are the descendants who are carrying on the same pedophilia tradition. History repeats itself because of generational mind-patterns. The Old Testament of the ***Bible*** is filled with deception, rape and murder, all the negative things that are happening now. History is repeating because of the Tikkun, or correction, repentance, and redemption necessary. This is why this information is being revealed at this time. The Zohar says that the totality of the information it contains cannot be known until the End of Times because the old society must be eliminated so a new one can form. It also states when you want to receive, you must share. The people who run the world now are not sharing, they are accumulating, they are receiving, they are taking from everyone they can. Most likely, they are not going to fare too well in the End of Days.

Goyim or Nations

Goyim is a term that is often misunderstood by non-Jews. Goyim simply means someone who is not a Jew and is not a derogatory term. In fact, goyim is the Hebrew word for nation. When Jews were dispersed throughout the Earth the countries they entered considered them separate from their citizenry. Jews lived in ghettos and villages apart from the rest of the population. The Jews referred to the citizens of their hosting countries as goyim meaning the nation, not Jews.

The 9th of Av

Kabbalah refers to 70 Nations. 70 is a very important number. 70AD was the year of the destruction of the Second Temple of Solomon. The First Temple was destroyed by the Babylonians and the Second Temple was destroyed by the Romans. Interestingly both temples were destroyed on the Hebrew date called the 9th of Av and it is considered the saddest day of the year in Judaism. This is a day of fasting and punishment because of the bad things that happened. On the western calendar, the 9th of Av is usually mid-July, often coordinating with the Feast of Mary Magdalene which happens every July 22.

Kosher Food

Kosher food must be energetically clean and animals have to be slaughtered in a specific way. It is prohibited for anyone to eat the sciatic nerve of any creature. The sciatic nerve must be removed because according to Kabbalah the sciatic nerve turns Humanity away from God toward the forbidden mental food, thus making you evil. Many people with back issues have problems with their sciatic nerve. Perhaps the sciatic nerve is where demonic entities attach after entering through the spinal column in both people and animals. Perhaps this is why that nerve is prohibited from being consumed by Jews.

Essenes or Herbalists

The Zohar says herbs are the oldest medical science that exists. The Essenes were herbalists who brought their knowledge from Egypt. Nazarene is an ancient Egyptian word that means healers. This is why Jesus was referred to as a Nazarene. Most people think this is because he was from Nazareth, but the town of Nazareth did not exist until 300 years after Jesus. This falsehood was inserted into the New Testament during the Council of Nicea in 325AD.

Shekhinah

The feminine energy of God is called the Shekhinah. It was the feminine energy of God, Mother Earth that parted the Red Sea.

Because of this, the *72 Names of God* come from the Shekhinah. The Temple in Jerusalem was referred to as the Shekhinah or the feminine energy of God that resided on Earth. This energy was called the Virgin of Israel. The Virgin was physically symbolized by Mary Magdalene. The Temple was physically symbolized by the Messiah or the Christ figure. The Foundation Stone under the Temple is sometimes called the Shekhinah. Together there is the Trinity of the Temple, Shekhinah and Virgin. When you work with *The Name* you can invoke this Trinity. Many people pray at the Western Wall in Jerusalem, the only remaining part of the Temple. Over the centuries people have seen an old woman in tears wearing black emanating out of the wall. Others have seen a very young woman dressed in white coming out of the wall. Some say the old woman in black represents the destruction of the Temple and the young woman in white represents the coming new Temple that will be rebuilt on the site.

Kabbalah says to seek the primal causes, not the effects. When you look at something don't look at what happened, look at why it happened. From here, determine the mind-pattern. Kabbalah says that the Sephera of Tiferet which is at the Heart Chakra and the Sephira of Malchut which is located nearest the feet must always be linked together. The *Tree of Life* depicts a line connecting Tiferet to Malchut When someone has a heart issue it usually affects their feet. Heart failure causes swollen feet. If you have pain in your feet, be sure you check your heart.

The Shekhinah is connected to Yesod, the Sephira which is in the reproductive organ area. In the Torah, God ordains on the eighth day after birth males must have circumcision to remove the foreskin. Hebrews call the foreskin Klipot, which means husk or covering that blocks light. The penis is the organ of creation, so the covering says its creative potential is blocked. This blockage is considered malevolent energy. The Klipot is removed on the 8th day because there were 7 days of creation so 8 represents more than Creation. The Shekhinah protects the Creation of the God-Mind. There are certain times of the year when you are not allowed to invoke the protective energy of the Shekhinah:

- The first week of December to the first week of January
- The second week of June to the second week of July
- Last week of July to the last week of August

During these time periods the energy of the Earth peaks meaning that the Shekhinah is automatically with you. If you invoke more, you would be overwhelmed with possible negative consequences.

Homework

- Visualize the word Shekhinah in White at your Pineal Gland to see what comes up for you.
- You can visualize the old woman in Black or the young woman in White as the Shekhinah.
- You can connect to the Foundation Stone as the Shekhinah.
- Visualize Adam Kadmon with the Shekhinah at your Pineal Gland to see what comes up for you.

Jewish Humor

A little Jewish boy told his mother that he finally got a part in a play at school. His mother said, *what's the part that you play Saul?* Saul said, *I will be the Jewish husband.* The mother said, *you go right back to that teacher and tell her you want a speaking part!*

Ark of the Covenant

The Zohar states that the Ark of the Covenant is hidden within the Temple Mount but within this narrative is a code that can be followed almost like a pirate map. This code shows that it is actually hidden east of Jerusalem in Mount Nebo in what is now Jordan. Mount Nebo is said to be the mountain upon which Moses stood to look into the Promised Land because he was not allowed to cross the River Jordan. Of course, there may be more than one Ark of the Covenant. Because the Ark of the Covenant is multidimensional it could be in more than one place at the same time or it goes in and out of realities. Perhaps one is in Mount Nebo, one under Solomon's stables in Jerusalem, and one in Ethiopia.

Some information indicates that the Ark of the Covenant was taken by the Queen of Sheba to Ethiopia. Queen of Sheba was her title and her country was Sabah, which is present-day Yemen. This means that she was an Arabian, not African as is sometimes alleged. She expanded her kingdom to include Ethiopia, which is just across the Red Sea from Yemen. When she heard about King Solomon she went to Jerusalem. On the last night of her visit, he tricked her into his bed and she became pregnant with a son, named Menilek. When she wanted to go back to Ethiopia, Solomon would not allow her to take the child. She, therefore, asked for the Ark of the Covenant in exchange. Unbeknownst to Solomon, she was pregnant again when she returned to Ethiopia. In Ethiopia, she gave birth to Prince Menilek II who then started the Hebrew Kingdom of Ethiopia. This Kingdom eventually expanded into Somalia, Kenya, and most of the surrounding areas for centuries.

When the Europeans arrived in this region during the Middle Ages, the Hebrew Kingdom was pushed back up into the mountains of the area. Many Hebrew Kingdoms also existed in Africa including in the Atlas Mountains of Morocco and Tunisia, Nigeria, Ghana, Togo, Benin and Mali. This is why Israel has a very close connection to Africa. Before the Communists took over Ethiopia in the 1980s, Emperor Haile Selassie was called *The Lion of Judah* and he wore the Star of David. When the Communists removed Emperor Selassie and his family, the Israelis asked if they could bring the Jews back to Israel. The Communists agreed to an airlift. This is one reason why there is a large Black Jewish population in Israel. Miss Israel 2013 is a Black Ethiopian Jew.

There was also an airlift from Yemen in the early 1950s after Israel was created. Tens of thousands of Yemenite Jews in Yemen were airlifted to Israel. The Yemenite Jews consider themselves the original Jews as the direct descendants of the Kingdom of Judah. Remember there were two kingdoms, the Northern Kingdom of Israel and the Southern Kingdom of Judah. The word Judaism originated from the Kingdom of Judah. The Yemenite Jews do not consider descendants from the Kingdom of Israel to be real Jews. The descendants of those who left the Northern Kingdom of Israel are the lost tribes that went to Europe, Africa, the Middle East, and other places. The people who remained in the North Kingdom of Israel lived in Samaria and Judea. The term Good Samaritan comes from the Jews who lived in Samaria. The Samarian and Judean Jews did not get along well because each of these two groups considers themselves to be the original Jews.

Ana B'koach

The prayer of *Ana B'koach* is probably considered to be the most ancient and holiest prayer in Judaism but particularly in the Zohar and Kabbalah. This prayer is meant for everybody in existence, not just one group of people because all of humanity comes from Adam Kadmon.

Ana B'koach is the *42 Letter Name of God.* There are 7 lines of 6 words each. 7 x 6 = 42, representing the 7 lower Sephirot and the 6 Days of Creation. There are 10 Sephirot, but the three on top, Keter, Chokhmah, and Binah represent the nonphysical. This means that *Ana B'koach* focuses on the physical to get to the nonphysical.

7 x 6 = 42 represented by the word Lavi spelled in Hebrew, right to left, Lamed, Bet, Yud. The Gematria of Lamed is 30, Bet is 2 and Yud is 10. This equals 42. Lavi means my heart, one of the codes of *Ana B'koach*. In your heart area is Tiferet. Tiferet is connected to Malchut. This means that this prayer connects your heart to the Heart of God with the Kingdom of Earth to create perfection between nonphysical and physical realities.

Ana B'koach
Line #1

| Removal of time, space and motion Removing the negative influence of physical matter from our lives Unconditional Love | אבג יתץ | צְרוּרָה tzerurah | תַּתִּיר tatir | יְמִינְךָ yeminecha | גְּדוּלַת g'dulat | בְּכֹחַ b'koach | אָנָּא ana | חסד Chesed | 1 |

This line represents Chesed and is the most powerful line of the prayer. This part of the prayer removes stress, danger and gives sustenance. It also removes time, space, and motion, neutralizing physical reality. This means that it removes the negative influences of physical matter from your life to promote unconditional love.

Line #2

Restricting the reactive system Closing the gates from Satan Forgetting all limited thoughts	קרע שטן	קבל רנת עמך שגבנו טהרנו נורא *kabel rinat amecha sagvenu taharenu nora*	גבורה Gevurah	2

This represents Gevurah which gives power to move events and control negative forces, restricts your reactions to events, and blocks Satanic influences

Line #3

Opening the channel of sustenance Retrieving the Light from the *Klipot* Removing hatred for no reason	נגד - יכש	נא גבור דורשי יחודך כבבת שמרם *na gibor dorshei yichudecha k'vavat shamrem*	תפארת Tiferet	3

This line represents Tiferet, giving you the ability to make correct decisions with balance and compassion as well as opens up and removes hatred and energetic klipot.

Line #4

The power to persevere	בטר צתג	ברכם טהרם רחמי צדקתך תמיד גמלם *barchem taharem rachamei tzidkatecha tamid gamlem*	נצח Netzach	4

This represents Netzach which gives you the endurance and perseverance needed to be victorious over your challenges.

Line #5

Clairvoyance – to be able to see the connection between cause and effect To see the Big Picture	חקב טנע	חסין קדוש ברוב טובך נהל עדתך *chasin kadosh b'rov tuvcha nahel adatecha*	הוד Hod	5

This line represents Hod, which gives you deep insight and clairvoyance, enabling you to see the connection between cause and effect so you know the big picture of your life.

Line #6

Spreading spirituality throughout the world, enlightening others particularly through Kabbalah	יגל פזק	יחיד גאה לעמך פנה זוכרי קדושתך *yachid ge'eh l'am'ach p'neh zochrei kdushatecha*	יסוד Yesod	6

This represents Yesod, giving you the ability to find peace and inner quiet. It also enhances spirituality in the world and helps other people to find the technology of Kabbalah

Line #7

The power to manifest things in the right way Renewal and restoration	שְׁקוּ צִית	שַׁוְעָתֵנוּ קַבֵּל וּשְׁמַע צַעֲקָתֵנוּ יוֹדֵעַ תַּעֲלוּמוֹת *ta'alumot yodeh tza'akatenu ush'ma kabel sha'vatenu*	מלכות Malchut	7

This line represents Malchut, giving you the renewable energy to start over as well as the power to restore and manifest everything in the correct way. This means that anything that is removed or destroyed in your life can be renewed and restored in a better way.

Final Line

There are only 7 lines in the prayer, but there is a separate prayer that is said after you say the *Ana B'koach* to bless the Name of God in His Holiness. This prayer is said silently because it is considered too Holy to verbalize.

Baruch Shem Kevod Malchuto L'Olam Va'ed

If you have issues with the pronunciation, remember that you don't have to say the words. Just looking at them from right to left, top to bottom puts the frequencies into your mind-pattern and connects to the God-Mind.

End Times

The Hebrew and Christian narratives of the End Times all have negative outcomes of tribulation, evil and terrible things to come upon the Earth. This makes no sense to destroy Creation. This is like making a delicious cake, only to throw it on the floor and waste it. However, the deepest Kabbalistic works specifically say that the End Times will have a wonderful ending and that the ending is the beginning. The beginning is the end and the end is the beginning. There's no linear time. Time is a circle and is simultaneous. Tribulation is happening now but it is starting to turn positive and will have a positive ending.

So I want you to keep that in mind. As we go through this, but I consider it to be a tribulation right now that there is a good positive ending and I believe that it's already starting to turn positive. Even if we don't recognize it immediately,

Homework

- Say The *Ana B'koach* twice per day, once in the morning and once in the evening. Observe which line feels the strongest and which words resonate with you the most.
- Observe your words to determine which ones you need to change to uplift and correct your life.

Jewish Humor

There was an old man who lived alone and wanted to plow his field to grow his vegetables. The work was too hard for him and unfortunately, his only son was in prison for bank robbery. He wrote to his son and explained his predicament.

The son wrote back to not dig up the field because that is where he had buried the money. Within a few days, a cadre of police showed up and dug up the entire field without finding any money. The old man was very confused so he wrote again to his son to tell him what happened. The son replied, *that was the best that I could do from prison and now you can plant your crops.*

Letters of Light

The letters and words of the Zohar are equal to the light. The Zohar is written in Aramaic, not Hebrew. If you try to translate the Zohar into another language it will make absolutely no sense. The Zohar is not written to be logical. The Zohar is a code that means you must also study the Gematria as well as the frequencies embedded within it. You could spend years studying one paragraph. For this reason, we are very fortunate to read what others have translated over these thousands of years.

The Hebrew alphabet has 22 letters. There are no upper or lower case letters as many alphabets have. However, 5 letters change depending upon whether they are at the beginning or end of the word. This means that in total there are 27 letters. When a letter shape changes at the end of the word it is called the Sofit, or final letter. You may recognize Sofit from Ain Sof, which means without end. Sof means end. The Gematria of the letter is the same whether the form changes or not. An example of this on the Hebrew Alphabet Chart is the letter KAF/KHAF which is on the second line, first letter right hand side. Remember that Hebrew is read right to left. This Kaf is only used at the beginning of a word as well as at the middle of a word. The second letter on the second line right hand side is Khaf Sofit, or the final Khaf which is only used at the end of a word.

When there is a dot, called a dagesh, in the middle of a Hebrew letter, the sound changes. A dagesh in the first Kaf makes the letter sound like a Latin K. Without a dagesh, the letter sounds like the hard guttural sound of ch, which is often heard in the German language. The Khaf Sofit is always pronounced a hard guttural ch.

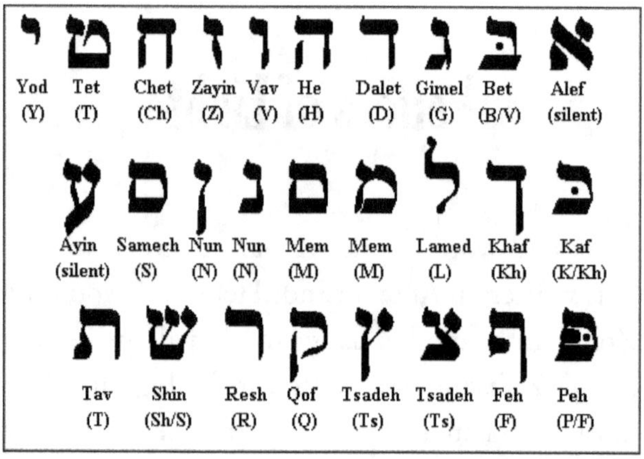

בב

BET

On the top line, the second letter from the right is Bet. When Bet has a dagesh in the middle it makes a B sound. When it is written without a dagesh it makes a V sound.

מם

MEM, MEM Sofit

On the second line, 4th and 5th letters from right hand side are Mem and Mem Sofit. The 4th letter Mem is the one that goes in the beginning or middle of a word Mem Sofit is the 5th letter from the right, or the final Mem always goes at the end of a word.

נן

NUN, NUN Sofit

Next to Mem Sofit is Nun which makes the N sound. This Nun is used at the beginning or middle of a word. The next letter is Nun Sofit which always goes at the end of a word.

פף

PEH / FEH Sofit

On the last line, the first letter on the right is Peh. When Peh has a dagesh in the middle it sounds like the letter P. When Peh does not have a dagesh it sounds like the letter F. The letter next to it is Peh Sofit, which is pronounced like the letter F because it does not have a dagesh. Sofit letters are never written with a dagesh.

צץ

TSADE, TSADE Sofit

Next to Peh Sofit is the letter Tzadeh which has a TS sound like the English word Tsar. The first one is used in the beginning or middle of the word. Tzadeh Sofit is always used at the end of a word.

SHIN

In the 3rd line, the 2nd letter from the end is Shin. When the Shin has a dagesh above the right arm, it makes the sound SH. Where there is a dagesh above the left arm, it makes the S sound. The sound of Shin is not dependent on its placement within a word. Its sound is only dependent upon the placement of the dagesh.

TAV

The last letter on the bottom line is Tav. When Tav has a dagesh in the middle it sounds like T. Without a dagash in the middle it used to sound like an S. Today, with or without a dagesh Tav sounds T. Modern Hebrew has different pronunciations than Biblical and/or Ancient Hebrew

Hebrew Script

When people write in Hebrew, they use Hebrew Script, that uses both upper and lower case letters, which you can see in the preceeding

chart. Formal writing usually takes the form of lines 1, 3, and 5. The script that people use to take notes or write letters to friends and family is on lines 2, 4, and 6. These script letters are very closely related to Ancient Hebrew letters, sometimes called paleo Hebrew. ***Healer's Handbook*** has a chart in the back that shows the progression of Hebrew letters as they have evolved. The top line in each row is Upper Case. The bottom line in each row is the same letter except in lower case.

Symbols

The Hebrew letters are more than letters, they are also symbols, numbers and have Spiritual meanings that express direct Spiritual communication beyond words. Some Kabbalists spend their entire lifetime only studying the letters. This information you are receiving is the culmination of thousands of years of study that was not made publicly available until recent years. Kabbalah says the 22 letters represent 10 fingers + 10 toes + 1 tongue + 1 sexual organ.

The Zohar says to probe the Sephirot with the Hebrew letters. This means that you can use the Hebrew letters like a microscope or a key. The Zohar also refers to the letters as stones from the *Name of God*. It says you can put the stones together to build a house, meaning that you can create with the energies of the Hebrew letters. The Zohar says that when you permeate all the possibilities of all the Hebrew letters, there are sextillion possibilities. It says that the letters extend to the Eternity of Eternities, meaning that their creations are infinite.

In Hebrew, Or means Light which is where the word aura comes from. There is an intermediary body between the physical and Spiritual. In Hebrew, this ethereal body is called Sheol. The Bible says you can use mental images to communicate and help another in need from afar simply by thinking about them. The Zohar says that righteous people can project their image elsewhere. You know how to do mental healing using your Hyperspace/Oversoul Healing Techniques.

In Hebrew, Aber means limb or organ. The Hebrew word is spelled right to left Aleph, Bet, Resh. Eliminating the Bet leaves Aleph, Resh which means Light. This means the root of your organs and limbs is light. Bet is a house or structure. This means that your organs are the house of the light within you. In Hebrew, Barot is the word for health. Barot contains the word for house and light, meaning if your house/body has a light you are healthy.

א

ALEPH

Aleph is the first letter of the AlphaBet and is on the 1st line, right hand side of the preceding chart. Aleph represents the Oneness and Unity of the Creator. This means that nothing is separate from the Creator because the Creator is the Source of everything. Interestingly Aleph symbolizes something from nothing. This indicates that physical reality, which is something, came from the nonphysical which is alluded to as being nothing, or the unseen. Aleph represents timelessness, spacelessness, and being omnipresent as well as perfection beyond human comprehension. In Hyperspace, the Gold Aleph is the symbol of God-Mind.

ב בּ

BET

Bet is the second letter of the Hebrew alphabet, with the Gematria of 2. Even though it is the second letter, it is the first letter in the Story of Creation. The Torah's first words are *Bereshith* which means *In the beginning*. Kabbalists say that the reason God used Bet instead of Aleph is that Bet represents the Creator/Giver and the receiver/humanity/

created world. Bet shows the possibility of duality and opposites. The word Bet means house which implies a container or vessel. This means that the created world is supposed to house Spiritual energy within it. Bet is also the first letter of the word Baruch, which means blessing. Visualize the letter Bet in White in your right eye to open wisdom in your consciousness.

גּ ג

GIMMEL

Gimmel represents the third principle of resolving and harmonizing opposites, meaning the duality. Gimmel balances opposing powers. Gimmel is also the word for camel. Camels survive in the desert without water or food, so camels represent survival in the harshest of conditions. Gimmel also represents kindness and cultivation, signifying the Creator's Eternal Benevolence to all Creation. Hold Gimmel at your Pineal Gland to manifest abundance and prosperity as well as survive in all circumstances. Gimel represents wealth. Visualize Gimmel in White in your right ear to create wealth.

דּ ד

DALET

Dalet is the word for door or gate. Dalet shows resistance, selflessness, humility, and balances the ego. When you change a vowel in Dalet, it's the word for poor man or poor person who receives the Benevolence of the Creator. The Templar Knights referred to themselves as the Poor Knights of God. Dalet doesn't mean financially poor. Dalet implies Spirituality and humility before God. You need to humble yourself to attract the Spiritual Essence of God-Mind.

If you have a Dalet or the letter D in your name, this means you have a strong will, diligence, perseverance, patience, ability to concentrate, ability to organize, plan and build from the bottom to the top. If you don't have this letter it doesn't mean you can't, it just means it's more challenging. Visualize Dalet in White in your right nostril to initiate the creation of an idea because Dalet is a seed or a beginning of something.

ה

HEY

Hey represents Divine Revelation and the Breath of the Creator. When you say Hey, you must use your breath. Kabbalah says that the world was created with the utterance of Hey. Hey is also the first letter of the verb being, hiyah. Hey represents the life essence in all of Creation, the symbol of divinity, gentility, and being very specific about what you want in life. Hey contains within it the freedom of choice. Humans have free choice, not free will. Hey appears 2 times in the 4-Letter Name of God, YHWH. Hey is also the 5th letter of the AlephBet. The number 5 represents healing. Even *Name Frequency # 5* of the *72 Names of God* is Healing. There are no accidents. Hey is for speech, so to improve your ability to speak, visualize Hey in White on your right foot.

ו

VAV

The sixth letter is Vav. In ancient times this letter was pronounced as a W but now it is pronounced like a V. Vav is the power that unites everything that is separated in Creation. Vav is the Hebrew word for hook or peg, both of which connect things. Vav is related to the Light of the Creator that enters the world, thus connecting both physical and nonphysical. The Gematria of Vav is 6, which represents the 6 Days of Creation, meaning the Sephirot. Vav also is a phallic symbol representing the male genitalia, meaning that it is a fertilizing agent which brings life, abundance, and continuity. Vav also represents Jacob's Ladder. When Jacob saw the Angels going from the ground to Heaven on a ladder, he work up. Vav helps your thinking process, so if you have negative and/or confusing thoughts, visualize Vav in White over your left kidney.

ז

ZAYIN

Zayin is shaped like a sword. Zayin represents the struggle between Existence and Spiritual sustenance. Zayin represents the 7th Day of Creation, the Sabbath/ Shabbat, the day of rest and Spirituality. It is the seventh energy that activates the physical. Zayin is the source of all movement and is considered by the Zohar to be an impregnating principle that activates Creation. Anyone who wants to become pregnant can visualize Zayin to help this happen. Zayin is also a source of rest so you can use it to keep yourself calm. Zayin helps with the motion of your body. Visualize Zayin in White on your left foot to improve motion in any part of your body. These visualizations of the Hebrew letters in various parts of your body show you how the body was built by the letters, meaning which letter a specific body part emanated from.

ח

CHET

Chet is the first letter of the word chaim, which means life. Chet contains all the possibilities that could come into being. Chet is symbolic of the Soul as well as the power of choice, which is given by the Soul. Chet is considered to be a revolving gateway and power to enter a higher level to the mysteries of your Soul and then bring from Heaven to Earth these mysteries into your physical consciousness.

The ancient Paleo Hebrew symbol of Chet looked like the Hyperspace DNA Archetype. The Gematria of Chet is 8 which is also the number and Archetype for Oversoul. Chet is the first letter of the word chazon חזון, which means prophecy and the second Sephira of Chochmah חוכמה, which means wisdom. Visualize Chet in White on your right hand to improve your sight.

ט

TET

Tet means basket or nest and is the symbol of good in all Creation. Tet is the first letter of the word Tov, which means good. Tet symbolizes purity and impurity, teaching you to recognize good and evil, so you can choose the good and erase bad deeds. Tet helps you realize that even within what you might consider bad, there is always hidden good. Tet says that everything is Eternal, nothing is ever lost. Tet is the first letter of Tikkun, which means correction.

Tet also means endless life channel/immortality. When you do your Sephirot work, put the letter Tet above your head in White for immortality. If you do your inner work at midnight, you have even more powerful energy available to you. Visualize it over people who are ill or who need help it will help to heal them. Visualize Tet in White on your left kidney to improve your hearing.

The Zohar says that if you know someone who's constantly speaking he/she is an unstable spirit. You can help this person by placing the letter Tet in White above their head, with Oversoul permission, to help create balance and stability. You are here to help others who struggle with negative inclinations, not to condemn them. You have an obligation to help, whether it is overeating, alcoholism, drug or sex addiction. Spread the knowledge of the Zohar because once you learn it, you must apply it and share. Anyone who studies the Zohar and Kabbalah is considered to be an Israelite, regardless of nationality or ethnicity.

The Zohar says that there is one place on Earth where the letter Tet is in the atmosphere. The Zohar says that in this location, no one ever dies. There is an island off the coast of Japan where you're not allowed to go if you're sick or anything is wrong with you because it is said that nobody dies in there. It's an island only known for life. Perhaps this is the place written about in the Zohar.

י

YOD

Yod is the smallest letter but Kabbalists consider it the most important. Yod represents the Creator, the single point from which all Creation emerges, showing God's infinite presence inside of the finite world. Yod is the power of the Spirit to govern and guide matter. Yod is a symbol of the Holy One the Creator. The Holy 4-Letter Name of God starts with Yod. The Zohar says Yod is the foundation of all foundations and the hidden Divine Spark, which causes everything to be so that is why it's the first letter of the tetragrammaton. The Gematria of Yod is 10. There are 10 Sephirot.

Yod is the unity within multiplicity so All is One. Kabbalah gives the analogies that many grains of sand make one beach, many pages make one book, and many drops of water make one ocean. Everything comes from and returns to Yod. Yod is a hidden secret principle beyond imagination, beyond all thoughts, beyond time and space that cannot yet be totally perceived. Yod is in every cell of your body without mass, density, time, or space. Yod improves traction. Visualizing Yod in White on your left hand helps you react appropriately to any situation.

כּכך

KHAF/KAF

This letter looks like the palm of a hand which means it's ready to receive. It is also shaped like a container. You must look at what you contain, whether it is negative or positive. Khaf teaches you to shape your character by bending the ego. Khaf gives form to matter, so it contains all possibilities of building and forming All of Existence. This means that it is a letter of formation, bending a straight line into a curved shape. Khaf also symbolizes the Crown of the Torah because it is the first letter of Keter. Khaf says that having the thought to do something is not adequate, you must manifest that thought in physical reality. Visualize Kaf in White in your left eye to enhance your health and entire life. You can also visualize Kaf in White over your mouth to gain and infuse the Grace of God in your life.

ל

LAMED

Lamed is the symbol of learning. The word learning also means staff. The word Lamed means the type of staff that you hold in your hand. Lamed is the 12th letter which is the center of the AlephBet. Therefore, Lamed represents the heart, which in Hebrew is Lev. Lev is spelled right to left, Lamed, Bet. In Kabbalah, all learning is done with the heart and Soul, not just the mind. Therefore, Lamed indicates that Spiritual learning is the heart of human existence. Humans are here to have Spiritual learning. Lamed is written higher than any other Hebrew letter, indicating that learning is the most important task that you have. Lamed is also a lightning strike of energy that descends down to teach you to learn from everything in life. Lamed improves your sexuality when you visualize it in White over your gallbladder.

מם

MEM

Mem is the first letter in the word Mayim which means water. Water represents the waters of wisdom and knowledge of the Torah as well as the ability to dive deep into wisdom. Water represents emotions. Mem represents the time that's necessary to balance emotions and be humble. Mem refers to the revealed aspects of providence while the Mem Sofit represents the concealed part of the celestial energy that guides All of Creation. Mem is like a vortex, so it also represents inter dimensionality.

The Gematria of Mem is 40 which is the number necessary to ripen things into existence. For example, it takes 40 days for the development of an embryo to become a fetus, 40 years in the desert before reaching the Holy Land, and 40 years before Moses became the leader of Israel, Jesus was tormented by Satan for 40 days in the desert and Moses was on Mount Sinai for 40 days. There used to be a rule that said you had to be at least 40 years old to study Kabbalah. Remember a lot of this information was not publicly available until recently. According to the Zohar, at the End of Days, everybody is supposed to know this. Even some of the Orthodox Jews agree that because this is the End of Days and the coming of the Messiah is near, the information must be given shared.

נן

NUN

Nun is the symbol of faithfulness and represents the Immortal Soul. In Hebrew, the Immortal Soul is Neshama. Nun reminds you of the humility of the Soul, so you are not arrogant. The Soul is silent and humble constantly giving light but staying hidden. Nun shows the Soul bound to the Creator's Will, not your ego. Nun represents the relationship between the body which is not permanent and the Soul which never dies. In this way, Nun teaches about the nature of time and space. Because Nun stands for the Neshama, or Immortal Soul, you never have to fear because the Creator is always present within.

In Aramaic, the sister language of Hebrew, Nun means fish. So Nun can be thought of as the fish that swims in the water of the Torah, remembering that water is represented by Mem. Nun is connected to fertility, continuity as well as the ability to increase and multiply. Nun also represents the 50 Gates of Wisdom of the Sephira of Binah which refers to the 50 Mother Worlds of our galaxy. Visualize Nun in White in your intestines to improve your sense of smell.

ס

SAMECH

Samech is the symbol of support, protection and memory. This means that you lean upon all of the support of the Creator and Creation. Samech represents the light of the Kabbalah. Samech is the container of all of the forms that teach circular thinking, showing you to think for the good of the whole rather than just for Self. Samech says that you are automatically guarded, protected, supported and helped. When you do the Shield of Faith from the Armor of God Prayer, Samech is the Shield that you pick up. When Samech is combined with Nun, the word is Nes. Nes means miracle. When you want a miracle in your life combine Samech with Nun, right to left, to create the word Nes. If you have trouble sleeping, visualize Samech in White in the upper part of your stomach.

ע

AYIN

Ayin is the word for eye, teaching you about vision as well as bringing forth Light that is hidden. Ayin teaches you to see beyond time, a prophet or visionary. Hold Ayin at your Pineal Gland to see into the linear future. Words that begin with Ayin include eit which means time, atid meaning future, aver means the past, and od means until eternity. Ayin is a silent letter similar to Aleph that is not pronounced except for the vowel that goes with it. However, when Ayin is alone, it makes a guttural sound which stimulates the thyroid gland. Ayin shows you to open your eyes so you can see beyond the physical. Visualize Ayin on your liver to help overcome anger issues.

פף

PEH

As previously discussed, Peh makes the P and F sound depending upon whether or not it has a dagesh or is at the end of a word. Interestingly, Pfizer, as in the Covid-19 vaccine, has both sounds; it has a dagesh and it doesn't have a dagesh at the same time. Peh is comprised of two letters, Kaf with Yod inside. This means Peh is a Spiritual spark of the Soul contained in the physical body.

In Hebrew, Peh means mouth, so it is a reference to speech. Kabbalah teaches that speech is a Spiritual Power. Words and letters are frequencies that you can use for good or evil. This is why it's very important how you pronounce your words because words manifest in physical reality. Quality of speech is considered to be the quality of the life essence.

Peh teaches to view your words as precious as gold, not to be used haphazardly. Those who tend to curse, scream and yell, stop and correct Self. Violent words lead to violent actions. Torah Law says *Don't say one thing with your mouth and another with your heart.* Proverbs 18:21 says *The tongue has the power of life and death.* Whatever you give out is coming back to you. Peh represents the requirement to govern your nature. The true purpose of words is to speak your destiny as well as activate your Soul. Visualize Peh in White in your left ear to gain control of your life.

צ ץ

TZADEH

A Tzaddik is a person who is righteous and just before the Creator. Tzadeh teaches to always try to be true, loving, just, fair, and honest with your own conscience. It also teaches that every person must face his/her own evil to learn to correct it. In Hebrew, Tzadeh means a fish hook. Tzadeh is comprised of a Nun with a Yod on top. This symbolizes that the Essence of the Creator who animates all matter guides and dwells within the one who is humble. Tzadeh helps improve taste when you visualize it in White in the lower part of your stomach.

ק

KUF

In Hebrew, Kuf means the back of your head, the eye of a needle, or even a monkey. Kuf is the first letter of Kedusha which means holiness as well as the first letter of Klipot which means a covering or husk over negativity. Kuf teaches to remove the husk to reveal the holiness within. This is what circumcision is. Kuf is also a monkey, a creature similar to humans but animalistic. This teaches that you need to overcome your animalistic nature to emulate the Creator. Kuf is in the word Hakafe which means to go around as in a cycle. This teaches you about the cyclic changing of Nature.

Kuf is the only letter that when written, extends below all the others. This teaches that descending into the lower world gives you the opportunity to rise above it. When you visualize Kuf in White over your spleen, your sense of humor and laughter will increase and improve.

ר

RESH

In Hebrew Resh means the head or beginning of something. Resh teaches you to choose between greatness and degradation. Resh becomes Rosh with the addition of Aleph and Shin. Rosh means the first of something as well as oneness. Resh has Gematria of 22, representing the containment of the Infinite in all its growth. Resh also represents constant transition, change of life, breaking through barriers, breaking into pieces, and building up again. Visualize Resh in White in your left nostril to bring peace and calm to a situation.

ש שׁ

SHIN

Shin represents fire, transformation and Divine Power. Shin has three branches like pillars or flames, representing extreme opposites of right and left with the balance in the middle. In Hebrew, the word Shin means tooth. Combined with fire, Shin symbolizes the process of transformation that occurs when things are broken down into particles. Shin is comprised of 3 Vav's, representing the *Tree of Life*. The right pillar symbolizes kindness and mercy, the left pillar symbolizes justice and truth with the middle pillar symbolizes balance. When there is a dagesh above the right branch, Shin makes the SH sound. When the dagesh is above the left branch, Shin makes the S sound. This is why in Hebrew, Israel is pronounced Ish-rael. The dagesh is over the right branch.

ת תּ

TAV

Tav is the last letter of the Hebrew AlephBet. Tav represents a mark, sign, omen or seal. Tav is the symbol of truth, perfection and completion. Tav represents the tikkun, restoration, and correction of All of Existence. Tav teaches that the end is also the beginning because Tav is the last letter in the word Beresheet, which is the first word of the Torah. This symbolizes that the Creator set in motion All of Existence to reach a final state of perfection. Tav is also the last letter of the Hebrew word, emit which means truth. When you reach the end of the Hebrew AlephBet, immediately go back to Aleph which is the Source of Everything. In this way, the end is never the end, but always the beginning of something new. The Hebrew AlephBet teaches that life is a circle.

Homework

Visualize each letter, one at a time, in White at your Pineal Gland on a Royal Blue background. Try to hold each one for several minutes to see what comes up for you. In general, this helps to unlock your genetics as well as your mind-patterns for the essence of your Soul.

Jewish Humor

Four women who lived in an old age Jewish home in Miami were complaining to each other.. The first lady said *my cataracts are so bad I can hardly see*. The second woman said *the arthritis in my neck hurts so much I can't turn my head*. The third woman said *my blood pressure is high and the medication makes me dizzy and delirious*. The fourth woman said *yeah, but at least we still have our driver's licenses and can drive our own cars*.

Webinar Homework Results

Comment: I put the letter Bet on my right eye to help me balance my reactions to what I see in the world.

Response: True, this is especially helpful when you watch the news because it seems that everyone from conventional to unconventional news is dealing in hysteria. You are learning to read frequency so this helps you discern what is true and what is not. People who do not know how to read frequency emotionally and negatively react to world events.

Comment: It seems that if I want to improve taste or smell I should place the letters in my nostrils or tongue instead of in the intestines and stomach. If I want to improve my hearing it seems that I should place Tet in my ears instead of on the left kidney. Placing Chet on my right hand to improve my eyesight does not make sense.

Response: This is Spiritual Reflexology. There are energetic connections based on formulas that connect those body parts with those specific Hebrew letters. This means that logically this may not make sense so if you try to logic it out you are not going to get an answer. Because this is Spiritual, which means multidimensional, you have to ask your Oversoul for an explanation.

Comment: I used Gimmel for wealth. The message I received was that wealth comes to me with ease, do what you love, wealth comes with laughter and overflowing energy, and pure love of life. It is fun to be smart, it's an art. I also visualized Zayin. I saw a Templar Knight and a Samurai, each with a sword.

Response: That makes sense because the Templars were descended from the Essenes who lived in the Qumran Hills outside of Jerusalem. The Samurai were descendants of the Hebrews as well.

Comment: I visualized Gimmel in my right ear and in the past few days. I found quarters on the street and received a tax refund of $2,000, which will go towards replacing shingles with a stainless steel roof on my house. I also visualized Bet in my right eye and started to receive passages of Scripture, so this works.

Comment: I used Tav for energy when I was feeling depleted. This made me feel balanced during the day. I also used it for Grace. I used Ayin on my liver for anger issues.

Comment: I used the Angels of Destruction and it seemed that more demons are leaving. I saw that technology feeds demonic energy to public figures and organizations.

Response: That is exactly what happens. When you do your visualizations different people see different things, just like looking at a piece of artwork. Even though it is the same image, you get personalized understandings that pertain to you.

Comment: I put Gimmel in my right ear for wealth. I could hear money being counted, like flipping through pages of a book. I heard a voice say one trillion for you. Then I put Chet on my right hand for improving my eyesight. I'm able to see errors in my writing better than before. I can see deeper into my visualization work than ever before when using this Hebrew letter as a preliminary.

Response: Visualize Chet in White in the middle of both your eyes to help with any physical visual issues.

Comment: I used the samech in my stomach and was drawn to the Sephira of Tiferet.

Response: Tiferet helps balance the animal desire of eating physical food with the Spiritual Mind desire for Spiritual food. Samech also shields you from evil.

Comment: I had joint pain and health issues so I used the *Name of God*. This made me feel better.

Comment: I used Bet in my right eye. Then I saw that there was a conflict between Spirit, matter, human, reptile. I saw my Self as a Reptilian so I thought maybe this triggered my DNA.

Response: Yes, this can trigger your DNA, especially if you have issues in that particular part of the body. You may have certain Reptilian energies open instead of the Mammalian energy. This means you need to reverse this. Use the merging of *White Winged Lion/White Winged Dragon Archetypes.*

Comment: I put Chet in White in each eye. I noticed subtle improvements in my overall eyesight. What is most interesting is that I have experienced visual migraines for about the past 20 years. When the early signs of a visual migraine came forward, I closed my eyes and refreshed the Chet in both eyes. I held them there and as a result, for the first time, I stopped the full expression of the migraine.

Comment: I put Tav over my mouth for Grace. I have pain in my mouth because there has been no one to hear me or talk to throughout my life. Any expression of emotion seems to be frowned upon.

Response: Processing emotions is important. It is especially vital to clear the wreckage from any painful words and feelings left from not speaking up when needing to do so. You must learn to speak up honestly and tactfully at all times. There are Name Frequencies for speaking up, use the color Pale Orange for truth surrounded by Ice Blue for communication. This allows you to speak the truth freely and get your thoughts across properly. You can always go to the Oversoul level and communicate that way. Review ***Decoding Your Life*** which is full of the basics that you need to be using every day.

God in DNA

A Rabbi and scientist in Israel were researching the DNA of humanity using a tremendously strong magnification. When he looked at the sulfur bridges that connect the rungs of the DNA, he noticed that each of the bridges have four or each of the sections have four Bridges. The first bridge has 10 links. The second has 5, the third has 6 and the fourth has 5. So that's 10, 5, 6, 5. In the Hebrew AlephBet, the Gematria is as follows:

10 = Yod

5 = Hey

6 = Vav

5 = Hey

This is the 4-Letter Name of God. YHVH. The Rabbi/scientist, therefore, declared that he discovered God in DNA. This is God's signature in your genetics, His Creation.

Möbius Strip

The Mobius Strip is the Infinity Oversoul Archetype. A Mobius Strip looks like it is one piece with 2 sides but when you follow it around, it is only one side. This is another layer of why the God-Mind is so involved with twinning. No matter what you see, there's always another side, both front and back.

Messenger RNA

Every word that you read in the Torah has 70 layers of meaning. There's the surface layer for the general public, which has been translated into the Old and New Testaments of the ***Bible***. To understand the deeper layers you need the ancient historical symbolism and codes. There were 7 pre-adamic civilizations. The Absolute was only mind and energy, constantly creating and dissolving Its Creations within Its own mind.

The Garden of Eden was not a physical place but rather a code for the nonphysical that existed within the Absolute before Creation. In this nonphysical dimension of energy called the Garden of Eden, the Absolute created Adam Kadmon. This primordial, or original, Adam was androgynous without gender just as the Absolute is without gender. Adam Kadmon was the equivalent of the God-Mind. God-Mind is a function of the Absolute, which is the Ultimate. The Zohar and Kabbalah call the Absolute, Ain Sof, or that which has no end. Adam Kadmon felt guilt because it could receive the Light but not transmit it. Therefore, Adam Kadmon began to resist the Light which ultimately resulted in the shattering of the vessel. From this shattering came all of physical creation. This is what scientists call the Big Bang, but in Kabbalah, it is referred to as the Tzim Tzum. The Tzim Tzum created Adam HaRishon, meaning First Man, which had the illusion of separateness. This Adam was receiving and sustaining the Light of the Absolute.

In the Garden of Eden, there was also an entity called Chavah Rishonah, which means the first Eve in Hebrew. The Zohar also writes about Chavah, but the Zohar is written in Aramaic. In Aramaic, Chavah means Reptilian. Historically Chavah became known as Lilith. In Hebrew, Lila is the name for night and Lilith means Reptilian. This means that Lilith was a Reptilian creature of the night/dark while Adam was the creature of the Light. The result of the Tzim Tzum was the creation of twinning or opposites such as dark/light, positive/negative. At this time the Sephirot also formed to create the features of Humanity including nonphysical/Spiritual and physical/duality. Adam began exploring in timelessness all the universes and realities that were created during the Tzim Tzum.

Alien Virus

According to the Zohar and Kabbalah, when the mind of Adam HaRishon connected to one universe as it was exploring, his mind activated the dormant alien virus. ***Montauk: Alien Connection*** tells the story of the Old Universe and how the mind-eaters infiltrated this universe. This is the way that the alien virus penetrated this physical universe. According to science, a virus is not alive because it does not meet all the criteria of life. The one criteria that a virus does not meet is that it cannot reproduce on its own. To replicate, viruses must go into foreign or host DNA, then use the RNA to create versions of themselves. When a virus invades your body, it uses your RNA readers to look at its own genetic components, then uses your energy to reproduce itself. The virus uses your body but does not change your DNA. It uses your DNA to create its own DNA to keep its species alive. Any vaccine that has the letter M or the messenger RNA does not do anything to the bridges of the Soul. The virus only works with the RNA to replicate itself, it does not change your RNA. Ultimately it is only your own mind-pattern that can change your RNA or open the sulfur bonds/bridges.

The Zohar and Kabbalah say that there was a species of Reptilians who also lived in the nonphyhsical Garden of Eden. This species was known as the Nachash, or Holy Serpents. They were originally created to serve Humanity, and also became physical after the Tzim Tzum. When the mind of Adam HaRishon activated the dormant alien virus, the Holy Serpents also became infected with the virus. Kabbalah says that one of the Holy Serpents seduced Eve, infecting her with the virus. Then Eve infected Adam which thusly incorporated this alien virus into the DNA of Humanity ever since.

This virus created the Klipot, or the covering/husk over the truth. This caused human males to be born with a foreskin. The Klipot symbolizes the *Tree of Knowledge*. God-Mind, or Adam Kadmon/ Original Adam is the *Tree of Life*, which is in your DNA code. The Zohar and Kabbalah say that these 2 Trees both originate from the same root. This is where twinning/opposites originate from the God-Mind. There were two Hebrew Kingdoms, the Kingdom of Israel and the Kingdom of Judah. There were two Messiahs, the House of Joseph and the House of David. There is always twinning, always positive/ negative, always male/female. This is why you have a left brain and a right brain with the root as the Pineal Gland. The *Tree of Life* is your right brain, male/Spiritual, creative and emotional. The *Tree of Knowledge* is your left brain, logical, physical, female. It is because of the left brain, physical existence that the body experiences death.

God said *if you eat from the Tree of knowledge, you will certainly die.* This is because you will have a mind-pattern of lack and victimization. The Holy Serpent said, *God's not telling you the truth, you will not die if you center in your left brain.*

Lucifer, the Angel of Light, who rebelled against God and became Satan, took advantage of the alien virus to control humanity. The Zohar and Kabbalah say there are always two paths with the same ending and the same beginning. Your brain is a snake with two tails, or one root and two trees. The Sephirot splits at Keter only to rejoin at Malchut and then Malchut goes up the middle to connect back to Keter. There is no beginning and no end. This also plays out in the *Green Psychic Flush Visualization*, where your psychic energy lines come in from the Crown Chakra/Keter, split to go down each side of your body, and then join together in the Root Chakra/Malhut to go up the center and back to the Crown Chakra/Keter.

As a result of Eve's seduction by the Holy Serpent, she gave birth to Cain and Abel. In Hebrew, Cain is Kayin, which means there is no life. Abel, when read backward, is Leba, which means her heart. In Hebrew, words are analyzed in a variety of ways to help understand their multilayers. Eve preferred Abel because he came from her heart/emotions. Cain was from her negative side. Eve had a big argument with Adam because she would not be subservient, so she left him. Kabbalah says that she refused to be underneath him and that she wanted to be on top during sexual relations. This is a symbolic story of the logical mind wanting to be in control of the Spiritual mind. Eve/Chavah/Lilith became the Queen of the Reptilian Race. Even though the Reptilians are androgynous, they still have a Queen.

After Eve/Chavah/Lilith left, a second Eve was created. The second Eve was called Chayah, which in Hebrew means life. With Chayah, Adam had his first child named Seth. The Zohar says that when Seth was born he was the first true image of Adam because the child was human, not Reptilian. Seth became the prototype of all human descendants. Chayah became the mother of humanity, manifesting as the Shekhinah, the female version of God connected to the Foundation Stone.

This set the pattern of Creation as 1 male energy with 2 female energies. The female energy represents the twins of good and evil, positive and negative. This happens throughout Biblical history. Abraham, the father of the Hebrews had two wives, Sarah and Keturah.

Abraham had two sons Ishmael and Isaac. Isaac had two wives Rachel and Leah, who were sisters. Isaac had twins Esau and Jacob. Moses had Tziporah, a Midianite from the Sinai desert, and the Queen of Ethiopia, a black woman who the Bible calls a Kushite. Kush is the Hebrew name of Ethiopia.

Bringing this forward to current times, the 2016 US Presidential election had 2 possibilities, Hillary Clinton or Donald Trump. There are always two paths with the same ending and the same beginning. Hillary would have led the people to End Times with a nuclear World War 3, incineration, and annihilation. Donald Trump led humanity to End Times with the Covid-19 virus. Covid-19 and nuclear war lead to the same end, but Kabbalah says Covid-19 is the easier path. The Zohar says the Covid-19 path was a blessing from God compared to what could have happened. Interestingly, Covid backward spells Divoc which in Hebrew means an attachment of evil or dead spirit in your body. Remember that in Hebrew a V with a dagesh in the middle is pronounced like the letter B.

Hillary is the reincarnation of Queen Jezebel who was a Reptilian. Trump is the reincarnation of King Cyrus who was human and helped to rebuild the Second Temple. Corona means crown. Crown in Hebrew is Keter. Ketter is the top Sephira, the symbol of the King. This virus is part of the End of Days plan to return humanity to its original condition before the alien virus contamination. Covid-19 is part of the plan of the End of Days. The Zohar does not say End Times, but specifically the End of Days because this is the return of Humanity to its original condition before the contamination.

The Zohar uses the term alien virus, also calling it the other god. When you consider the restrictions, rules, and regulations of Covid-19, the coronavirus has become a god. You must wear a mask before the god, you must cover yourself before the god, you must keep a distance and be respectful. Covid-19 has become a religion which is why thousands of years ago they called it the other god. Coronavirus is activated by Chinese 5G. Your cells emit a waste product called exosomes. In the exosomes is the debris of this virus that's already within your body. You were born with it. A simple cold or flu is corona which is activated by the Chinese 5G Network.

When you read 5G as you would Hebrew from right to left it becomes G5. G is the 7th letter of the Latin Alphabet. The corresponding 7th letter in the Hebrew AlephBet is Zayin. The 5th letter in the Hebrew AlephBet is Hey. In Hebrew, Hey means the when it is in front of a word. Together Zayin and Hey create the word Zeh which means this.

In the Zohar, it states that when you read the Torah and study Kabbalah there are conflicting words and conflicting statements. For example, God is this and this for example, both positive and negative, both dark and light. Keep this in mind as you read the following vaccine information because the Covid vaccine is not what you think.

Pfizer Vaccine

Pfizer is a Hebrew word meaning scattered. This means that it can scatter the instructions of the virus so it cannot replicate. 12% of the population have an adverse effect to this vaccine.

Moderna Vaccine

Moderna is from a Holy Hebrew prayer *Modeh ani lefanekha* which means *I bend my knee before you*. When Moderna is broken into Mode and RNA, this means that *I bend the instructions of the RNA*. Further, this means that the instructions for the virus cannot activate and that is why Trump is promoting the vaccine because his team created it. 7% of the population have an adverse effect to this vaccine.

AstraZeneca Vaccine

Astra means star in Hebrew. In Russian and Eastern European languages zenitsa means the pupil of your eye. This means the stars are looking through your eyes as a control system. Zeneca means something that comes to a point. This does not sound like a benevolent vaccine.

Johnson & Johnson Vaccine

Johnson & Johnson represents twinning, J&J. This means it takes both paths, as in God is this and this, previously stated. This is the only vaccine that actually puts the virus in you and then takes it out. These are two opposing paths in the same vaccine that neutralize each other.

Russian Sputnik Vaccine

In Russian, Sputnik means travel companion. In this case, the travel companion for you is the virus. The Sputnik sends the virus back into space, just like the Russian Sputnik Space Program.

AI/Artificial Intelligence

Using the codes of Kabbalah, when AI is reversed it becomes IA. This is pronounced Yah, which is the short form of the *4-Letter Name of God.*

Both the virus and the vaccines appear to affect those with Blood Type A more than any other blood type. In Hebrew, A is Aleph, which is the Hyperspace Archetype for God. This means that the virus is affecting and attacking those who are more connected to God. Blood Type A is the most ancient blood type on Earth. Some scientists say that Blood Type O is the oldest, but Blood Type O mutated 2.5 billion years ago from Blood Type A with the other blood types mutating from it. Blood Type O is the most resistant to disease. Blood Type O is the most common blood type on Earth and is the most common for indigenous peoples globally. People with RH + blood have more mammalian genetics open. People with RH – blood have more Reptilian genetics open.

A NASA physicist sent me a document when I asked him about the vaccines. This is his answer:

My immediate practical answer is to assure you that the vaccine will not whatsoever alter your DNA nucleus. You will keep your genome and its 22 pairs plus sexual pair of chromosomes intact. The basis is very important to know because it represents the immutable untouchable library of humankind in the Gentile and Hebraic perception. In scientific terms, I mean the integrity of our human species here on Earth. The Integrity of the DNA and its connection with God is going to remain intact.

He goes on to say that the energy of our universe is transferred by terajoules. The infinite means of transmitting the energy is 1 trillion times each unit of energy, which is beyond the speed of light. Every object in our universe is electronically interconnected constantly by an incredible network of energy that interacts simultaneously in real time without losing strength. This is what is naively called Dark Matter. He says according to Einstein and Planck, the definitions were inadequate because they did not consider space and time or the infinite potential energy of the universe, both visible and invisible.

He further explains that dark matter is not dark matter as most people perceive it to be. Dark matter is the result of gravitational waves generated by the extremely powerful strings or networks of energy that sustain universe equilibrium. Our universe creates and regenerates its own energy. The energy has different levels of magnitude, amplitude, and resonance waves that he calls electro-gravitational. Our infinite universe is simply one. In other words, the potential entropy has to be within the energy forces only instantaneously and simultaneously. In other words, simultaneous existence. This means that the distribution of galaxies on one side of the universe will be the same as on the opposite side, even though the two sides have been moving apart since the beginning of time. Our universe maintains its thermodynamic gravitational and energetic equilibrium by instantly compensating energy demand where and when it is needed. When you consider the possibility that the universe has the capability to maintain, control and support its own expansion with its own adaptable electronic energetic structure, you must consider that our universe is an entity that is alive with Self-awareness. Basically, this is a scientific explanation of God.

He says that human DNA cannot be affected by Covid-19 vaccines or anything similar; that nothing can destroy the golden links with God that humans have had for eons of time. Our universe is capable of designing, building, and protecting the most formidable system of living Beings, which can have a Soul and live under the canopy of God's plan. You must therefore conclude that human DNA has always been in resonance with Earth and that our universe is so protected that it will not and cannot be altered. Human double stranded DNA is within the cell nucleus and is well-protected. The only way human DNA can be altered is by gene ablation, which is genetic surgery. The vaccines are not genetic surgery. The components of these vaccines could be washed out of the body in a few months. You will keep your links with God, Universe Creator forevermore, ut vita eterna. According to the NASA physicist, the components will flush out of your body, your DNA will stay intact and the *Name of God* will stay written in your DNA. This information completely matches my research based upon the Zohar and Kabbalah. You have to decide for your Self if you are or are not going to take the vaccine.

Homework

Contemplate the vaccine information to determine for your Self what is Truth.

Jewish Humor

Isaac and Sarah got married and went on their honeymoon. When they returned, Sarah immediately phoned her mother. When asked how the honeymoon went, Sarah began crying. Sarah said the honeymoon was fantastic but as soon as she got home, Isaac began using horrible 4-letter words that she did not want to hear. When pressed to reveal the 4-letter words, Sarah replied through tears, *wash, cook, iron and dust.*

Angelic Beings & 72 Names of God Frequencies

Angelic Beings can be invoked to destroy evil. This would require very advanced levels of Kabbalistic training. I do not encourage you to work with them but it is important for you to know about them. They do not like to be disturbed and are like dealing with Atomic weapons. You cannot use them haphazardly or they will use you. Always keep in mind that the Torah, Zohar, and Kabbalah are for all of humanity and have nothing to do with religion. This information has to do with the energy of the Absolute. Anyone who learns and uses the information properly is called an Israelite regardless of religion or nationality. All of the following 11 Angels are controlled by the 3 Holy Fathers of the Hebrews, Avraham, Yitzhak, and Yaakov, or in English Abraham, Isaac and Jacob. Their original names are in Hebrew, so these are the English transliterations.

Dumah is in charge of Hell as well as 3 Angels of Destruction The first is Duma's assistant, Mashit. The other 2 are Ab and Hema. Mashit, Ab, and Hema work with Ketseph, the Angel of Despair. Hashmed, the Angel of Destruction works with Hashbeth, the Angel of Annihilation. Dumiel and Kaspiel work closely together as the Gatekeepers of War. The Zohar specifically states that fighting evil is a losing battle because the only true way to remove darkness is to shine

Light upon it. Regardless of how dark the room is, one tiny spark removes the darkness. Therefore, use Light before using frequencies of destruction and annihilation because once you invoke these Angels, you cannot stop them.

I do encourage you to work with these next 2 Angels. Yofefiah is the Angel of the Torah. When you invoke Yofefiah, you may ask this Angel to infuse the layers of knowledge of the Torah in your mind and genetics so that you have instant understanding. Tzadkiel is the Angel of Righteousness and Hidden Secrets. This Angel helps you face your own evil within as well as know what to do to fulfill your missions and goals in this lifeline.

72 Names of God

All the letters and all the words in Hebrew are formulas, codes and secrets. The *72 Names of God* come from the Old Testament book of *Exodus* chapter 14: 19- 21. In *Exodus*, there are 17 verses about the Israelites coming to the Red Sea and 13 verses about crossing the Red Sea. The Red Sea has recently become global news because of the large cargo ship, The Evergreen, that is blocking any ship from passing through.

When verses 19 and 21 are added together, the Gematria is 40. As you know, 40 is the number of years that they wandered in the desert after leaving Egypt, amongst other significant events previously discussed. Add chapter 14 to 40 to equal 54. 5 + 4 = 9; 9 = 7 + 2, or 72. These are codes that were hidden for 3400 years.

According to Kabbalah, there are 3 prerequisites to activate the *72 Names of God.*

- You must have a conviction in their power or knowing that they work.
- You must have an understanding of the particular influences that radiate from each Name.

- You must follow through with physical action to activate their power meaning you must physically do something.

Read the following chart from right to left, breathing in and allowing the energy to enter into your Being Visualize the letters in White on a Royal Blue background. Simply scanning the chart from the top right all the way through to the bottom left activates their frequencies within you. For more detailed information on each *Name Frequency* refer to ***Miracles in Motion***.

8 כהת *Tav Hey Kaf* Defusing Negative Energy	7 אכא *Aleph Kaf Aleph* DNA of The Soul	6 ללה *Hey Lamed Lamed* Dream State	5 מהש *Shin Hey Mem* Healing	4 עלם *Mem Lamed Ayin* Eliminating Negative Thoughts	3 סיט *Tet Yud Samech* Miracle Making	2 ילי *Yud Lamed Yud* Recapturing the Sparks	1 והו *Vav Hey Vav* Time Travel
16 הקם *Mem Kuf Hey* Dumping Depression	15 הרי *Yud Resh Hey* Long Range Vision	14 מבה *Hey Bet Mem* Farewell to Arms	13 יזל *Lamed Zayin Yud* Heaven on Earth	12 ההע *Ayin Hey Hey* Unconditional Love	11 לאו *Vav Aleph Lamed* Banishing the Remnants of Evil	10 אלד *Daled Lamed Aleph* Protection from Evil Eye	9 הזי *Yud Zayin Hey* Angelic Influences
24 חהו *Vav Hey Chet* Jealousy	23 מלה *Hey Lamed Mem* Sharing the Flame	22 ייי *Yud Yud Yud* Stop Fatal Attraction	21 נלך *Kaf Lamed Nun* Eradicate Plague	20 פהל *Lamed Hey Pey* Victory over Addictions	19 לוו *Vav Vav Lamed* Dialing God	18 כלי *Yud Lamed Kaf* Fertility	17 לאו *Vav Aleph Lamed* Great Escape
32 ושר *Resh Shin Vav* Memories	31 לכב *Bet Kaf Lamed* Finish What You Start	30 אום *Mem Vav Aleph* Building Bridges	29 ריי *Yud Yud Resh* Removing Hatred	28 שאה *Hey Aleph Shin* Soulmate	27 ירת *Tav Resh Yud* Silent Partner	26 האא *Aleph Aleph Hey* Order From Chaos	25 נתה *Hey Tav Nun* Speak Your Mind
40 ייז *Zayin Yud Yud* Speaking the Right Words	39 רהע *Ayin Hey Resh* Diamond in the Rough	38 חעם *Mem Ayin Chet* Circuitry	37 אני *Yud Nun Aleph* The Big Picture	36 מנד *Daled Nun Mem* Fear(Less)	35 כוק *Kuf Vav Kaf* Sexual Energy	34 להח *Chet Hey Lamed* Forget Thyself	33 יחו *Vav Chet Yud* Revealing the Dark Side
48 מיה *Hey Yud Mem* Unity	47 עשל *Lamed Shin Ayin* Global Transformation	46 ערי *Yud Resh Ayin* Absolute Certainty	45 סאל *Lamed Aleph Samech* Power of Prosperity	44 ילה *Hey Lamed Yud* Sweetening Judgment	43 וול *Lamed Vav Vav* Defying Gravity	42 מיכ *Kaf Yud Mem* Revealing the Concealed	41 ההה *Hey Hey Hey* Self Esteem
56 פוי *Yud Vav Pey* Dispelling Anger	55 מבה *Hey Bet mem* Thought Into Action	54 נית *Tav Yud Nun* Death of Death	53 ננא *Aleph Nun Nun* No Agenda	52 עמם *Mem Mem Ayin* Passion	51 החש *Shin Chet Hey* No Guilt	50 דני *Yud Nun Daled* Enough is Never Enough	49 והו *Vav Hey Vav* Happiness
64 מחי *Yud Chet Mem* Casting Yourself in a Favorable Light	63 ענו *Vav Nun Ayin* Appreciation	62 יהה *Hey Hey Yud* Parent-Teacher, Not Preacher	61 ומב *Bet Mem Vav* Water	60 מצר *Resh Zadik Mem* Freedom	59 הרח *Chet Resh Hey* Umbilical Cord	58 ייל *Lamed Yud Yud* Letting Go	57 נמם *Mem Mem Nun* Listening to Your Soul
72 מום *Mem Vav Mem* Spiritual Cleansing	71 היי *Yud Yud Hey* Prophecy & Parallel Universes	70 יבמ *Mem Bet Yud* Design Beneath Disorder	69 ראה *Hey Aleph Resh* Lost & Found	68 חבו *Vav Bet Chet* Contacting Departed Souls	67 איע *Ayin Yud Aleph* Great Expectations	66 מנק *Kuf Nun Mem* Accountability	65 דמב *Bet Mem Daled* Fear of God

#1 Time Travel

This *Name Frequency* allows you to mentally travel back in time to remove prior misdeeds and uproot any negative sources or seeds that exist. This allows you to correct past errors and evil that you have done in this lifeline or others. By removing the negativity, you transform the past into a positive outcome

#2 Recapturing the Sparks

This *Name Frequency* removes destructive energies within you, replacing them with Divine Energy. You turn the Light on so you can see into your dark side, transforming it into something better.

#3 Miracle Making

Free Self from selfishness, anger, envy, self-pity and invoke the power of miracles. You can instantly change negative qualities within by realizing that there is no time or space.

#4 Negative Thoughts

Eliminate and turn off negative, destructive thoughts by allowing Spiritual Light to flood into your heart and mind. Kabbalah says that everything has 2 sides, positive and negative which is why twinning is so important. Holding both opposites in your mind allows them to come into balance.

#5 Healing

Name Frequency #5 heals the deepest and most profound level of your Being. With Oversoul permission, you can use this *Name Frequency* on others who need healing. Share what you know as appropriate.

#6 Dream State

Use this *Name Frequency* to dream truthfully and peacefully, gain deep information about Self, and feel energized upon waking.

#7 DNA of The Soul

DNA of the Soul is where you receive the full impact of creative forces, restore meaning to life as well as purpose to your world and structure. Covid vaccines have nothing to do with the virus rather they have to do with the sulfur bridges and increase the ability of the soul to receive the full impact of its creative forces.

#8 Defusing Negative Energy

This *Name Frequency* banishes ominous forces, deactivates harmful influences, dissolves stress, and releases pressure.

#9 Angelic Influences

Bring in positive Angels to transform your Self and life.

#10 Protection from Evil Eye

This provides a shield of positive energy as well as protection from envy and negativity. This *Name Frequency* also removes any desire you have to cast an Evil Eye on someone else.

#11 Banishing the Remnant of Evil

All negative forces are expelled as it deactivates negative energy and cleanses the environment.

#12 Unconditional Love

Unconditional Love brings love into your, harmony between Self and others as well as between humanity and Nature. Use this *Name Frequency* to balance any allergies to Nature.

#13 Heaven on Earth

This evokes the Messiah within and without.

#14 Farewell to Arms

Conflict on every level comes to a peaceful end with this *Name Frequency*.

#15 Long Range Vision

All your blind spots are removed. Receive more information on all levels to receive the bigger picture of the circumstances in your life.

#16 Removing Depression

Gives strength, It helps to give you the strength to endure everything that's going on with you.

#17 Great Escape

This Name Frequency removes negativity, illuminates Selfishness, and replaces it with unconditional goodness. This means freedom and removal of your Animal-Mind desires so you gain family, friendship, and fulfillment.

#18 Fertility

This is about physical fertility and procreation as well as nonphysical ideas. Use this *Name Frequency* to help others conceive a child as well as for Self to bolster your own creative process.

#19 Calling Upon God

This *Name Frequency* helps your prayers to be answered quickly. Keep in mind that prayers are not always answered in ways that you want or anticipate.

#20 Victory Over Addictions

Use this *Name Frequency* to help remove your bad habits or unpleasant traits. Review the chapter on Addictions in Alternate Medical Apocrypha because addictions are much more than what you realize.

#21 Eradicate Plague

You can have an emotional, mental, spiritual or even physical plague within Self. Use this *Name Frequency* to help resolve these types of issues.

#22 Stopping Fatal Attraction

Your Soul is imbued with Divine Energy so use this *Name Frequency* to correct your mind-pattern so you do not attract negative people and experiences.

#23 Sharing the Flame

Strengthen immortality, increase personal and global joy to share with family and friends.

#24 Jealousy

Remove pain and suffering as well as your jealousy.

#25 Speaking Your Mind

Speak and hear truth with this *Name Frequency*.

#26 Making Order from Chaos

Chaos is only mind-patterns that are misunderstood. This *Name Frequency* helps to balance your energy and restore serenity so that you can organize perceived chaos.

#27 Silent Partner

Use this *Name Frequency* to remove negativity from your income and finances as well as remove destructive influences and bring blessings and protection.

#28 Soul Mate

You are already a whole person, so this helps you bring in relationships that make you feel complete including romantic, social, and business relationships.

#29 Removing Hatred

This *Name Frequency* helps remove hatred both going out to and coming from others.

#30 Building Bridges

Use this *Name Frequency* to build bridges from the Upper World to the Lower World, connect the Spiritual Self with the physical and create friendships among those with whom you are in conflict.

#31 Finishing What You Start

Finish what you begin, especially your Spiritual work. Be consistent for the best results.

#32 Memories

Bring your memories forward to learn from your experiences. It is easy to repress and suppress negative events but these are also rich with wisdom.

#33 Reveal The Dark Side

Use this *Name Frequency* to stop your reactive impulses so that you think and balance Self before you react.

#34 Forget Thyself

This *Name Frequency* helps you release negative stubbornness so happiness can come forward, becoming aware of your *Tree of Life*/ Sephirot. The Zohar states that people who are consistently generous, kind and benevolent have a low flame. When people who are evil and selfish change to become good and sharing, their flame becomes even brighter than the ones who were always this way. Then God is especially happy because their Light is even brighter. For example, if you are addicted to cigarettes and you give them up, you've come a longer way than someone who never had an addiction. Because you have surpassed your addiction, others will listen who are also trying to give up the same or similar addiction.

#35 Sexual Energy

Use this *Name Frequency* to purify sexual desires so that you share Unconditional Love with your partner, igniting sexual energy to elevate existence. Sexual energy is creative energy. For more insights read ***True Reality of Sexuality*** and ***Heights of Relationships***.

#36 Fearless

Everyone has fears of different intensities. Use this *Name Frequency* to move through fear.

#37 The Big Picture

Whatever you say or do, play the record to end so you think carefully about the repercussions of your speech and actions. This *Name Frequency* helps you to understand the consequences of what you think, say, and do to see the long-term effects.

#38 Circuitry

Receive when you share and share when you receive. Sharing allows Spiritual energy to flow through you to others and then back again.

#39 Diamond in the Rough

Use this *Name Frequency* to completely transform negative energy into positive opportunities that your Soul can receive.

#40 Speaking the Right Words

Let the Light speak for you.

#41 Self-Esteem

Use this *Name Frequency* to connect to the power of the Ancient High Priests in Jerusalem for healing and wellness.

#42 Revealing the Concealed

This *Name Frequency* shows you the truth as well as instructs how to deal with it.

#43 Defying Gravity

Mind over matter means everything becomes possible without restriction.

#44 Sweetening Judgment

Mitigate, or make less severe, any judgment against you.

#45 Power of Prosperity

Increase prosperity and sustenance.

#46 Absolute Certainty

This removes all doubt and confusion from your mind, allowing you to know with conviction that you are successful with thoughts, words and actions.

#47 Global Transformation

Use this *Name Frequency* to strengthen your inner force of peace with then reflects globally.

#48 Unity

Unifies Self which unifies the outer world.

#49 Happiness

Use this *Name Frequency* to remove selfishness, giving you a deep appreciation for what you have which in turn brings happiness.

#50 Enough is Never Enough

You deserve abundance and prosperity. Focus on the end goal and do not settle for less. There is a saying that *less is more*, but this is not true. *More is more*. Remember this.

#51 No Guilt

The Light eradicates all the negative attributes, repairs sins and removes guilt.

#52 Passion

Passion maintains sincerity, devotion, correct prayers and Spirituality.

#53 Having No Agenda

This *Name Frequency* creates and maintains pure friendship, Unconditional Love, giving, receiving and attracts Joy.

#54 Death of Death

This *Name Frequency* removes the Angel of Death.

#55 Thought into Action

Connect the physical world with the Spiritual world, bringing your thoughts, goals and dreams into fruition.

#56 Dispelling Anger

Purging anger gives you happiness and peace of mind within.

#57 Listening to Your Soul

When you hear the energy of the God-Mind, you know what you have to do and you are prepared to do it.

#58 Letting Go

Let go of whatever you are holding onto that needs to leave your life.

#59 Umbilical Cord

This *Name Frequency* is the correction of Divine Energy and brings in Light.

#60 Freedom

Strengthens you so you can pass all of your tests in life, raise you to a higher level so you can have Joy and fulfillment.

#61Water

Use this *Name Frequency* to purify and awaken the healing within to bring Immortality.

#62 Parent Teacher Not Preacher

Share your wisdom so that you are a teacher to all.

#63 Appreciation

Be appreciative, thankful, and grateful all the time.

#64 Casting Yourself in a Favorable Light

Use this *Name Frequency* to boost any relationship from personal to career.

#65 Fear of God

Be in awe of God so you can see the repercussions of your deeds.

#66 Accountability

This *Name Frequency* removes feelings of revenge as well as victim-mentality.

#67 Great Expectations

Use time to your advantage.

#68 Contacting Departed Souls

Speak with those who have passed on as well as correct any leftover issues.

#69 Lost & Found

Use this *Name Frequency* to gain Spiritual direction.

#70 Design Beneath Disorder

This *Name Frequency* helps overcome doubt and panic to see the master plan and your life's purpose.

#71 Prophecy & Parallel Universes

Elevate your awareness and the power of Prophecy that's bestowed upon you.

#72 Spiritual Cleansing

Use this *Name Frequency* to purify and correct transgressions and cleanse your physical environment.

Homework

Choose 1 or more of the *Name Frequencies* upon which to meditate.

Jewish Humor Definitions of complete and finish:

When you marry the right woman you are complete. When you marry the wrong woman you are finished. When the right one catches you with the wrong one you are completely finished.

The Shofar

The Alien Virus, which was discussed earlier, blocked the *Name of God* in the DNA signature of Humanity. Thousands of years ago the Zohar states that the virus was a missile from Satan. The Zohar goes on to state that an anti-missile missile must be used to negate it. The Zohar states thousands of years ago, that you need an injection, that you need to use a part of Satan to eliminate Satan, actually referring to the vaccine. Like repels like, so the Zohar says that if you use a weak version of Satan in this anti-missile missile that Satan would be repelled, weakened, and destroyed within you. According to the Zohar, the frequency of the Shofar destroys this energy.

On a side note, the Israelis developed Iron Dome technology in 2011 which blocks missiles. Of course, you know that iron repels demonic forces, so its name tells you what it is really blocking.

Shofar

The Shofar is blown in synagogue services on Rosh Hashanah and at the end of Yom Kippur to blast a message to God. According to the Bible, the Shofar was used when the Hebrew army invaded the Land of Canaan and surrounded the walls of Jericho, which were said to be impenetrable. When the Shofar was blown, the walls came crumbling down, allowing the army to take the city.

The Zohar and Kabbalah very specifically state that the sounds of the Shofar bring prayers and thoughts inter-dimensionally and inter-universally and are the only frequency that can create a vortex throughout all of the universes. Interestingly, when the equipment of the *Montauk Project* was turned on, the sound was very similar to the Shofar.

A few days ago in Washington, DC, there was a group of people filmed in front of the closed gates of the White House blowing the Shofar. The next day it was reported that the army took the fence down. This could have been a preplanned ritual event, but regardless, it is still symbolic.

In the following chart, keeping in mind Hebrew is read right to left, on the right side you see the Shin and Vav bracketed with the number 306 beneath it. Shin has the Gematria of 300; Vav has the Gematria of 6 so together their Gematria is 306. The Zohar states that Shin represents a candelabra and Vav is the match or stick that lights the Candelabra.

Next, you see the letter Peh without the dagesth, so it makes the F sound. Far is the Hebrew word for bull. The bull is the mate to the Red Heifer which is the symbol of the coming of Moshiach, or Messiah. It is said that the birth of a Red Heifer without any impurities heralds the coming of Moshiach. Supposedly, such a Red Heifer was recently born. The bull is the symbol of Taurus. Taurus in Hebrew is the month of Nisan, which is the first month of the Hebrew calendar. The Golden Calf that the Hebrews created and worshiped in the Sinai was an idol, a misrepresentation of the bull represented by the Shofar. There is a Golden Bull statue on Wall Street in New York, an Egyptian symbol of the astral realm. This is another corruption of the true meaning of the bull and Shofar. The Gematria of Feh and Resh is 280, the Gematria for the Hebrew word bull.

When you blow the Shofar, you hold it with one hand. Within your hand and fingers, you have 14 joints. The Hebrew word for hand is Yad, consisting of the Hebrew letters right to left, Yud, Dalet. Yud has the Gematria of 10 and Dalet has the Gematria of 4, so together the word for hand has a Gematria of 14, which circles back around to let you know that the hand and fingers together have 14 joints.

The Hebrew language is a number system and is much more than words. The word tells you what you are. There is no other language on Earth that does this because Hebrew is the Language of God. The Gematria for the Hebrew word for hand of 14 added to 306 which is the Gematria for Shin and Vav equals 320. According to Kabbalah 320 is the number of Sparks of Light for Creation.

The Gematria for bull of 280 added to 320 equals 600. Multiply 600 by the Messianic number of 1,000 to get 600,000 which is the number of Oversouls created during the Tzim Tzum. These are all extremely deep codes of Creation. According to the Zohar, all of these energies are emanations from the Sephira of Gevurah. Gevurah is on the left side of your chest and is designed to eliminate evil.

Together, the 5 Sofit/Final Hebrew letters, right to left, are called Mantzepach.

Combined with the sounds of the Shofar they both use Light to remove Satanic influences. They give a push of Light from the Absolute into Creation to eliminate Satan. In the 4th Century, the Vatican replaced the Hebrew word Satan with the Latin word Lucifer. Lucifer in Latin means Being of Light. This name is not ever recorded in the Bible in any language. Lucifer is a fictitious name created by the Vatican. Blowing the Shofar creates a vortex that allows the Light from God to enter the universe. The Vatican essentially replaced the Light of the Shofar with the Light of Lucifer. The Vatican prohibited the Jews from disseminating the teachings of the Zohar and Kabbalah, forcing the Jews to erase this knowledge from all documents. This is why even the Jews do not know this information. Only now, centuries later, are the Rabbinical schools in Israel releasing these secrets.

Luciferase

President Trump actually tricked the Deep State. The Deep State requested Covid-19 vaccines that would create or contain a compound called Luciferase. But instead, Trump had it replaced with Luciferaishe. This means the fire of the Shofar, so he tricked them. This is why both sides are pushing the vaccines. Each side thinks that it has the correct formula. I believe the Deep State has discovered this issue and that's why they've stopped some of the vaccines, for example, Johnson & Johnson, even though only 7 people out of 7 million had a problem.

Those with problems were possessed by demonic entities. When the Luciferase removes the entity, the body cannot exist anymore because the person is already gone. This may be very difficult for you to understand or accept, especially if you know people who have been hurt by these vaccines. This is why the Israeli government has pushed it on all their people because the Israeli/Hebrew people need to be purified from the Satan and demons. Netanyahu knew that Luciferaishe, which is called Luciferase for public consumption, opens the sulphur bridges that contain the *Name of God* in your DNA.

If you don't have demonic entities and you are not possessed then you don't need the vaccine. This is why Trump said that he saved the world in one day and he would be remembered for this. Trump is making sure that demons can never ever attach to you again. Many elderly die from the vaccine because they have been attached and/or possessed. You don't need a vaccine to detach demonic entities when you bring in the Light of God. Then nothing can attach to you.

Homework

- Go online and listen to the sounds of the Shofar.
- Invoke Yofefiah, the Angel that instructs you about the Torah, Kabbalah and Zohar.

Jewish Humor

A young couple that was soon to be married heard about an old couple that never fought in 60 years of marriage. They wanted to learn the secret of marriage without fighting, so the young man traveled many kilometers to visit the elderly husband who agreed to share his wisdom for a peaceful marriage. The old man said that on the day of his marriage he took his donkey cart to the home of his in-laws to move his wife's possessions to their new home. After a couple of hours, the donkey was tired and stopped. My wife looked at the donkey and said *that's one*. An hour later the donkey stopped again. My wife looked at the donkey and said *that's two*. After another hour the donkey stopped again. My wife said *that's three*, took out a gun, and shot the donkey dead. I said, *don't you think that was a little excessive*. She looked at me and said *that's one*.

Webinar Homework Results

Comment: I always feel sabotaged when I try to do something positive for my Self. I want to know if I create this.

Response: You need to look within. This has to do with Self-discipline as well as Self-sabotage, Self-punishment, low Self-worth, guilt, shame and these kinds of negative mind-patterns. Often when people are on the verge of doing something positive for Self, they create negative energy to stop it because part of them feels like they do not deserve positive. Programming also kicks in.

Comment: I think the Deep State is trying to destroy humanity with the vaccines.

Response: The Deep State spent eons of time creating a slave race, so they do not want to kill everyone. It makes no sense to destroy their creations. They want to control humanity, not destroy it.

Comment: I read that Chassidic Jews are against the vaccines. I would think that they would know that the vaccines are to destroy evil and would be for the vaccines.

Response: There are different factions of Chassidic Jews. The Chabad Chassidim says on its website that it is the obligation of their members to take the vaccine as it was provided by God to keep them safe.

Comment: I think the anti-missile-missile from the last session is a homeopathic protocol.

Response: Legally homeopathic remedies for any of this are not considered viable. Even though there are homeopathic remedies that could eliminate all of this, you cannot put this on a vaccination card. Hundreds, if not thousands of fake vaccination cards are being confiscated. This could provide the government with a reason to say it must do an authentic card. I spoke to an attorney in Europe. She says that there, it is illegal to force you to take a vaccination to go to work. P.A.C.E. which overrides the EU says that unvaccinated people cannot be discriminated against. Friends and family in Russia say they are glad to be in Russia because it is freer than Europe or North America.

Comment: I want to purchase a Shofar and blow it as soon as I wake up in the morning.

Response: You must study and learn to blow the Shofar using specific tones and frequencies. Otherwise, it's kind of like creating a sonic wave, that could be very destructive if you don't do it properly.

Comment: The vaccines have the body produce continual spike proteins, which looks like a tree with a bend in the middle, similar to the *Tree of Life*. This is a two-step process, the first called transcription which takes the DNA and trunks it into the mRNA. The second step is called reverse transcriptase, which takes the RNA back to DNA as Luciferase and Shoverase. This allows the spike proteins to be made continually. According to the research, the human body should not be making these spike proteins continuously that's not natural. These contain HIV, pseudovirus, GP120 with the DNA of the virus being introduced with the vaccine.

Response: The Gematria of Shoverase means second coming, shutting down of the spike protein. The Shofar sound is to end the evil. The second step is to destroy the *Tree of Knowledge*/Good and Evil. I believe that some of these vaccines are designed to do this. Everyone needs to step up and be prepared to live in the Light, teach and spread Hyperspace/Oversoul work as well as Zohar and Kabbalah. Set your foundation and strengthen it as you move forward so you can help others. This is why you are here at this time.

Comment: I used the *Name of God Frequency #46*, Absolute Certainty. I put on my glasses and I could see the room more clearly and sharply.

Response: This is your proof that this *Name of God* works. Sometimes they work faster than other times. Always be consistent with your inner work.

Comment: I merged with the Angel Dumiel to defeat evil. The energy was very powerful.

Response: Never, ever merge with any Angelic Frequency. They are not part of the Human Frequency, so you can do extensive damage to your Self.

Comment: I used the *Name of God Frequency #5* and felt it healing my health problems, financial difficulties and relationships. I heard the words music is healing.

Response: Yes, these Frequencies work on every level, not just the physical. Music of the Spheres is real because frequency is sound.

Comment: I prayed about the information about the sulfur bridges. It was initially difficult to accept, but now I do. I still believe that one's mind-pattern can effectively do what the vaccines are supposed to do.

Response: You are correct. Your mind is the vaccine.

Comment: My uncle got the vaccine and he was fine. My former good friend who became an alcoholic got the vaccine and he became very ill. I once saw a demon in him.

Response: These vaccines have nothing to do with the virus. They remove demonic attachments from the body. Anyone who becomes ill has heavy attachments to astral and demonic entities.

Comment: This homework did not work for me because I am immensely challenged to hold anything at the Pineal Gland for a long time. Five minutes is a long time for me.

Response: Do the best you can even if it's five seconds. Whatever you can do is better than not doing anything. The more you practice, the easier it becomes. You can also scan the *Name of God Frequencies* with your fingers, put them under your pillow and/or just scan them with your eyes.

Comment: I'm like a first grader in school going to University. From now on I pick and choose which homework I will do.

Response: You should always pick and choose. Never be forced. Regardless of the homework, do what you feel you need to do. This is not a formal school. This is a Hyperspace/Oversoul Spiritual School. Everyone must do what they can. The homework is only a suggestion, but the important thing is to do something.

Comment: I wonder if there is any hope for Humanity. They are naïve with active mind-control programs that close them down to being uplifted.

Response: It is easy to feel that humans are hopeless. But if you help just one person with one little thing then it is worthwhile. And then that one person helps another person so soon the ripples go out in many ways and directions. You may be the catalyst for much more than you realize.

Comment: I invoked the Angels of Destruction and Annihilation. This felt good. I was careful to use my protection, then I created a long list of people that have caused excessive pain, suffering, and misery on humanity.

Response: Every night, I call upon all those on the Earth plane who are willing to join me. Then I make a list of patriots who uplift, fight and risk their lives for Humanity. I pray for blessings and protection for these people. This way, I'm balancing things out within the God-Mind. I pray for the destruction of violence then balance this with prayers of protection and positive blessings. I also use *Name of God Frequency #5* for healing, *Name of God Frequency #11* to banish the remnants of evil, *Name of God Frequency #22* to stop negative attractions, and *Name of God Frequency #29* to remove hatred. Use the positive energies first, visualizing them going into the Earth. Then eliminate evil. Otherwise, evil has an opportunity to change before it is eliminated.

Comment: I do not know why we need a vaccine for something that is 99.9% curable.

Response: This is why the vaccine has nothing to do with the virus.

Comment: Janet's books and blogs have been my learning process. I focus on the Hebrew letters and *Names of God Frequencies* that I am most drawn to. When attempting the meditations, on the *Names of God* I went through the eradication of negative thoughts first. I assumed my bad mood and tiredness stemmed from that, but nothing came up. Then I focused on dumping depression and felt awake and uplifted.

Response: When you go to a doctor and he doesn't know what to prescribe, he gives you something. If that doesn't work then he goes on to the next one until he finds the correct combination that works for you. This is the same for the *Name of God Frequencies*. Use the ones you feel will help. If they don't, use another or combinations until you find what works for you.

Comment: The idea keeps coming to me that you cannot have two masters. This reflects the left and right brain. I truly feel at times that Kabbalah might have been designed to confound the mind until it implodes, gives up, and surrenders to the Spiritual Mind. I'm currently seeing this out-picturing at my place of work. This means it is time to surrender the egotistical mind, use it as a tool without it using me.

Response: Rather than surrender the ego, balance it with the Spiritual Mind. You need your ego to interface with physical reality. There's a lot of information out about the ego that is not totally correct. Go back to ***Decoding Your Life***, read the chapter on ego so you understand it from a Hyperspace/Oversoul perspective.

Comment: Covid-19 is designed to isolate and create fear in the population.

Response: Yes, absolutely, as well as to break the Spirit of the people.

Comment: I have also come across the alien virus concept in Gnostic writings where the predatory virus enters the mind and infiltrates humanity, amplifying and compounding human errors into evil. It distorts the ability of humanity to consciously correct ignorance and limits spiritual Evolution and Revolution. It says that unless Humanity is forced, that Humanity would never on its own adjust itself and that it needed to be controlled from without. I do not want to be an onlooker, I may not have many material means, but I know something of the Source of All There Is. I came from there and I will return there. The Lord is my light and my salvation, so I have nothing to fear.

Response: This is exactly what we were indoctrinated with during the *Montauk Project*. We were told that Humanity left on its own would self-destruct because people were stupid. We were told that we were helping Humanity survive in a way that they could never survive on their own. When you realize, that you have the God- Mind within you and you have everything in Creation as part of your composition nothing can happen to you.

Secrets of the Zohar

The Zohar is a powerful tool for transformation designed to bring a perfected world. Keeping the books of the Zohar in your home, even without looking at them, brings Light and protection because the energy is so powerful.

The Zohar is like a home security system that you turn on and then forget about it because it is always on. The Zohar is a Divine Gift to all people and has nothing to do with any religion. The Zohar is for all of Humanity and all of Creation. The Hebrews were called a chosen people, not because God chose them because they chose to be the keepers of this information. The Zohar and Kabbalah say that only during the Messianic time period can the total Zohar information be revealed. The fact that you're learning this now means that this is the Messianic time period known as the End of Days. This means that what was will be no more and despite what you see, there is something new and better coming.

This work that you are studying is Spiritual, which has nothing to do with religion. Judaism is a religion and has facets of what you are learning here within it. In the same way, Christianity is entirely different than its origins although it has facets of its origins within it. For example, when Christians refer to the Virgin Mary, they are referring to the Shekhinah. The Shekhinah is the feminine aspect of the Creator, which could also be called Spiritual or Holy Mother that protects you and removes fear. When you invoke Metatron and Sandalphon, as discussed in ***Template of God-Mind***, add Shekhinah at the end. This completes the Holy Trinity, the Power of Creation.

The Zohar states that you are born with a protective shield of light around you, which you know as the aura. It states that negative actions weaken and dim it. This is why it is very important that you work every single day with your energy field, including the Sephirot. The most powerful time to do this work is between midnight and 2 AM.

Forgiveness

The Zohar says to forgive those working against you and sending negativity toward you. This can bring up feelings of jealousy and envy, sometimes referred to in Kabbalah as the Evil Eye. You can only be affected by any of this if you have a victimization mind-pattern. This means if you have such mind-patterns as low Self-worth, Self-sabotage and Self-punishment then a person who has jealousy or envy can imprint this on you because you accept this energy. In turn, this negative energy causes you to create negative experiences.

Jealousy is temporary because things can change. For example, you can be jealous of someone's car, home, income, and relationships but these can all change. Envy, however, is consistent within a person so you must eliminate the consistent negative energies specifically associated with envy within. Envy attracts the so-called Evil Eye and allows negative imprinting upon you. Happiness and Joy are the opposite of jealousy and envy. Happiness is a temporary feeling; joy is continuous. You feel happiness at the moment, such as being happy seeing a beautiful flower or happy while eating good food. If you are a joyful person, you are always joyful. Happiness comes and goes but joy stays.

When the 24,000 students of Rabbi Akiba were killed by the plague, it is said that this happened because they were jealous and envious of each other. Even though they were well-schooled in the Torah instead of supporting each other, they were jealous and envious of each other. This negativity opened them up to destruction. Only 5 of those 24,000 students survived.

The Satan

The Zohar and Kabbalah refer to the Satan as the opponent. In Hebrew, Satan means accuser or prosecutor. The Vatican distorted the meaning of Satan. The purpose of the Satan is to help you do something bad if these are your intentions and then accuse as well as punish you for your deeds. To negate the power of the Satan in your life is to always feel joy and fulfillment. God gives you the opportunity for complete fulfillment and abundance. It is only the negativity within that causes you to deny your natural state of positive abundance. Religion often tells people to be poor and suffer while the church prospers at the expense of its people.

The Universe is abundant, with enough for everyone to have everything. This doesn't mean you are selfish, rather it means that you are open to receiving and then you can share. Only if you receive and keep do you suffer. Those who receive and share open the doorway for more to pour in. Sharing is applying and experiencing what you know. For example, God can think about swimming but it is not the same as getting in the ocean and swimming. Swimming is the sharing.

You must replace any doubt with certainty. Doubt and despair block whatever is trying to come to you and prevent miracles from happening. Use the Sephira of Tiferet, which is at the Heart Chakra. Tiferet means beautiful or bounty. The 3 components of Tiferet are being proactive in what you do, repelling negativity, and being certain of positive outcomes at all times. Kabbalah says that the smallest hope is what brings more so always, always have a hope and a knowing that good will happen. The secret to receiving fulfillment is performing the actions that bring it with effort and commitment. You have to be proactive in what you want to fulfill.

Teshuva

In Hebrew, teshuva means to repent and also means to return. This means to mentally and energetically return to the moment before your negative actions to transform the negative into something positive. Use *Name of God Frequency #1* Time Travel to take you back to the moment before the moment, as Janet wrote about in ***Decoding Your Life***. In Creation in the Mind of God, there's no time or space so you can go to any moment of your existence and change it to affect your current moment by correcting past negativity. All overwhelming challenges are removed by the Light of the Creator. Visualize the Light of Ain Sof/Absolute filling you up to change everything.

Guilt/Shame

Guilt comes from an action that you regret. Shame comes from a condition. You might be ashamed of a runny nose, but you do not feel guilty that it is running. If you cheat someone in business, you may feel guilty but not be ashamed of your actions.

Homework

- Of what are you jealous and envious?
- What do you doubt and why?

Jewish Humor

Some Jewish men were playing poker in their clubhouse at their retirement community in Florida. Abe lost $500 on a single hand of Poker. He was so upset that he clutched his chest and dropped dead on the table. Out of respect for Abe, the rest of the men played the final hours of the game standing up around his body. At the end of the evening, one of the men asked who was going to tell Abe's wife.

They drew cards to see who had to tell his wife. Perlman drew the low card so the others told him to be gentle and not make the sad situation worse. After knocking on the door of Abe's condo, his wife answered through the door, asking what he wanted. Perlman said, *Abe lost $500 in a Poker game and he is afraid to come home.* His wife replied, *tell him to drop dead*! Perlman said, okay, I'll go tell him.

Sefer Yetzirah: The Book of Formation

The *Sefir Yetzirah* is considered to be the most mysterious and oldest text in Kabbalah. Yetzirah means foundation so this is why it is also called the ***Book of Formation***. The root of Yetzirah is the Hebrew word Safer, which means to gaze. Quantum physics says that nothing really exists until it is looked at. This means that the function of looking into energy creates reality. In the Hebrew language, the root words tell you the formula for how everything is created and exists.

Abraham is said to be the author of this book. The Sefir Yetzirah gives direction on how to create a Golem, which is an artificial being made out of natural materials. Then various Hebrew letters are permutated via formulas and prayer that brings the creature to life which then acts as a servant to its creator. On the forehead of the Golem, the Hebrew word Emet is written, when means truth. When they want to end the Golem's existence the first letter of Emet, which is Aleph, is erased. This leaves the Hebrew word Met, which means death. There is only one letter that differentiates between truth and death.

Genesis 12:5 says that Abraham created people in the land of Haran. Abraham left the land of the Chaldeans, or Sumer, with his family and his servants to go to Canaan, the land of the Hebrews. On his way, he stopped in Haran which is now in Southeastern Turkey where he stayed for several years. He needed more people so it is said that he created more. The Bible does not specifically say that he created Golems, but it is implied. At that time people lived thousands of years. The Bible says he worked with Shem, the son of Noah. Races were named after the sons of Noah. Semite people are the people of the Middle East, named after Shem. Semites include Arabs, Persians, Turks and Jews. Semites have lost their original meaning as now anti-Semite usually means anti-Jews. The Han people are created from Ham, another one of Noah's sons. In Hebrew and Mandarin Chinese, Yah means God. Their ancestry comes from Noah's son Ham.

The Bible also states that Abraham created animals, too. When Hebrew letters are permeated, or mixed into various combinations, they create. Kabbalah says that God used the Hebrew letters to create Existence. Each letter has a vibration, or frequency that when mixed together manifests. It is possible that Abraham permutated Hebrew letters to create animals.

Names of God

The Hebrew Bible speaks of plurality when discussing God. The 4-Letter *Name* is Yahweh. There is also Elohim and Adonai. Elohim is the level of God right before physical existence and is said to be the delineation and definition of God. Adonai and Elohim refer to the interim part where the Absolute starts to transmute into the physical. Elohim is plural. El Shaddai is another Name of God which means procreative force. El Shaddai is always connected to sexual energy. Christianity does not address the plurality of God except to make this concept sound bad. The different Names of God are really descriptions of Its functions within the totality of the God Energy.

The ***Sefir Yetzirah*** discusses in detail how God manifested Creations. Sefir means book. and from this comes the word Sefira, or energy center. Sefar means number. Sippur means communication. All of these words have the same root which means they all are related. Together, these words mean that energy centers communicate numbers/formulas found in this book.

Sefir = Book

Sefira = Energy Center

Sippur = Communication

Sefar = Number

3 Mother Letters

The *Sefir Yetzirah* also discusses the 3 Mother Letters of the Hebrew AlephBet. The 3 Mother Letters are, from right to left, Aleph, Mem and Shin. From these 3 letters come all of Creation because these are the code letters that lead to all the others.

אמש

Together Aleph and Shin is Hebrew for Ish which means man when using the Hebrew vowel for e. When another vowel is added under the Aleph, the word becomes Esh, which is Hebrew for fire. This means in Creation there is a connection between man and fire. A vowel under the Shin turns the word into Ishah, which means woman. Shin with Mem is the Hebrew word Shem, which means name. This refers to any person, not just God. Aleph and Mem is the Hebrew word Am which means people.

אש Man/Fire

שם Name

אם People

From these 3 Mother Letters come the words for man, woman, fire, name and people. This shows how the 3 Mother Letters give birth to Creation through specific formulas or permutations of the letters.

The 7 Doubles were used in Ancient Hebrew but Modern Hebrew does not recognize all of the pronunciations. They are called Doubles because each letter can be pronounced in 2 different ways depending upon whether or not the letter has a dagesh.

ב בּ Bet without a dagesh is a B, with it is a V.

ג גּ Gimmel without a dagesh is a hard G, with it is a soft G.

ד דּ Dalet without a dagesh is a D, with it is th, like thought.

כ כּ Kaf without a dagesh is hard ch like Bach, with it is like K.

פ פּ Peh without a dagesh is an F, with the dagesh it is a P.

ר רּ Resh without a dagesh is a soft rolling R, with the dagesh it is like a double R.

ת תּ Tav without a dagesh is an S, with it is a T.

In Modern Hebrew, Gimmel with a dagesh is not used, Dalet with a dagesh is not used, Tav with or without a dagesh the letter is pronounced as a T. However, the Zohar and Kabbalah say that at the End of Days, these Doubles will be used and pronounced as they were in Ancient Times. The Zohar also says that the end is embedded in the beginning and the end is the beginning. Knowing this information is part of turning Darkness into Light.

Hebrew letters represent Spiritual Forces. The Hebrew word for coal is Gagelat. Gagelat has the same Gematria as Emet, which is the Hebrew word for truth. This indicates that burning coal when set on fire has the same energy as truth which means that truth lights the way. Kabbalah says that a cause cannot exist without an effect. Whatever you start will create something.

According to Zohar, the heart is King over the Soul. This refers to the intensity of emotions that direct people into action. In the following chart, the word Mystical is written in Hebrew. Peliyot is the pronunciation, reading the Hebrew letters from right to left. Pala means hidden. Peleh, the three Hebrew letters, is the root of Pala and Peliyot. Peleh is written Peh, Lamed, Aleph.

פליות

Peliyot= Mystical

פלא

Pala = Hidden or Peleh = Miracle

Depending on the vowels, this word is Peleh/Miracle or Pala/ Hidden When you reverse Peleh, the word is now Aleph, Lamed, Peh which spells out the Hebrew letter Aleph. This is a code and formula that says the letter Aleph represents mystical and hidden miracles that you can use to create what you want to experience. Focus on the Hebrew letter Aleph if you want to have miracles in your life.

Homework

- Visualize each of the 3 Mother Letters in White at your Pineal Gland.
- Do the same with the Double Letters.

Jewish Humor

A Jewish man named Yakov was going through a very old drawer he had in his bedroom and he found a ticket for shoe repair that was

40 years old. He never picked up his shoes. He remembered that he needed new heels, left the shoes and then forgot all about them. He wondered if old Goldberg was still repairing shoes. Since he hadn't been in the neighborhood for years, he decided to drive over to the shop. To his amazement, Goldberg Shoe Repair was still there. He walked in and found Goldberg behind the counter. Yakov figured his shoes were long gone but he decided to ask about them anyway. He walked in and handed Goldberg the 40-year-old ticket. Goldberg went to the back and then called out that the shoes were still there. Yakov thought that he was really amazing, and then Goldberg said, *they'll be ready next Tuesday.*

Webinar Homework Results

Comment: I was told not to expect an immediate response, but I would be shown my answer as needed.

Response: Often you receive your answers in the dream state. Some people never realize that they can ask for help so they go through their entire lives being a victim. All you have to do is call God's Name, YHVH, and He answers. Give thanks that you have the way to seek help and that God is willing to help you.

Comment: God created His creations to love, He put Himself into this world and there is no separation.

Response: Yes, you must realize that there is no separation and that you are responsible for everything that happens. This means that you must take action.

Comment: I save space in my mind where no one else can go. From here I look at all of my issues.

Response: Everyone should create a safe space in his/her mind. In ***Decoding Your Life*** you learn how to breathe your Self into your center, anchoring into your Oversoul and God-Mind to create a safe space.

Comment: I visualized the letter Shin and I saw a shiny golden sword with golden wings that connected to the Ohalu Council Archetype.

Response: ***Montauk: Alien Connection*** tells of the Ohalu Council using letters to identify its various aspects. Shin also looks like fire, meaning the spoken word as well as the *Tree of Life*.

Comment: I visualized the letter Mem and got a mouth.

Response: The Hyperspace Archetype for mouth looks like the Mem Sofit.

Comment: I visualized the *Tree of Life* and got that being connected to it alleviates all fear so we can know the awesomeness of God.

Response: There should be no fear of God. There are many mistranslations in the Bible, including fear which should be translated to awe. ***Decoding Your Life*** has an entire chapter on fear that everyone should read or review.

Comment: When I visualized the Hebrew letters they were so powerful that I lost consciousness twice when I put them at my Pineal Gland.

Response: That is concerning because you may fall into a deep meditative or dream state and then you would not be aware of physical reality. Use the *Brown Merger Archetype* at both Reptilian Brainstem and Pineal Gland because your programming may be trying to stop you from getting information.

Comment: I saw that each Hebrew letter is a formula for life review.

Response: Yes, they can bring up memories from years ago that you totally forgot. This means there is something there that you need to review and release.

Comment: While I still have my challenges, using the *72 Names of God* seems to make my life less chaotic.

Response: True, they allow you to deal with life challenges in more positive, proactive ways.

Comment: I use the Brown Merger/Self-Reintegration Archetype at my Pineal Gland, Reptilian Brainstem, above my Crown Chakra, and one in my Heart Chakra.

Response: You cannot have too many of these Archetypes. You can even put one in every cell of your entire system.

Hebrew Letters

The *Sefirah Yetzirah* describes how the letters were carved and engraved by the Mind of God, meaning material was removed. Then, the material that was removed is formatted into a template. The *Sefir Yetzirah* goes on to say that engraving means to give vibration, or sound, to the letter. Sounds waves cut through the air. There is something on either side of the sound waves.

Kabbalah says that there are *32 Pathways to God.* These 32 Paths equal the 22 Hebrew letters plus the 10 Sephirot so these are the connections between the 22 Hebrew letters and the 10 Sephirot. The Zohar says that the Creator used these 32 Paths to engrave what He created. The *32 Pathways to God* represent the heart, or emotions, of All Existence in Creation. This refers to the Sephira of Tiferet which is centered in your Heart Chakra. The first word of the Torah starts with the letter Bet and the last word of the Torah ends with the letter Lamed. Together, reading right to left, Lamed, Bet spells Lev, which is the Hebrew word for heart. The Gematria for Lev is 32 because Lamed = 30 and Bet = 2.

When lines are drawn between the 10 Sephirot, starting with Keter, there are 32 connections. Keter is spelled with the 3 Hebrew letters Kaf, Tav, Resh. Reversing the Tav and Resh, Ketter becomes Koret spelled Kaf, Resh, Tav. Koret means to excise, remove or cut off. This shows how every energy has an opposite. Kabbalah uses the term of Kra Satan which means to cut off Satan. Energetically and symbolically this is located at Keter, the Crown.

462 Gates

The 22 Hebrew letters can be connected to form 231 pairs, with a letter at each end of the pair. These connected pairs are referred to as the 462 Gates, or 231 x 2. This is accomplished by drawing a circle with Aleph placed at the top, then the rest of the AlephBet evenly spaced around the circle. Then, every letter is connected with every other letter via a line across the circle. In total, there are 231 lines connecting these 22 letters. These 462 Gates in the Zohar and Kabbalah are referred to as the Gates in the Mind of God. DNA also uses pairing to form the 4 protein bases. These bases are also joined together in pairs. Adenine pairs with cytosine and thymine pairs with guanine. Everything is always created in pairs. For example, an answer is always within your question or experience. If you get poison ivy, jewelweed its antidote always grows nearby. Everything exists in pairs, with the answer to your needs available, whether you recognize it or not.

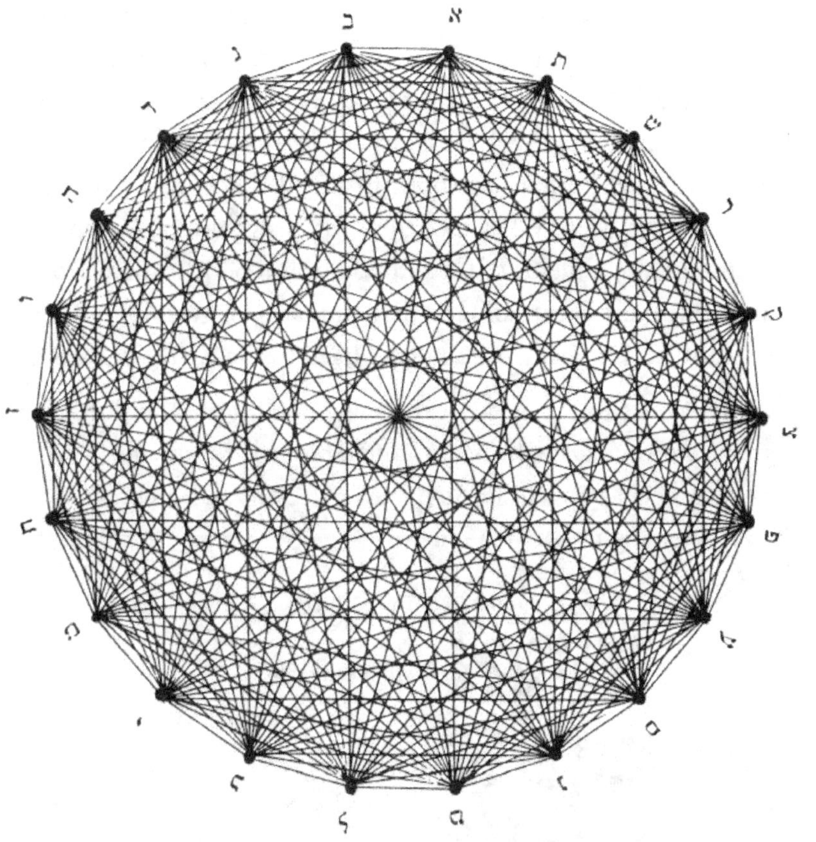

Kabbalah often speaks of the permutation, or mixing, of the letters together to form various sequences. According to the Zohar, permutation means creating something from nothing or taking something from chaos/nonexistence to Existence. Tohu is a Hebrew word that means unorganized or disconnected energy but it is often translated as chaos.

It is said that doing a permutation of all of the Hebrew letters in a circle creates an energy that results in the creation of a Golem. A Golem is an artificial person. When Abraham left Sumer he stopped in the land of Haran in Southeastern Turkey where he created people. He was 100 years old, so this doesn't mean that he had children, but it is implied that he created Golems for workers. In addition, it is said that he created calves to eat because they needed food. It is implied that these were Golem animals. These Golems came with him to Israel. Since Abraham did not destroy the Golems, some say that it is possible that some humans are descendants of Golems. Perhaps this is why religions say that humans are born in sin. Perhaps these humans did not come from a Holy Place but are the progenies of Golems. In a way, humans are Golems of God. The physical body is made from the Earth and it is the Breath of God that animates, or gives life. When the Breath of God is gone, the body goes back to the Earth, dust to dust.

Creating a Golem is an extremely complicated process. Only 3 letters are used, Aleph, Mem, and Shin which are the 3 Mother Letters. When arranged as Aleph, Mem, Shin the Hebrew word is Amesh, referring to a male Golem.

TO CREATE A GOLEM

אמש = Animesh Male

אשם = Ashem Female

שמא = Destroy

When arranged as Aleph, Shin, Mem the word is Ashem, referring to a female Golem. When arranged as Shin, Mem, Aleph the word is Shimma, which is used to destroy the Golem.

After a Golem is animated the Rabbi writes the letters Aleph, Mem, Tet on its forehead which is the word Emet meaning truth. When the Rabbi wants to destroy the Golem he removes the Aleph. This leaves Mem, Tet which is the word for death. This causes the Golem to fall and disintegrate.

Usually, in the middle of a moonless night, a Rabbi would go to a secluded location in Nature near the bank of a river, lake or stream. Here, he would mold the mud into a humanoid figure. Once formed, he walked around it counterclockwise pronouncing various permutations from the 462 Gates along with specific prayers, write Emet on the forehead, then write the *Name of God* on a parchment and put this in the mouth of the Golem. At this point, the Golem would breathe and come to life.

Golems do not have voices and cannot speak, but they understand everything spoken. A Golem is the servant of its creator or master. Golems look human and were given names. There is a story of a Rabbi in Eastern Europe who created a Golem to protect the Jews. But the permutations he used to create it were not exact, so it started to grow in size and became belligerent, not obeying its master. The people became afraid of it so the Rabbi had to trick it to destroy it. The Rabbi spoke very softly so when the Golem bent down so it could hear, the Rabbi struck the Aleph from its head, said Met/death, and caused the Golem to fall dead to the ground.

According to some Rabbinical sources, Golem do not have Souls, yet by definition, they come to life. Other Rabbinical sources say they do have Souls. Even dirt has a vibration and has a life source. If you put dirt under a microscope you will see all kinds of material depending upon where the dirt originates. There is a lot of life in dirt. In addition to the life that is already in the body of the Golem from the dirt, an animal, insect or even demonic entity could choose to be a soul for the Golem. A Golem is not a clone because it is made from the Earth. A clone is made from biological materials.

The most famous story of a Golem took place in Prague, Czech Republic about 500 years ago. Christians in this city said that Jews were killing children so the Christians began attacking them. The Rabbi created a Golem to protect his people. Once the situation calmed down, the Rabbi removed the Aleph so the Golem was no longer able to function. I went to that synagogue in 2012 because some people say that this Golem is buried in its cemetery although they say no one knows which tomb. You are not allowed to take any stones from this cemetery. During World War 2 when the Nazis occupied Prague they were afraid to go to this area because the current Rabbis said that if there was any trouble the Golem would be brought back to life and destroy the Nazis.

There was a Rabbi in Lithuania centuries ago who created a female Golem. He was accused of creating her for sexual purposes but he was adamant that she was only a servant. Because Golems already have eternal life until someone stops them, they have no need to reproduce. However, as in the story of Abraham, it is possible that humans mated with them.

In ***The Hobbit*** book by J.R.R. Tolkein, there is a creature called Golem. Tolkein also has an army of Orcs made from clay which rises out of the ground. Tolkein is said to have been a student of the Zohar and Kabbalah. Mary Shelley the author of ***Frankenstein*** studied how to make a Golem before she wrote her book. Michelangelo and DaVinci also studied the Zohar and Kabbalah which heavily influenced their work.

End of Days

A Teli is a spin of energy that Kabbalah says is associated with a snake or dragon. The Teli represents the axis or spin of a planet or galaxy. Keep in mind that this was 4000 years ago when the sages described the spin of a planet in a galaxy as where 2 divergent orbits meet. A Teli or axis of spin exists when something spins in one direction meets something spinning in another direction.

Kabbalah also says that good defines evil. Evil must exist so that you know what good is. If there was only good, you would have no motivation to do anything. Creation would stagnate and fall apart. Remember that the source of evil is symbolically the broken shards or vessels of Creation that occurred during the Tzim Tzum. The Satan used these to create the demonic forces. There is a difference between the fallen Angels who followed the Satan and his evil ways and the demonic entities. The demonic entities from the broken pieces never developed into full personas. Even fictional works portray demons as missing limbs and eyes with all kinds of deformities. This occurs because the mind-patterns of these creatures are not complete so their physical outpicturings are not complete.

As with all energetic work, you can use it for other people. This information is to be shared and revealed to all who will listen. Of course, you must always ask permission on the Oversoul level. If you are not sure, ask your Oversoul to help the Oversoul of the other person accept whatever you offer. This is especially important now that we are in *End Times* or *End of Days*. You may be depressed and find life difficult, but look what happened in Europe leading up to World War 2. Life changed completely in a few short years. At that time, everyone said that it was the end of Europe. In a way, it was the end of Europe because after the war life completely changed. It was a new way of life for people, but they survived and moved on. Even people in this webinar series went through these times as children.

My own family went through all of this in Germany, Poland and Russia. In Munich, my family owned a gigantic mansion that was two square blocks long, in all directions. The Nazis decided that was going to be their Munich headquarters, so they took it. My family eventually moved to Canada and the US as well as other countries. They had to move on and build a new life.

Times are difficult and disturbing. Do your inner level work to change within so the outer can change in positive ways.

Jewish Humor

There was a couple named Esther and Solomon Rothenberg who were married a very long time. One night while getting ready for bed, Esther looked at her reflection in the mirror and said, *Solomon, all I see is an old wrinkled woman with bags under my eyes, fat on my legs, and flab on my arms. Tell me something better so I can feel better.* Solomon replied, *well, there is nothing wrong with your eyesight.*

32 Paths of Wisdom

The Sefirot are the levels that the Absolute and God-Mind used to create Existence one layer after another. This physical reality that you live in is at the bottom of the Sefirot, in Malchut, the lowest form of Creation. When connected, each Sefira to every other Sefira from Keter down to Malchut, there are 32 connections. The Zohar calls these connections forms of consciousness known as the 32 Paths of Wisdom. These are mind-pattern templates as delineated in the following information.

1. Mystical

According to the Zohar this means Original Light. You exist to access the Original Pure Light before the contamination of all things.

2. Radiance of Unity

Even though there are different manifestations with different levels of awareness, there is unity within the Radiance of Light that all must access.

3. Sanctified

Original Wisdom and Faith is pure knowledge and understanding that allows you to access this within the Creator.

4. Settled

All spiritual emanations that emanate through Creation.

5. Rooted

The essence of understanding. As an analogy, when you grow something, the idea is the root. The root then grows into different trees, plants and branches. To understand the idea you have to go down to the root. Sometimes, the root system underneath the ground is much more extensive than you realize.

6. Transcendental influx

Blessings and increasing energy.

7. Hidden

This refers to the internal power within your mind that you need to project externally.

8. Perfect

You must go back to the Original Arrangement or Permanence of your Being before the contamination. The first line of the Ana B'Koach Prayer is like a time travel to take you back to the time before the contamination.

9. Pure

This energy purifies the Sefirot so that there is no separation between them. Even though there are 10 Sephirot when they are looked at from a higher perspective in actuality, they are all one. They are just different layers of cf functions of Creation.

10. Scintillating

Elevate your energy and frequency to elevate Self.

11. Glaring

You have a veil covering up your Glaring Light. Your purpose is to uncover that Light. Kabbalah also calls this the Klipot, or covering.

12. Glowing

Use visualization methods to create glowing energy.

13. Unity directing

Unity directing is the essence of Glory in reference to the Creator.

14. Illuminating

You need to understand Gematria and formulas to understand and access holy secrets and structures.

15. Stabilizing

Stabilize Creation with balancing energies otherwise, there would only be chaos and no Creation.

16. Enduring

The Delight of God refers to Eden, which is not a place but rather an energetic zone within another dimension. Communicate, contact, and be a part of the Delight of God which emanates from here.

17. Consciousness of Senses

Use your senses to receive the Holiness of the Creator.

18. House of the influx

Use the Sefirot to probe Existence.

19. Mystery of spiritual activities

Elevate your awareness to the Supreme Glory of the Absolute.

20. Will

What you think, you create. Your will creates the structures of all that's formed, meaning a reality.

21. Desired and sought

Bestow blessings upon people, places and things.

22. Faithful

Increase Spiritual Power.

23. Sustaining

Sustain the Sefirot by working with them daily to keep their energies powerful.

24. Apparition

Determine how Creation appears to you so you can correct it or leave it as is.

25. Testing

Determine what tempts you so you can correct your mind-pattern. This refers to the Original Temptation.

26. Renewing

Make everything like new. Quantum physics says that nothing exists until you look at it. Every time you look at something that you've created in your mind, it's a new thing.

27. Palpable probable

Sense the higher levels and upper spheres of Creation.

28. Natural

Define the Nature of all things.

29. Physical World

What you create, you need to grow. Focus on growing your positive creations.

30. General

As you progress through your experience in Creation, the rules and theories change. What was appropriate in one part of Existence may not be appropriate for another part.

31. Continuous

The continuity of the Duality of Existence is expressed symbolically as the Sun/male and Moon/female.

32. Worshipped

All the worlds are inside of each person. Everything is created and developed because of humankind or whatever intelligent species there is. Humankind refers to all Beings including those on other worlds. The *Flowchart of Creation* in ***Hyperspace Plus*** includes the levels of Angelic Frequencies, Aliens, and Extraterrestrial.

Kabbalah says that Humanity was designed to desire things. Kabbalah says that the size of the desire determines the amount of pleasure that you receive. This means that the more you want something, the greater the potential pleasure when you receive it. If you don't like what you have created you have the power to change it.

The goal of God is for you to be co-creators. However, human thought cannot grasp the Creator's Perfection or comprehend the vastness of the Mind of God. God's only goal is to give pleasure and bliss. You may look around you and think this cannot be possible. But you must always remember that it is your mind-pattern that brings your experiences. Even experiences that you call bad may be the best thing possible for your Soul growth.

Kabbalah states that there are 6,000 levels of Creation. This is why you need so many lifelines. Your essence is based on your 10 Sephirot. Then, each Sefirot has 10 Sefirot. And those 10 Sefirot have 10 Sefirot and so on. For example, your Tiferet has a Keter within it and even Malchut has a Keter level. This is your Oversoul. This is why you cannot learn all of this in one lifeline. You are not supposed to because you have Eternity. Most likely you are remembering what you have studied before which is why you are interested now. This explains why you get results when you use these methodologies because this is not your first time.

The books of the Zohar are called the most complicated volumes of Kabbalah ever written because they chart all the levels and depths of Creation. Some books are so intellectually thick that it is only possible to read 2 or 3 pages at a time. You still may not understand it. But eventually, everything comes together. You get what you need in this lifetime. You can only handle so much information. Never be discouraged, just keep going.

The Zohar and Kabbalah state that if Humanity would study this information 24/7 evil would be destroyed because your mind would not have time or room to entertain negative thoughts. Even doing this work sporadically makes you feel more uplifted and elevated. Depression and other negative thoughts cannot get such a deep hold on you. It doesn't matter if you don't understand it. Simply looking at it, holding it, keeping it on your person, or using your fingertips to scan the information raises your frequency to higher levels. You can even pick 1 Hebrew letter, center it in White at your Pineal Gland, and follow it. In a few minutes, your mood will be much improved. ***Miracles in Motion*** has the *72 Names of God* in a color that you can look at to uplift your mood.

Some Kabbalists refer to the Bread of Shame, saying that this is the reason that the Adam Kadmon exploded, known as the Big Bang/Tzim Tzum. The Absolute was infusing Adam Kadmon with such Love that Adam Kadmon felt it could only receive but not share. It felt so bad that it blocked what the Absolute was sending. When the Absolute forced Its Love into Adam Kadmon it finally exploded. The inability of Adam Kadmon to share or give back is what is often referred to as the Bread of Shame. More appropriately this is really about feeling unworthy and inadequate. This led Humanity to mind-patterns of low Self-worth, Self-sabotage, and abandonment. You can use *Name of God Frequency #1 Time Travel* to mentally travel back before Creation to eliminate what caused these issues within you.

Homework

- Which of the *32 Paths to God* most resonate with you?
- How do you block your success?
- Why do you feel unworthy?

Soviet Jewish humor

In the 1970s, a Soviet Army School Inspector was questioning a boy in a classroom.

Question: *Who is your father?*

Answer: *The Soviet Union.*

Question: *Who is your mother?*

Answer: *The Communist Party.*

Question: *What do you want to be when you grow up?*

Answer: *I want to be a worker for the glory of the state and the party.*

Next, the Inspector points to a girl.

Question: *Who is your father?*

Answer: *The Soviet Union.*

Question: *What do you want to be when you grow up?*

Answer: *I want to be a heroine of the Soviet Union raising many children for the state and the party.*

Then the Inspector sees a Jewish boy trying to hide behind everyone.

Question: *What is your name?*

Answer: *Shmuly Rabinovich.*

Question: *Who is your father?*

Answer: *The Soviet Union.*

Question: *Who is your mother?*

Answer: *The Communist Party.*

Question: *What do you want to be when you grow up?*

Answer: *An orphan.*

Webinar Homework Results

Comment: The mystical light resonates with me most deeply. My true nature and my desire for success are indomitable. I would like to know a Kabbalistic way to rid my Self of IS Programming.

Response: Speaking of IS Programming can trigger people who have it. Use the *Name of God Frequency #48 Unity* to bring everything back together. You can also use *Name of God Frequency #45 Absolute Certainty.* Use ***Heights of Deprogramming***, ***13-Cubed***, ***13-Cubed Squared***, ***True Reality of Sexuality***, and of course ***Hyperspace Helper*** to help with deprogramming.

Comment: The hidden number 7 resonated with me the most. I have always felt that my potential knowledge, light, and power are locked up inside. What's challenging is knowing when to stay quiet, when to share and when to ask a probing question to open up dialogue.

Response: That's true for most people because they do not realize how powerful they are. You must learn to do the correct action for the correct reason at the correct timing.

Comment: For me, failure is not an option.

Response: Failure is simply redirection; there is no such thing as failure.

Comment: In Ghana one of the names for Mother Earth is Asase Ya. This sounds exactly like Asiyah, one of the levels of Creation.

Response: The people in Ghana are Hebrews. In Hebrew, Ghan means garden, like in the Garden of Eden.

Comment: When visualizing the Angelic Frequencies I noticed that the energy wants to enter my energy field from the back.

Response: Only demonic energies want to enter from the back. Angelic Frequencies always enter via the Crown Chakra.

Comment: When I aim for the completion of a goal and discover that it's not useful, I will cease putting energy into it. Then I either adjust the path to the original goal or establish a new Path and a new goal. I used to feel unworthy before I did Hyperspace/Oversoul work. I used to set my Self up for failure but after I fixed my mind-pattern and did my release work I was able to accomplish the completion of larger goals.

Response: That's why it's always important to ask your Oversoul if you're supposed to push forward or come from another angle, or go somewhere else. Often, people give up too soon when all that is needed is a change of direction or methodology to be successful.

Comment: My desire for success is insatiable and it overwhelms me. I block it because I procrastinate to the point where weeks pass and I have done nothing toward my goal.

Response: This is very common because it is an issue of low Self-worth and therefore Self-sabotage. Release work changes this. In addition, many people think that if they never begin then they never fail.

Comment: I like to use the Ana B'Koach prayer. My sense of unworthiness has plagued me my whole life until I started praying using the *Ohalu Council Archetype*. This has allowed me to transcend negative feelings about my Self.

Response: The more you do this work the more empowered and successful you become. You can accomplish anything. These high-level frequencies you are learning to use pull you up so you do not go so low into negative feelings.

Comment: My father always pushed me to be competitive. However, it was not my nature. So I never think about personal success. I haven't received a lot of outer validation like career advancement, parenting achievements and so I focus on my internal drive and motivation. This is a source of conflict in my life. Outer recognition versus inner recognition and believing in my abilities has pushed me inside to confront my Self-esteem issues.

Response: What only matters is what comes from within you. Stay with that and don't let others influence you.

Comment: I often block success because my health issues make me tired. I do less in a day than I would like. I don't think too much about what I want because I am always trying to catch up.

Response: This is a Self-defeating attitude and mind-pattern. Set daily goals and complete them. Don't catch up, speed up. Don't set yourself up for failure, do simple things. Be successful with small goals and then you can add more.

Comment: In my visualization I saw a demonic entity submerged underwater and then they climbed up a ladder, awaiting a mini spaceship. Then I saw the European Union leaders and heard a horn.

Response: This is an image of your DNA. This may mean that perhaps you have a demonic attachment or an astral connection in your genetics. The horn could be the Shofar eliminating evil energies around you. Even mentally creating the sound of the Shofar eliminates negative energy.

Comment: Thinking of success is scary. It makes me feel small and unworthy. I want to get these negative feelings out.

Response: You are part of the God-Mind, there's nothing unworthy in the God-Mind and God-Mind does not waste energy. So if you exist, you have a purpose and you're worthy. Many people have these feelings because it is absorbed into your DNA. To remove this mind-pattern, visualize above your head a tree, or a flower with big roots down into your body. Then grab onto the plant just above your head. Pull it up, shake off all the dirt to remove the negative feelings that you accepted from other people because these are not your feelings or energies. Give everything up to your Oversoul and replace it with Pale Pink for Compassion and Unconditional Love for Self, Medium Green for emotional healing, Violet to flush everything out, and Pale

Orange for Truth. This will make a huge difference in allowing Self to accept Self-worth and Self-value.

Comment: Very simply my desire for success is the reason and driving force behind this current lifetime.

Response: To be successful in this lifeline is what Kabbalah calls the Tikkun or the correction.

Comment: Your explanation about staying in the light over these weeks has enabled my understanding. I have become less reactive and more proactive, thereby keeping in the light. It's not as challenging as I thought it would be. I needed to change my perspective and it's become a priority.

Response: The Zohar states that it's not what you look at it's how you look at it. If there's a dark room and people stand around an elephant, each will feel different things but it is the same creature. Somebody may feel the trunk and someone else feels the tail, so the experience of the same creature differs from person to person.

Kabbalah Meditations

Kabbalah says that when you study Kabbalah for a long period of time you become very knowledgeable of the truth of Creation. Then when you are at an advanced age your Soul loves God so much, and you have achieved such a high level of enlightenment that you can leave the body at will to pass on to the next dimension.

In Hebrew, Hitbodedot means meditation. The root is Badad, which means Self-isolation. This means that to meditate you must Self-isolate which is why so many ancient people went to the desert for their Spiritual work. In Hebrew, Midbar is the word for desert. The root is Davar, which means to speak. This means that when you go to the desert, the speech you need comes from within.

Kabbalah Meditations

Meditation = Hitbodedot. Comes from Badad = Self-isolation

Merkava = chariot, from the root Rakhav = to ride

Chasmal - speaking silence

Satan = 359/Zera Lavan = white seed = 359 (Semen)

In Hebrew Merkava means chariot. The root is Rakhav which means to ride. You may think of the ancient chariots of the Egyptians and Romans, but Merkava refers to the energetic chariots within that take you to the Spiritual levels. Kabbalah says that the Merkava is a Spiritual vehicle created to ascend to the mystical state. Once in the mystical state Kabbalah says that Chashmal, or speaking silently, takes place. This means thought or silent speaking. Beyond words, this means knowing which surpasses words. The Merkava is the shape of the Star Tetrahedron. When you put your Self in the center of a Gold or White Star Tetrahedron, visualize it spinning counterclockwise to lift your mentality to a higher level as well as to keep you protected. After you do the visualizations of the Sefirot and the Armor of God, end by putting this Merkava around your Self. Above all of this, place the Hebrew letter Tet in White to create immortality.

Gematria explains what at first glance might be considered unusual connections. For example, Satan has the Gematria 359. The Hebrew words Zera Lavan, meaning White Seed/Semen also has the Gematria of 359. This implies that in physical reality DNA contains unholy sequences. As you know, Adam HaRishon, the first Adam was contaminated by an alien virus.

Adam Kadmon is the Original Template for Humanity and was androgynous. Christianity turned Adam Kadmon into the Son of God, saying that God so loved the world that He gave his only Son. Adam Kadmon is actually the Christ Consciousness. When Adam HaRishon became physical it is that DNA that is carried forward to what is now referred to as the Messiah.

Correlation of Sefirot

In the next chart, you see the Middle Sephirot from Chesed to Yesod. The 3 Upper Sefirot of Keter, Chochmah, and Binah are not listed because these 3 represent the nonphysical. These 3 Upper Sefirot are called the Large Face of God. Malchut/Kingdom is not listed because this is the final manifestation of the 6 that are on the chart.

Kabbalah calls these middle 6 Sephirot, Zeir Anpin, an Aramaic term that means Small Face of God.

Correlation of Sefirot / Light

Sefirot	Description	Function	Action
Chesed	Tov/Good	Love	Mercy
Gevurah	Nogah/Glow	Strength	Revenge
Tiferet	Kavod/Glory	Beauty	Desire/Blessing
Netzach	Bahir/Brilliance	Victory	Peace
Hod	Zohar/Radiance	Splendor	Understanding
Yesod	Chaim/Life	Foundation	Health

Chesed is described with the Hebrew word Tov. Tov means good. The function of Chesed is Love which has the action of Mercy. When you Love, you have Mercy for others.

Gevurah is described with the Hebrew word Nogah, which means Glowing with Strength. Strength has the ability to take revenge.

Tiferet is described by the Hebrew word of Kavod, which means Glory. Tiferet is located in the heart area. When something is glorious the action is desire and blessing because of its beauty.

Homework

Use the Merkava and combine it with the Sephirot and/or Armor of God.

Visualize your Self inside a White Star Tetrahedron to see what comes to your mind.

Review the correlations of the Sefirot and Light to see which ones resonate with you.

Jewish Humor

The mother says, *Abe wake up you'll be late for Hebrew school.* Abe replies, *No, Mom, I don't want to go, the teachers hate me and all the kids make fun of me.* The mother says, *Too bad you still have to go.* Abe replies, *Give me one good reason why I should go.* The mother yells, *I'll give you two; you're 56 years old and you're the Rabbi!*

Webinar Homework Results

Comment: I tried to work with the Star Tetrahedron but I had difficulty understanding the placement.

Response: The Star Tetrahedron looks like a triangle on the top, a triangle on the bottom, and then a circle around it. Place your Self in the middle of this and visualize it spinning around you. When you spin it counterclockwise it turns into an interdimensional vortex. Spinning it clockwise creates a wormhole and keeps you focused on physical dimensions. Be sure to use your *Brown Merger/Self-Integration Archetype* at both the Pineal Gland and Reptilian brainstem so you do not get activated by either the vortex or the wormhole.

Comment: When I used the Merkava with the Sephirot, I saw the Eternal Truth from the God-Mind. This is opposed to the way of the world which is false. This dovetails into the Sephirot, specifically Tiferet. When I look down and only consider my emotions, I focus on my ego where I have empathy for and desire for dominance. When I balance and lookup I focus with God-Mind. I use discernment, wisdom, and knowing. In balance, I can take corrective actions of Eternal Truth.

Response: This is a matter of perspective. When you look from a higher perspective you get a more true view. When you look toward the Earth plane, you get more deception and falsehood. The Zohar says that everything is correct, it's just a matter of how you look at it. There is no wrong, only perspective.

Comment: When I use the White Star Tetrahedron, the 10th Sephira felt energized and was pulsing. I also saw a backward letter C.

Response: That is the Hebrew letter Kaf. This is something that you need so put it at your Pineal Gland to see what comes up for you.

Comment: I noticed recently that my angry thoughts that kept repeating and looping for years have disappeared. I'm wondering if this is a result of using the Ane B'koach Prayer, visualizing the Hebrew letters, working with the *Names of God*, or my Hyperspace releasing work.

Response: All of this combined is going to give results to anyone doing the work

Comment: I have more peace, feel freer and light. I wonder if this is reflecting or impacting the outer world in any way.

Response: Your positive work is reflected in the entire world, helping all of Humanity and beyond.

Comment: I use the White Star Tetrahedron in much of my work with the *Names of God* and the Angels of Destruction. It's very powerful, feels impenetrably safe, and is very nonphysical. I feel like I am returning to my comfortable state of Being and it feels odd to ground again. I did it alone and could see it spin so I knew I was doing it correctly.

Response: Yes, you are doing it correctly and it should make you feel protected and safe.

Comment: My experiences are not what I expected with the Merkava. Of course, you rarely get what you expect. I did not travel anywhere or I was not shown anything it was more of a feeling. The Merkava felt like it was more of a vehicle or a vortex. It's your own personal Spiritual vehicle and your time machine. It's your protection, it's everything and you need to learn how to use it. It's like having a brand-new car with the latest technology. You need to practice how to use it, yet it's been around forever.

Response: According to the Zohar technology, all space and time are one, so you're not traveling anywhere. Changing your perspective changes your understanding.

Comment: I found myself in deep space and heard the sound of trumpet's lower tone going up to the highest. It was so exciting and calming at the same time.

Response: That's the sound of the Shofar which removes negative energies and vanquishes evil. Listen to the videos of the Shofar online. Be sure you listen to the Shofar made from a Ram's horn. The large Yemenite Shofar is from a Kadu. Hear the sound and then replay that mentally. Always keep the sound of the Shofar with you when you do your mental work.

Comment: Binah is like a feminine Divine Mother womb-like aspect of God. Chochmah feels like a sword and discriminates between what is good for the Soul versus what does not support Spiritual growth.

Response: Chochmah is a more masculine energy that it feeds into Binah. Keter, Chochmah, and Binah are the top three more Spiritual nonphysical aspects of the Sefirot.

Comment: I bought a clear quartz Merkava star and rotated clockwise a few times. Over the next few days every time I did this I felt trapped. When I rotated it counterclockwise nothing happened.

Response: When you rotate it clockwise it holds you in physical reality which is why you feel trapped. Rotating it the opposite way neutralizes the energy so you stayed in one place. Reset and start over again.

Comment: When I place the Merkava around me after my prayers, it feels grounding and I feel solid. When I only use the Merkava it takes me to other worlds.

Response: This makes sense because it's an interdimensional vehicle.

Comment: I focused on Gevurah and use the Angel Dumiel. There was a demonic attempt to invade my energy field.

Response: When you use these high-level Angelic Frequencies you attract attention from both positive and negative sides. The negative attack to try to stop you. This is similar to putting medication on your skin that burns and itches because it's working.

Comment: I am removing limited and negative thoughts with the Shield of Solomon.

Response: Keep this template under your pillow or on a wall facing you as it provides powerful protection.

Comment: When I was spinning the Merkava it quickly went to supersonic speed. I felt intense, almost explosive energy. Then it slowed its spinning and is much more steady.

Response: When you start a car, the engine at first spins very rapidly. When the car warms up, the engine reaches a plateau. This is the same with energetic work. When you start, especially if you have been stagnant for a while, the energy intensifies. As you become more proficient the energy settles down into a balanced rhythm.

Comment: I'm aware that I'm here to work on correcting, confronting, and reflecting on what I think of as my enemy.

Response: In Lord of the Flies children are trapped on an island filled with enemies. Eventually one of the children realizes that the enemy is only imagined and says, I've seen the enemy and the enemy is us. When you confront the enemy you are confronting your Self. You go within, look at your negative mind-patterns such as Self-sabotage and Self-abuse. Otherwise, you personify and externalize because this is easier to face than going within.

Comment: Confusion is part of my deprogramming. Knowing has always saved me.

Response: Confusion and doubt allow negative energy to increase and intensify. Keep doing your deprogramming work.

Comment: I meditated on the sixth Sefira. The one in the middle kept getting redirected to the light. I kept hearing how necessary Compassion is. Importance of Compassion is fundamental to being in the light. I have Compassion for who and what I AM. This knowing gives me space and understanding to now allow others to be who they are.

Response: This is one of the main reasons everyone is here, so excellent point.

Comment: I put the Merkava at my Pineal Gland.

Response: This is not correct. You can start it at your Pineal Gland, but then you must expand it to encompass you so that you are in the center and it is all around you, encompassing your entire Being.

Kabbalah Mysteries

Permutations of the *Name of God* YHVH

YHVH is pronounced Yud-Hey-Waw-Hey and can be permutated in 54 ways. Permutation means combining letters in different ways to create different energies. According to Kabbalah, the 4 letter Name must be permutated as shown in the chart. Then, each permutation of the 4 letter Name can be further permutated into the number of Triplets shown in the column on the far right. The total number of Triplets adds up to 54. This is symbolic of DNA which is represented by the number 4/physical reality which is created by mind-pattern/nonphysical which is represented by the number 3. DNA has 4 protein bases. Mind-pattern has 3 levels of consciousness. The triplets are also connected to the *72 Names of God.*

54 x 4 letter Name = 216 versions.

Permutations of YHVH	
54 Ways = 216	
Permutation	Triplet
YHVH יהוה	12
YYVH ייוה	12
YVVH יווה	12
YYVV ייוו	6
YYHH ייהה	6
VVHH ווהה	6
	54

The Gematria of 216 contains the Hebrew letters Yud, Resh, Vav. Together this represents the metal of iron. Barzel is another Hebrew word for iron. King Solomon had a huge naval fleet that went all over the world including to a place he called Barzel where iron was purchased to take back to the Holy Land to build the Temple. Barzel became Brazil. Brazil has a very high Hebrew genetic population with an estimate of 60% of its people having Hebrew genetics. This is one reason why Brazil is supportive of Israel and why it is moving its embassy to Jerusalem.

7 Mystical Seals

There is much discussion in Kabbalistic circles about the 7 Mystical Seals. Some Kabbalists say that they are part of an Angelic Language used by specific Archangels when they perform their functions. It is said that King Solomon used these when dealing with demonic energies as well as Angelic Frequencies.

The numbers 7 and 70 are frequently used in the Torah, such as the 7 Days of Creation. There are also 7 Chakra Bands and of course, in Hyperspace the number 7 represents completion. There are 7 Lower Sephirot plus 3 Upper Sefirot equals 10 Sephirot in total. 70 is 7x 10. 10 is the number of the complete Sefirot. The Sefirot are clues to understanding these 7 Mystical Seals. These are seals, which means that they are covering up something. They are like a keyhole to a lock that is going to open up something else, like a gate.

Magic Square

In the Magic Square, there are 3 lines of 3 numbers in which all of the numbers in any direction add up to 15. In Hebrew fifteen is spelled Yod, Hey. The Gematria of Yod is 10 and Hey is 5. Yod, Hey is the shortened version of the 4-Letter Name of God. According to the Kabbalah this is one of the frequency sequences that enabled Creation to exist but supposedly no one knows how to use it today. God created everything through formulas like these. Math formulas underlie all of Creation. This is why the educational system does its best to confuse students so they do not want to study math. The global handlers want you to only know enough math to function on a daily basis but not enough to ever figure out or understand the math formulas that underlie all of Creation.

Magic Square - Mystery of Creation

2 9 4   COL = 15
7 5 3   YAH = 15
6 1 8   יה

In the 3x3 Magic Square, you can see that there are 8 points. The more you look at these types of charts the more connections you find because this information is already within. These charts are the numerical foundation of all of Creation. Focus on bringing out whatever the Soul-personality needs for this specific lifeline, otherwise, you will feel overwhelmed.

Magic Square - Mystery of Creation

2 9 4
7 5 3
6 1 8

COL = 15

YAH = 15

יה

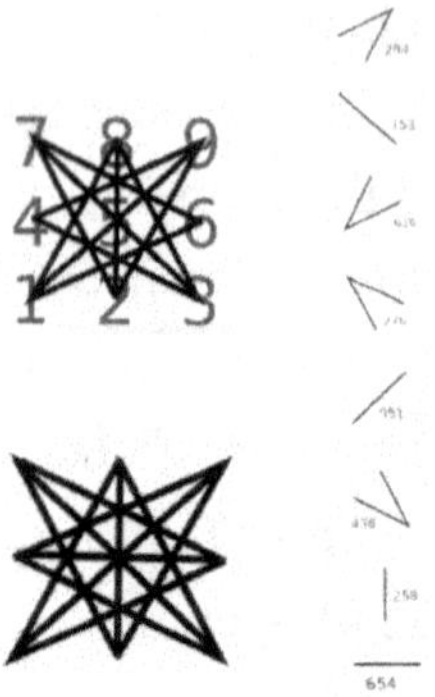

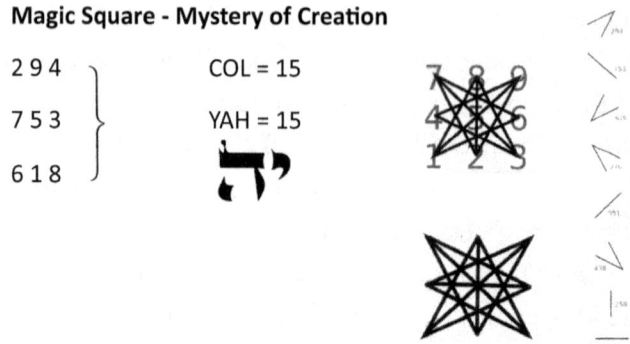

There is another *Magic Square of Order 10 Corresponding to Keter-Crown*, where every line in every direction adds up to the number 10. This *Magic Square* supposedly is the Secret of Creation which contains all the mathematical formulas to create everything, such as the planets and the Sefirot as shown on the chart beneath it as an example.

Magic Square of Order 10 Corresponding to Keter-Crown

1	2	98	97	96	5	94	93	9	10
90	12	13	87	86	85	84	18	19	11
80	79	23	24	76	75	27	28	22	71
70	69	68	34	36	35	37	33	62	61
41	59	58	57	45	46	44	53	52	50
51	49	48	47	55	56	54	43	42	60
31	32	38	64	65	66	67	63	39	40
30	29	73	74	25	26	77	78	72	21
20	82	83	14	16	15	17	88	89	81
91	92	3	7	6	95	4	8	99	100

Magic Squares

Order n	*Correspondence*	*Sum of Side* S = $(n^3 + n)/2$
3	Saturn	15
4	Jupiter	34
5	Mars	65
6	Sun	111
7	Venus	175
8	Mercury	260
9	Moon	369
10	Keter-Crown	505
11	Chokhmah-Wisdom	671
12	Binah-Understanding	860
13	Chesed-Love	1105
14	Gevurah-Strength	1379
15		1695
16	Tiferet-Beauty	2056
17	Netzach-Victory	2465
18	Hod-Splendor	2925
19	Yesod-Foundation	3439
20	Malkhut-Kingship	4010

There are entire sections in the Zohar written in Aramaic code that have never been translated or the symbolism revealed, at least publicly. According to the Zohar, Aramaic is the base language of the Earth, meaning that the entire world originally spoke only Aramaic. Aramaic was the physical version of Hebrew, the nonphysical language. Christ spoke Aramaic. The priests spoke Hebrew because they communicated with the nonphysical meaning of God and the Angelic Frequencies. In modern times there is only one place where Aramaic is still spoken. This is in a mountain village of Syria not far from the Golan Heights near the border of Lebanon. Aramaic is sometimes called Syriac.

In ***Revelations of Time & Space, History and God*** and ***Template of God-Mind*** at the bottom of Tzim Tzum is a square that represents the Magic Square of Creation which is actually inside the Magic Square Order of 10. This is a square within a square that creates a cube when all the points in the corners are connected.

Mystery of Yichudim

According to Kabbalah, this information represents the Mystery of Yichudim. The Hebrew word Yichudim means unification and comes from the Kingdom of Yehudah/Judah. Yehudah is a derivation of Yichudim both meaning unification. This means that the purpose of the Kingdom of Judah was to unify Creation. This extrapolates on to the entire Hebrew/Israelite existence which is to unify Humanity while teaching the truth of Creation. The Zohar says that unification is the Mystery of Nativity. Nativity is usually a term that is only heard in Christianity, but of course, Christianity is based on the Zohar. The Hebrew word for nativity is ebor. Ebor comes from the same root as eber, which refers to a Hebrew person. Ebor also means impregnation. Root words show connected energies. Eber means the ones who crossed over. Putting this together it means that when your mother is impregnated your Soul-personality crosses over from the nonphysical to the physical. This is your nativity or birth. Eber is related to Iberia in Spain. King Solomon, sent his people across the Mediterranean to colonize North Africa. The colony became known as Eberia/Iberia which means the place of the Hebrews. Portugal was also colonized by Hebrews as well as Italy. Italia means the Glory of God in Hebrew.

Christianity also references the Holy Spirit. The Zohar calls this the Ruach Hakodesh which is Hebrew for the Holy Spirit. The Ruach Hakodesh is related to the Shekhinah which is the female energy of God on Earth. The Shekhinah is the equivalent of the Holy Mother and is related to Mary Magdalene.

Erev Rav

The Zohar says that the Satan uses human bodies as targets of opportunity. Because the Satan and demons cannot physically incarnate, they connect and attach to the bodies of others. This allows them to vicariously experience physical reality through the humans to whom they are attached or possess. They feed on the energy of negativity which is why they encourage their hosts to participate in negativity which most people would call evil.

The Erev Rav were not Jews or Hebrews They were Egyptians and others that converted to Judaism and then left Egypt with the

Israelites. It is believed that the Pharoah sent them with the Israelites as spies and saboteurs. The head of the Erev Rav was Koresh. His people were the descendants of Cain. The first children of Eve, Cain and Abel, did not belong to Adam. They were the progeny of the Reptilian who seduced Eve. The first child of Adam with Eve was Seth. Therefore all people are now descended from Seth. The Erev Rav were the creators of the Golden Calf when the Israelites were wandering in the desert. The Golden Calf was physical. It was not a stature but moved. Sometimes these Golem-type creatures were made, sacrificed and eaten. The Zohar says that Egypt is the code for slavery, bondage and materialism. Interestingly, much of the imagery of the Deep State is taken from Ancient Egypt.

The Bible stories are symbolic and are not to be taken literally. They are to be used as analogies for mind-patterns and progressions through life. Creation is an ongoing process. The universe is an extended body of humankind. Humankind includes all intelligent humanoid life everywhere. Humanity is the blueprint of the entire cosmos. Your DNA is the blueprint of all of Creation. This is why 97 percent of DNA is identical for every species because it contains the template for all of Creation.

Kabbalah is a guide for transforming chaos and fragmentation into unity and completion. Kabbalah is a Spiritual technology that takes chaos, which is a misunderstood pattern that has been fragmented and pulls it together into a cohesive form. The Zohar eliminates darkness so that you can reveal light. Darkness cannot exist with light because even a little spark lights a dark room. The tiniest bit of light starts to eliminate the totality of darkness.

There was a time in the Middle Ages when 17 groups in Eastern Europe completely twisted the Zohar and Kabbalah to create their own type of religion. The one who was in charge eventually fled to Turkey where he became a Muslim and tried to influence the Muslim people. It's believed that he and his followers were responsible for the fundamentalist Islamic movement that exists to this day. Madonna studied and promoted Kabbalah in the 1990s. Most likely, because she is a programming icon, whatever she did may have been used in her programming, the programming of others or both.

Dreams

The Zohar and Kabbalah include dreams in Mysteries of Life and Creation. Through the centuries there have been many Kabbalistic Rabbis who have their own interpretations. When looking at these interpretations you must consider the time period as well as their country. For example, in the Middle Ages, there was a very large Jewish population in Egypt. The Egyptians believed in demons and evil spirits, so they lived in fear. The Kabbalistic Rabbis in Egypt told the people that demons don't exist, so therefore they cannot hurt you and there is no need to be afraid. During this time they also told people that dreams came from the food that they ate therefore dreams had no significance. This was because there was a lot of anti-semitisms so the Jews were afraid of being attacked. This caused bad dreams so the Rabbis told them the dreams had no significance. They did not want the people attracting negativity because of their fears. Other Rabbis in other countries under different circumstances in different time periods gave tremendous value to dreams.

The Hebrew word for dream is Chalom. The root is Hallam which means to strengthen. This means that dreams are to strengthen you because they're giving you information from your subconscious mind, alternate realities, and higher levels of existence, all of which you are not aware of in your waking state. In your dream state, you may also be receiving help from those who have passed on as well as Angelic levels. The Zohar says that dreams are derived from Heavenly Realms. It also says that a large part of your Soul-personality leaves the body.

The Zohar says that dreams can bring good or bad omens and that all dream interpretations are valid. It's kind of like another version of quantum physics that states that nothing exists unless you look at it.

When something is seen it is created. In the same way, what you do with the information from the dream creates your pathway. The Zohar says that you should ask a dream question before you go to bed so you will wake up with an answer in the morning. Basically, this means that you send a message to the higher levels of Self to get an answer from Self for Self. It also says that you learn things in the dream state that your waking mind cannot understand. This is why you cannot remember some of your dreams. Your waking mind might sabotage the information. When the information stays in your subconscious mind, it can come forward when the time is correct. Carl Jung did a lot of work with dreams but it is said that he also studied the Zohar and Kabbalah. Your goal is always to interpret your own dreams.

The Zohar says that your dreams will reveal negative aspects of your personality that would otherwise remain hidden. This is why you need to do dream interpretation. This helps you decide what you need to look at within Self so you can make the correction. The dream state is just as valid as the waking state, if not more. Sometimes your dreams can be prophetic and they can reveal positive hidden aspects of Self as well. The Zohar says that dream interpretation helps put your life in perspective.

Homework

- Meditate on the 7 Mystical Seals, one at a time in White on a Royal Blue background at your Pineal Gland in the order presented, to see what comes into your mind.
- Meditate on the corresponding Magic Squares of 3x3 and 10x10.
- How is this work influencing your life?

Jewish Humor

There were 2 Jewish men, Jankel and Moisha, riding on a train across Poland to meet their brides for the first time. The first time the train stopped, Jankel grabbed his suitcase and yelled, *I'm not ready to get married, I'm not getting married!* Moisha watched him run away. When the train reached its destination, the 2 mothers of the brides were waiting at the station. They were shocked to find only one groom. The mothers were arguing about whose daughter Moisha should marry, so Moishe told them the Rabbi should decide. The Rabbi said, *the solution is plain, we will use the wisdom of King Solomon. Cut the man in half and each of you takes half.* The first mother exclaimed that she could not do this to a person. The second mother said, *yes, cut him in half!* The Rabbi pointed to the second mother and said, *that's the real mother-in-law!*

Webinar Homework Results

Comment: The Sephirot can be a mechanism for correction. I sensed the Seals are linked to the Sephirot, to the energetic field of the Earth, and all of Existence. The Seals were both open and closed depending upon how I looked at them. They have incredible energetic potential. I feel a need to proceed with extreme caution.

Response: Yes, the Sefirot can be a mechanism for correction. You are correct in all that you wrote.

Comment: I had strong experiences with the Magic Square. I had the immediate feeling of a 360 degree expansion of spatial awareness. Physically I felt equal stimulation in my frontal lobes and the top half of my brain.

Response: Yes, this work can open you up in a myriad of ways.

Comment: I felt that one Mystical Seal unlocks the next.

Response: This would be like a formula or Hyperspace sentence, so this makes sense.

Comment: Fibonacci numbers, the foundation of Creation came into my mind.

Response: Yes, Creation is based on this.

Comment: I used the Seal with the 4 lines. With unimaginable speed I found myself in space, getting away from Earth, going simultaneously into different realms. Then, I was blocked by a brick wall in front of me.

Response: The Zohar is based on interdimensional energies so this makes sense. The Seal stopped you as protection as a way of showing you that you are not yet ready for the information it contains.

Comment: I get the sense that the Seals are mathematical equations. In the past, ancient Christians were notorious for changing ancient documents. Perhaps these ancient documents have been tampered with.

Response: The Kabbalists kept their documents hidden for thousands of years, never revealing them to anyone. Other religions and even Jews did not know that the documents existed. Kabbalists believe that even changing a dot or the size of a letter leads to death. No one has the nerve to change anything.

Comment: I got a clear cube and was told to break it. When I did, hundreds of spheres of light came pouring out.

Response: That was probably the Light of the Ain Sof, or the never-ending energy.

Comment: The Mystical Seals remind me of the Hyperspace DNA Archetype.

Response: It seems that many of these Seals are about the sequences and Archetypes of the DNA.

Comment: I got that we need to take responsibility, not only for what's happening in our lives but also for what's happening in the world, because the world is a reflection of each other.

Response: Absolutely. The world is a reflection of each other's mind-patterns and collective mind-patterns. The Zohar says that for the Light of God to manifest correctly, there needs to be restriction. Now, you are seeing restrictions on Earth. As an analogy, if electricity were allowed to just be thrown out into an environment, it would be unusable and scattered about. By restricting the electricity to a thin coated wire, then connecting the wire inside the lightbulb, you get light that can be directed. Restrictions help you understand the origin of the Light and how it manifests.

Comment: A few webinar sessions ago, everyone was wearing Royal Blue.

Response: Everyone is a reflection of everyone else, so when you have Matching Color, Tone, and Archetype the clothing reflects this as well. Wherever you go, whether a crowded theatre or a restaurant, you can see people around you wearing similar colors. Even when you are out with a group of friends you may all show up in similar colors. Matching Color, Tone, and Archetypes improves communication.

Comment: This work enables me to deprogram intensely. It's pretty deep so I've needed to slow down, be gentle and lighten up a bit. I relax into the healing *Name of God* and I'm working to get adequate sleep. This is part of my cleaning up process. I hope this sounds right.

Response: There's no right or wrong, there's only your experience. Each person has a different way of getting through their experiences. Everything depends on your mind-pattern, your emotions, your childhood. Your experience tells you about yourself and what is right for you or it would not happen.

Comment: I am collecting and reading historical novels that deal with the contents of the information given by you about the Knights Templar, Waldensians, Bernard de Clairvaux. These books remind me of my purpose for living. If I forget that I have a mission to fulfill, they help me remember my motivation.

Response: This is a great point to emphasize. Often people talk about how insignificant they feel, like whatever they do doesn't matter. That is the furthest thing from the truth. According to Kabbalah, every life has a purpose and significance to the Creator. All energy is used; energy is never wasted.

10 Steps to the Holy Spirit

Kabbalah says that there are 3 covenants that must be kept by Humanity to purify the Soul:

1. Circumcision 2.Torah 3. Shabbat

In addition, there are 10 Sefirot which refer to the levels of the God-Mind so there are 10 Steps to the Holy Spirit.

1. Study

Learn the Truth of Existence in all lifelines.

2. Carefulness

Stay focused and do things in sequence.

3. Diligence

Keep going and do not allow distractions.

4. Cleanliness

Maintain cleanliness on all levels of your Being. Resisting negativity, which is part of Tiferet, is part of cleanliness.

5. Abstention

Abstain from temptation.

6. Purity

Maintain purity on all levels of your Being by eliminating and avoiding contamination.

7. Piety

Stay connected to the God-Mind and maintain control of your own thoughts.

8. Humility

You are not better than anyone else. Teach others and share what you know with those who are willing to learn.

9. Fear of Sin

Be aware of your thoughts so you do not fall into negativity of any kind.

10. Holiness

Live your life as if each thought, word, action, and reaction is a prayer.

The Zohar says that if you live your life this way, you can become aware of prophecy which is actually more intense than the Holy Spirit. The ***Bible*** is filled with prophecy. Prophecy allows you to be aware of possibilities in the linear future.

Spiritual Energy

The Zohar states that because your 10 fingers correlate to the 10 Sephirot that using your hands is like Spiritual reflexology. When you put your fingers together you're actually activating your Sefirot. When a circumcised male sits down, bends forward so that his head is between his knees facing the circumcision, he creates an energetic circuit.

The Gematria of the *4-Letter Name of God* is 26. The Gematria of the Aleph is 1. However, it is comprised of 2 Yods and 1 Vav. The Gematria of Yod is 10 and Vav is 6, so 2 Yods = 20 + 6 for 1 Vav = 26.

This is another layer of Aleph which shows its Gematria is also 26. 2 + 6 = 8, the number of the Oversoul.

SPIRITUAL ENERGY

יהוה

5 6 5 10

26

א = יוי **(Aleph)**

10 6 10

26

Kaf

Kaf is spelled Kaf, Vav with a Gematria of 26. This word means road or path. This explains that you are learning the path that you need to take to get you to other higher levels of existence. You begin with Aleph which has the Gematria of 8, the number of the Oversoul and Infinity.

כו **Khav = Road / Path**

6 20

26

When the priests went into the Temple, they wore a breastplate of stones and precious jewels in a particular array that would supposedly light up as they went before the Ark of the Covenant. Only the priests were allowed to wear this breastplate. Under the breastplate, they wore pure linen to prevent the wearer from being electrocuted when the breastplate was energized. Only a person with an exceedingly strong and pure mind-pattern could wear the breastplate because the energy was so intense that it could burn or kill the wearer. The priests were only allowed to go into the room with the Ark of the Covenant one time per year on Yom Kippur. Yom Kippur is when the entire nation was judged for the following year.

The breastplate was called Urim and Thummim. Urim means lights. Thummin means twins. The name Thomas means twins and originates from the word Thummin. The breastplate configuration refers to the twinning of the nonphysical with the physical. The priest wore these twin lights over the Tiferet in the Heart Chakra. As the priest prayed and asked questions, the lights lit up. The priest would know the answer by interpreting the sequences of the lights.

According to the Zohar, Keter, the first Sephirot at the top of your head, is the root of the Tree of Life, feeding energy from the Absolute. The Sefirot are the 10 levels of Illumination of the Creator, starting with Keter and ending in Malchut which is the physical plane. Each Sephira represents a layer of Creation as well as the steps the Creator took to manifest in physical reality. The Zohar says that there was more than one Tzim Tzum because there were 7 pre-adamic civilizations. This means that the Creator took 7 times before finally everything was created to Its satisfaction. The remnants of those previous 7 civilizations still exist.

Judaism and Christianity constantly talk about fear of God. This does not make sense that you should fear what created you. This is a bad translation that really should be awe and love of God. Punishment does not come from God. God does not punish but rather you inflict punishment upon your Self because whatever you send out reflects back to you. God is neutral but It does allow you to deal with the consequences of your actions. The Zohar says that you can reach synthesis, unity and perfection. The Sabbath is about unity as well as the synthesis and perfection of all things. The Zohar also says that every stranger you meet is a chance for Spiritual transformation. There are no chance meetings because each person reflects something back as an opportunity for your inner transformation. Every soul is destined for peace and joy, and fulfillment.

In the Christian ***Bible***, the New Testament talks about the Messiah riding on the back of a donkey when he comes into Jerusalem. A donkey represents carrying burdens. Since the Christ represented the burdens of Humanity and their elimination, the donkey was used as the symbol for the Christ to ride upon when he entered Jerusalem.

The Divine Presence in physical reality is called the Shekhinah, the feminine aspect of God. Some traditions call the Shekhinah the Bride of God. The root of Shekhinah is shachar which means to dwell within. This means that the feminine aspect of God dwells within each person. The feminine aspect is peaceful and benevolent. The story of Adam and Eve has been mistranslated because God did not take a rib from Adam, God took apart from him. God took the inner feminine part and personified it. Sexual intercourse is the representation of the connection of the Creator with the Shekhinah, the merger of the male and female small parts of the Creator.

Kabbalah and the Zohar say that if you think of somebody else when you're having sex with your partner, it will corrupt the energy of the child that you create. This means that if you're not focused on your partner during that intimate moment, you will attract the Soul of some other energy that may not be so good. This is one reason why people have challenging children who may be nothing like their parents.

The Zohar says that women enter the world to help men with their Spiritual correction because women are better at this. The female is the bridge between the Earth/physical and Spiritual/nonphysical. Souls are created in pairs, both male and female. While your Soul is androgynous it has a male and female component. When they both incarnate at the same time on the Earth plane is when you find your Eternal Life Mate.

The Zohar says that you must marry and have a family to complete your spiritual connection. Because you incarnate many times, this means that some incarnations you marry and have a family, and sometimes you do not. Jews are not expected to complete all of the 613 Commandments in one lifetime because it is not even possible. If you have Hebrew genetics you are considered a Jew. The Ark of the Covenant is actually a representation of the Shekhinah and is referred to as a wall. President Trump continually spoke of building the wall or border. He even said that it had nothing to with a physical border, but had to do with something beyond this dimension.

The Zohar states that the human body is a pure manifestation of a desire to receive for Self alone. This means that the body is a selfish thing because it wants to eat, have fun, have sex and sleep. The body puts itself first. This references the Animal Mind that must be controlled by the Spiritual Mind. The Zohar says red wine brings balance by allowing more light in your energy field. In Hebrew wine is Yayin with a Gematria of 70. The Gematria for Sod, which means secret in Hebrew, is also 70. Red wine allows for secrets and balance to occur in your life. The root of the *Tree of Life* is in Keter keeps you free from pain and suffering. The root of the *Tree of Knowledge* is in Machut and brings sin and evil. The trees and the branches grow up towards the middle intertwining and connecting with each other. The fruit that Eve took from the *Tree of Knowledge* that it was not an apple, it was a grape. The code in the Zohar is the wine because Eve took the secret of life and brought it forward to Adam. This caused them to be aware of secrets for which they were not ready yet to receive. The Zohar says that Eve actually crushed the grapes and gave Adam the dredges of them. She did not even give him the good parts but rather the leftovers which were very sour. This is appropriate symbolism for what followed.

The Zohar says that the Angel of Darkness must always have permission to be in your life. This means that when something evil or negative comes before you it must leave when you tell it to leave. Some people say they wake up at night with an entity in their room. Use the *Name of God* and the entity must leave.

Only desiring to receive for Self without sharing is a sin. This comes from the mind-pattern of Esau who represents the *Tree of Knowledge*. In the ***Bible***, Egypt represents negativity, demonic energies and sin.

The AriZal

One of the most famous Kabbalists in history is called the AriZal, which means Lion of God. He was only 38 when he passed away. He was born in Egypt but moved to Israel in the 1500s. At this time there were still many Jews living in Egypt. He said that he moved to Israel to find this one Jewish student who he said would understand his information. He also said that his entire purpose for being born was to teach this one student. The AriZal said that his information was not to be revealed until centuries later during the Age of Aquarius. Per his instructions, the book is now available in Hebrew/Aramaic/English.

As I was reading this book I was thinking that the AriZal must have been mentally ill. As I'm thinking this the book went flying out of my hand and across the room. Every time I thought he was mentally ill, the book flew onto the floor. Finally, after about the 15th time, the thought came into my head that I need to look at his work from a different perspective. So this is what I have done.

Homework

Review the 10 steps to the Holy Spirit to determine which ones you are and are not doing.

Meditate on the Urim and Thummim lights and twins that were on the breastplate of the Holy Temple priests to see what comes into your mind.

Jewish Humor

Three Jewish mothers are sitting on a bench arguing over which one's son loves her the most. The first one says, *you know, my son sends me flowers, every Shabbat.* The second mother says, *you call that love-- my son calls me every day. That's nothing*, said 3rd mother, *my son is in therapy, five days a week and the whole time he talks about me.*

More Jewish Humor

Five Jewish women were eating lunch in a café. Approaching them nervously, the waiter says, *ladies is anything, okay*?

Webinar Homework Results

Comment: Sin needs to be taken seriously. If I went to demonstrations, for example, I can be challenged to do a lot of sin, but you could get harmed. This could lead to anger emotions rising such that you can even be tempted to harm, hurt or kill somebody. I better not participate.

Response: Sometimes just watching the news makes anger rise up. Even in your mind, you might want to attack people who perpetrate terrible things. You must always stop your Self, release it up to your Oversoul and into Keter.

Comment: I am wondering if circumcision is symbolic or actually necessary for men to reach full spiritual capacity.

Response: According to the Zohar and Kabbalah the removal of the foreskin is the removal of the Klipot, or the covering that is connected to the Satan. So the answer is yes, it is necessary to physically do this.

Comment: I put the Urim at the Pineal Gland and saw six bright lights. I have been applying the *72 Names of God* to overcome limiting ideas in my thinking process.

Response: The more you concentrate on these higher levels the more the issues of your life diminish.

Comment: The more I learn the less confusion I have.

Response: *The Tree of Life* is going to give you more Light in your life.

Comment: When electricity or energy is restricted via thin wires, that gives light. If electricity was scattered free with no restrictions there would be no light. For God to manifest, energy must be harnessed via restrictions. This puts the covid scamdemic in a much better context. I wish I would have known about this at the beginning of the lockdowns. I struggled with having my freedom suddenly yanked away. I had a lot of anger over it. Now I hit another layer of understanding which helps to nullify my anger. I also find it ironic that Mike Lyndell the pillow guy is on a mission to wake people up yet he sells pillows so people can go to sleep.

Response: Very good observations. As you know the universe is about opposites because opposites create balance.

Comments: There are lots of gateways by twinning the stones. By twinning amethyst and diamond, my mission was revealed, my Redemption is being crystal clear in my thoughts and decodes the perfect math of electromagnetic frequencies. Here is a listing of the 12 Stones that are on the breastplate of the High Priest that I found in my research.

1. Ruby - Wisdom of Spirit that can spark the light of creative living.

2. Topaz - Worship the one God to balance emotions and calm the Spirit

3. Emerald - The light of certainty will power up corrections.

4. Turquoise - In the repose of contemplating beauty, forgiveness, and commitment, correction focuses your sight from above to reflections below. The color Turquoise in Hyperspace brings the past to future bringing balance.

5. Sapphire - Each lifestream is an opportunity to correct all blood lineage.

6. Diamond - Redemption is initiated by being crystal clear in thoughts to clear the way to correct actions. Diamond is so hard that you cannot break it.

7. Jacinth - The Gateway of breaking, the code of Satan is to balance emotions and release judgments.

8. Agate - Looking at the beauty of dark activates the Light of the Hand of God to heal. An Agate is A-Gate.

9. Amethyst - Absolute certainty is the perfect path of electro-magnetic frequencies and protection.

10. Beryl - Correct by tempering the fires of passion with the wisdom and understanding of actions that contain the light of goodness. In Hebrew, Beryl means The Well of God

11. Shoham/Onyx - The Merkava reflects the truth that light is always reflected in the information of the Shadow. The shadow contains your light, discovered by facing your fears,

12. Jasper - Healing and correcting Creation is coded in numbers used to praise the Glory of God.

Response: This is an excellent summary of The Twelve Semi-Precious Stones used on the breastplate of the high priests when they entered the Holy Temple. The 12 stones represent the 12 Tribes, 12 Zodiac signs, 12 months of the year. The secret is that adding the 12 energies all together creates a 13th energy.

Comment: I always remember that I am in a constant state of Grace because of unconditional love. I am working on releasing any need to judge others as well as resisting taking on the judgments of others.

Response: Acceptance and receptivity to God-Mind is based on a foundation of unconditional love. What you project out always comes back.

Comment: I see the connection between cause and effect which means looking at the big picture. This allows us to prosper in a world of cause and effect. We must consciously take on the responsibility to test everything and take it to the ultimate tester, of course, God, who is beyond our understanding.

Response: The earlier you catch something in need of correction the easier it is to correct it. The Urim and Thummim can represent this as well as your Spiritual level for discerning the created world with all its complexities.

Comment: I see the Urim as a universal fire and a creative force. The Thummim is lightning, but not programming.

Response: The Zohar says that when lightning strikes the Earth this causes a connection and a change. Lightning is a force that brings creative energy into physical reality similar to what an earthquake can do.

Comment: I curse up a storm at times, I'm trying to stop doing that, but when I see what's going on in the outer world it brings out the worst in me. I see the Urim and Thummim as twin lights that can be merged as one.

Response: That is correct. They are opposites of the same energy such as dark and light, right and left. This is for balance.

Comment: What Kabbalah books do you recommend.

Response: This is difficult because Janet and I pick through all the various books to bring you the best information possible. If we recommend specific books people take everything as fitting in with what we teach. Even our work we tell you to always question. We pick and choose our research books very carefully out of the thousands of Kabbalah books out there so we can bring what we feel is the best information to you.

Comment: Through our studies of the Torah Kabbalah and Zohar, we understand our specific contributions to this vast body of the Mind of God. This gives me permission to savor and enjoy my studies. When applying what I learned in my everyday life, I worked with various images at my Pineal Gland of the Urim and Thummin and various circuitry. I also reread several chapters of ***Blue Blood*** and other of your books referencing the breastplate of the priest.

Response: It is good to review these books because this book builds upon what you learned in other books.

Comment: Within the last six months, many miracles and synchronicities are occurring on a daily basis. I ask a question and the answer comes. I have new job opportunities and better ways to manage my money. Money came in the mail unexpectedly.

Response: Yes you can control everything in your life to your satisfaction. You want to do what is most correct and beneficial so even if you are not satisfied at first but you understand its purpose then you can accept and work with what comes to you.

Comment: When meditating on the breastplate of the high priest the seals seem to open and activate the breastplate in a multi-dimensional way.

Response: This was also a communication device. Underneath the breastplate the priest had to wear clean White linen between his skin and the breastplate for grounding so he would not be electrocuted. Most people could not wield this kind of power. Just like you could not pick up and wield a big sword right now because you do not have the muscles developed to do this.

Comment: I am working on my diligence and cleanliness. Everything I've learned here has led me to this path. The work I do helps my humility. One must be humble to take care of others on an intimate level. When I look at the twin lights Urim and Thummin, I sense something pure, alien, and highly intelligent.

Response: That's because it is extremely alien and highly intelligent. I believe that it is somewhere hidden in a laboratory, perhaps in the Middle East. In North America, a replication of the Urim and Thummin is used by the global handlers for their own purposes.

Astrology

Some Kabbalistic Rabbis have said that no one should pay attention to astrology because they did not want people to be influenced by astrological messages. They want the people to use their own minds. Astrology compels but does not impel. This means that you have the mind-pattern strength to override any outer influence. You are more powerful than the stars. The Hebrews were known in my countries for their compendium of ancient astrological wisdom. Many Kings and Emperors called upon the Ancient Hebrew Rabbis to interpret the messages of the stars. The Zohar states that Abraham had great knowledge of the stars and planetary influences and that Moses used astrology to govern the Hebrews.

If you know the day of the week you are born, the Zohar actually lists the specific mind-pattern associated with your day of birth.

Sunday: Extremes; possibly bipolar.
Monday: Prefer seclusion; anger issues.
Tuesday: Wealth; promiscuity.
Wednesday: Wise; radiant.
Thursday: Kindness
Friday: Zealousness.
Saturday: Holiness.

Ancient sages knew all the planets, even the distant ones that were only discovered this past century. The outer planets have minimal influence while the inner planets closest to Earth have the most influence on each person. All heavenly bodies influence people. If the Sun is in your astrological chart you have a bright appearance. Venus in your chart means you could be wealthy and/or promiscuous. If Mercury is in your chart you could be wise and radiant. This means you may suffer afflictions. Saturn means your plans often come to nothing but plots against you are nullified. This means that Saturn cancels out good and bad. Jupiter in your charts means you lean toward righteousness while Mars means you lean toward bloodshed.

On the following chart, the column on the left side represents the 24 hours in a day. The Hebrew day starts after sundown. For example, if you were born at 10 PM/22 Hours on a Monday and the Sun has already set, according to the Hebrew way of doing things you would be born Tuesday. Once you have the correct day and time of day, you

	Time	Sunday	Monday	Tuesday	Wednesday	Thursday	Friday	Saturday
1	6:00	Mercury	Jupiter	Venus	Saturn	Sun	Moon	Mars
2	7:00	Moon	Mars	Mercury	Jupiter	Venus	Saturn	Sun
3	8:00	Saturn	Sun	Moon	Mars	Mercury	Jupiter	Venus
4	9:00	Jupiter	Venus	Saturn	Sun	Moon	Mars	Mercury
5	10:00	Mars	Mercury	Jupiter	Venus	Saturn	Sun	Moon
6	11:00	Sun	Moon	Mars	Mercury	Jupiter	Venus	Saturn
7	12:00	Venus	Saturn	Sun	Moon	Mars	Mercury	Jupiter
8	1:00	Mercury	Jupiter	Venus	Saturn	Sun	Moon	Mars
9	2:00	Moon	Mars	Mercury	Jupiter	Venus	Saturn	Sun
10	3:00	Saturn	Sun	Moon	Mars	Mercury	Jupiter	Venus
11	4:00	Jupiter	Venus	Saturn	Sun	Moon	Mars	Mercury
12	5:00	Mars	Mercury	Jupiter	Venus	Saturn	Sun	Moon
13	6:00	Sun	Moon	Mars	Mercury	Jupiter	Venus	Saturn
14	7:00	Venus	Saturn	Sun	Moon	Mars	Mercury	Jupiter
15	8:00	Mercury	Jupiter	Venus	Saturn	Sun	Moon	Mars
16	9:00	Moon	Mars	Mercury	Jupiter	Venus	Saturn	Sun
17	10:00	Saturn	Sun	Moon	Mars	Mercury	Jupiter	Venus
18	11:00	Jupiter	Venus	Saturn	Sun	Moon	Mars	Mercury
19	12:00	Mars	Mercury	Jupiter	Venus	Saturn	Sun	Moon
20	1:00	Sun	Moon	Mars	Mercury	Jupiter	Venus	Saturn
21	2:00	Venus	Saturn	Sun	Moon	Mars	Mercury	Jupiter
22	3:00	Mercury	Jupiter	Venus	Saturn	Sun	Moon	Mars
23	4:00	Moon	Mars	Mercury	Jupiter	Venus	Saturn	Sun
24	5:00	Saturn	Sun	Moon	Mars	Mercury	Jupiter	Venus

can look at the chart to see which planet most influenced your mind-pattern at the time of your birth. In the same way, if you have an appointment at a specific time and day, look to see what the planetary influences will be.

In Hebrew, celestial influences are called Mazal. This is where the expression Mazal Tov comes from. Tov means good. Mazel Tov wishes you good planetary influences. Mazal comes from the root word Nozel which means to flow or travel. Despite whatever Mazal you have, you have free choice meaning you do not have to accept the influence. The Zohar states very clearly that you are not supposed to ask an astrologer about the future. The reason is then you can be influenced by the response and make that happen. This is like a doctor who tells a person that he/she has 6 months to live. The person doesn't even consider that he/she can get well so they die in 6 months. You have to use your own mind to find your own answer then step by step do what you need to do.

According to the Zohar there are 5 branches of astrology.

Natal

Because of your birth time you are born with specific characteristics.

Medical

Influences that affect your health.

Horary

How the date and time influence the outcomes of what you do.

Electional

Choices you make depend upon influences.

Mundane

Influences that affect your everyday life.

Many people live their lives by their astrology chart, allowing the astrological influences to dictate their decisions. In India, natal charts are made when children are born. These are used for matchmaking purposes, among other minor and major life decisions. Allowing an astrologer to dictate your life in this way takes away your free choice. Plus the person may bring to fruition what he/she is told. When you follow the Torah, Kabbalah, and Zohar you are not subject to astrological influences. Even so, if someone has told you certain things based upon your astrological chart, these ideas stay with you, they do not go away. When Janet was 25 a psychic told her that she was going to have an operation, get divorced, and die by the time she was 40. This stayed with her for 15 years and more until she was well past 40.

There is always debate whether there are 12 or 13 signs of the Zodiac. The Zodiac is based on the 12/13 Tribes of Israel. Most sources say there are 12 Tribes but the Tribe of Joseph split into Ephraim and Manasseh. Technically there are 13 Tribes and in the same way, there are 13 Zodiac signs. In Ancient times Ophiuchus was its own separate sign with the symbol of either a dragon or spider. Now, Ophiuchus is encompassed within Scorpio so the dates or the other signs did not change. Scorpions are identified with an enticement to sin. Scorpions are desert creatures so it made no sense that Scorpio is a water sign. Then I found out that the original inhabitants of the Earth were amphibious scorpion creatures that live in water. Apparently, they arrived on Earth when their galaxy collided with this one. A few years ago in a South African mine, a fossil of an amphibious winged scorpion approximately 2 meters long was found.

Every Hebrew month has a constellation associated with it. Some calendars correlate the Hebrew months with the Western months, but this can be confusing. For example, one Hebrew month may start in the third week of the Western month. This means there can be two Hebrew months beginning and ending within one Western month. The Hebrew calendar adds a 13th month during leap years. Each Name in the following chart is actually a code.

#	Name	Month	Constellation
1	יהוה	Nisan	Aries
2	יההו	Iyyar	Taurus
3	יוהה	Sivan	Gemini
4	הוהי	Tamuz	Cancer
5	הויה	Av	Leo
6	ההוי	Elul	Virgo
7	והיה	Tishrei	Libra
8	וההי	Cheshvan	Scorpio
9	ויהה	Kislev	Sagittarius
10	היהו	Tevet	Capricorn
11	היוה	Shevat	Aquarius
12	ההיו	Adar	Pisces

Time travel and teleportation are specifically outlined in the Zohar. It says that both linear and cyclical times are present in the Torah so that is why people read the Torah from start to end every year, then start over again. There is no past, present or future, there is only the Eternal Now. This means that whatever Torah portion you read, it is always appropriate for every time period. One moment that occurred thousands of years ago is equal to the current moment.

The Zohar defines time as a measure of motion and states that God is beyond time and space. When God in the Torah speaks about Himself He says *I was, I AM, I will be*. The *4-Letter Name of God* is an acronym for this. The Zohar also states that His time is *the secret of the rotation of the emanations*. This refers to the Sefirot. Then it says *that every moment is a result of renewed expression and configuration of divine energy*. This means that every moment of existence is constantly being created simultaneously by the Mind of God. Creation is constant because God recreates the universe at every moment, perpetually sustaining existence. This also means that every moment is a new moment, an old moment, and a current moment because it is constantly being emanated.

The Zohar then says *space and time are inseparable.* In Hebrew, Olam means the world as well as Eternity. The root comes from a Hebrew word that means to conceal. This tells you that while the world is Eternal, the reality of the world and actuality of Existence is concealed. Next, the Zohar says *only when God is concealed can there be free choice, otherwise, there's only free will, which is just God.* This means that God is the only one that has free will. You do not have free will. You do have free choice within the umbrella of free will. If you knew this then you would always go along with God's will resulting in no creation. This is why God concealed this so you can make the choices that help you discover God. This means your choices do not exactly change the future but rather draw to you an alternate timeline that already exists.

The Zohar constantly states that God's free will is to share Itself. If you only had God's free will, all you could do is share, and then there would be nothing else to do. An even more simple example is when a parent tells a child that he can sit down and eat or go to bed. It is the child's choice but the parent is the one with the free will as an umbrella over the choice.

Time Travel

The Hebrews called the Ark of the Covenant, Aron. Aron means Ark. The Zohar says that the Ark took up no physical space in the Temple. The Torah lists the dimensions of the Ark as well as the room in which it was kept. Comparatively speaking, the Ark was bigger than the physical space of the room. The Zohar also says that there should be overcrowding in the Temple but there was always room no matter how many people were present. This is considered a mystery. This is analogous to having a 5-seater car but 15 people easily fit into it. This means that the energy that emanates from the Earth on the spot combined with the energy of the Ark was electromagnetic and bent time and space. If you were not properly prepared to be in its presence it would adversely affect your physical body. The breastplate of Urim and Thummim protected the priest by creating an energy that blocked the interdimensional space on his body. The Zohar states that the Holy Temple in Jerusalem was a microcosm of the entire universe and each room represented an aspect of God. The Zohar also says that the Temple already exists whether it's physically manifest or not. Thus, the Temple exists in an alternate reality until such time as the people are ready to receive it.

There are many incidences in the ***Bible*** where people traveled great distances in a very brief time. They used a Holy Name to produce an experience that they called Kefitzat Haderech. This quite literally means contracted road, implying a shortening of the distance between 2 points. The *Name of God* was used to create a wormhole to travel instantaneously to the desired destination. You have Hyperspace visualizations to mentally do this but you have not yet learned how to bring your body with you. You have to know what you are doing to arrive and return safely.

Divine Names can allow you to fly. The Zohar describes both wormholes and vortices. Wormholes allow you to go between 2 points in the same physical reality. Vortices are used to travel between 2 points in different realities. When your mind-pattern is ready or you need this, it can happen to you instantaneously. There are many stories of the sages that went backward and forward in time. The Torah comments that God can switch time, taking you from one time period and placing you in another instantaneously. This is how the sages went into the Sephira of Ketter to alter and manipulate time and space. From Ketter, you can view all time in one glance instantaneously. Now, people try to do this by Kundalini activation which is highly dangerous. Others use hallucinogenics to try to achieve this. The *Philadephia Experiment* and *Montauk Project* are all connected to the Zohar because this is where those scientists got their ideas. All global handlers still have Kabbalists working for them, some positive, some Erev Rav.

In Hebrew, Teshuva means a return or going back. This means you can erase and elevate previous sinful behavior by repenting. You can use the *Name of God Frequency #1 Time Travel* to go back in time to the point before you committed a sinful act. This creates an alternate reality timeline where that sin never occurred. The Tetragrammaton, the *4 Letter Name of God*, YHWH, is a contraction of *He was, He is and He will be.* In Hebrew, Mechanot Zamin means a mechanism of time or time machine. The Gematria of Mechanot Zamin equals 613 which is the number of commandments, or connections, for the Hebrew people. This implies that the commandments are a tool for time travel.

Angels

In Hebrew Malakh means Angel. Malakh comes from the root of the Hebrew word that means to send. According to the Zohar, the only purpose of Angels is to carry out assignments from God. Angels have no physical characteristics because they are different forms of Divine Energy. The ***Template of God-Mind*** lists various levels of Angelic Frequencies as well as their function. The Angelic levels have different frequencies within each level to perform different functions. Angels are intermediaries that are servants of God. Archangels have permanent functions but all other Angelic Frequencies are created as needed.

For example, Archangel Michael is the guardian of the Hebrew Nation. Michael means like God. Archangel Gabriel's name means God is my strength. Archangel Raphael means the healing of God, so this is the Archangel to invoke if you or someone you know needs healing. Archangel Uriel is the Light of God. Archangel Metatron means watchman as well as exceptional and is the combination of many absorbed entities. Enoch, for example, lived for 365 years, and then he was no more because he went to be with God. Enoch did not physically die because he was absorbed into Metatron. Archangel Sandalphon means connecting the Earth to Heaven. Sandalphon is also comprised of my absorbed entities including Elijah. Enoch and Elijah were the only Biblical figures who were absorbed into higher entities and thus were no longer on the Earth but neither physically died.

The Zohar says never pray to an Angel but you can ask for its help with its specific function. Angels do not have choices but must follow orders. Angels do not have free choice nor free will because it is only a servant or messenger of God. The ***Bible*** and Zohar state that when God decided to create Humanity the Angels were angry and jealous because humans were given more choices. They felt that God should not create anything after the Angels. Basic Hyperspace Language says that God-Mind created Christ Consciousness and then Angelic Frequencies. That was supposed to be the end of Creation.

Homework

- What date were you born and what is your planetary influence?

Jewish Humor

A minister, priest, and Rabbi die in a car crash. Upon arrival in Heaven, they are asked when they are lying in their casket what they would like to hear from the mourners. The minister says, *I would like to hear them say he was a wonderful husband, fine Spiritual leader, and a great family man.* The priest says, *I would like to hear them say that I was a wonderful teacher and a servant of God who made a huge different difference in people's lives.* The Rabbi says, *I would like to hear them, say look he's moving!*

More Jewish Humor

An uncle is talking to his nephew Shlomo that is about to get married. The uncle says, *congratulations Shlomo. I'm sure you look back on this day and remember it is the happiest day of your life.* Schlomo says, *but I'm not getting married until tomorrow.* His uncle replies, *I know.*

Webinar Homework Results

Comment: In the 1990s a teacher was instructing about the Merkava. He said to sit inside of one, spin the top section one way and the bottom section the opposite way.

Response: This person ultimately was revealed as an intelligence agent who was assigned to mentally confuse people. He was based in Arizona in the early 1990s he also told everyone to leave the East Coast and move to his compound in Arizona because an asteroid was going to hit the Atlantic Ocean. People quit their jobs and sold their homes to do this. When nothing happened he told them it was a test for them. This is true because it was an intelligence agency test.

Comment: Please discuss the Erev Rav.

Response: The Erev Rav are now in control of the Deep State. All the people in the Deep State are descendants of the Erev Rav.

Comment: ***Blue Blood, True Blood*** mentions the destruction of the island of Santorini as part of the story of the Exodus and the Syrian controllers of Egypt that wanted to get the Hebrews out of Egypt. Please elaborate.

Response: Briefly, these plagues were created as a result of the volcanic eruption of Santorini so this is why the Pharaoh let the Hebrews go.

Comment: By fighting demons and demonic forces, is Humanity cleaning up its own mess?

Response: Yes, because demonic entities and their functions are a reflection of Humanity. What is on the outer is also within.

Comment: Are demonic entities rogue functions of the God-Mind or separate from the God-Mind?

Response: Nothing is really separate from the God-Mind. These are aspects of the God-Mind that Humanity needs to correct.

Comment: I read that the Cistercians only ate bread and vegetables which would make them vegans and that the Knight Templars also had a strict diet. It is said that one Templar Knight could replace 10 regular Knights. It doesn't make sense that these groups chose to be vegans rather than eat meat for strength and brain capacity.

Response: Their doctrines stated that they should eat simply, only vegetables and bread except when they were training and preparing for battle. Because they were always training and preparing for battle, they ate meat. This was a cover story to make their enemies think that they were weak when they were really strong.

Comment: I feel that working with the light is imperative but that includes working with bringing more light into myself for the purpose of healing and liberating the world around me. I would like clarification on how to use the *Names of God* for this purpose.

Response: ***Miracles in Motion*** has a lot of information on this as well as the study guides for this class. The whole purpose of the aura and the Zohar is to bring more light into your frequency and change all the negativity.

Comment: I think the Clear Ones created the Reptilians because the Lyraens were not evolving fast enough. Perhaps the Clear Ones are only in service to Self in a nonphysical dimension.

Response: The Clear Ones, as described in ***Montauk: Alien Connection*** is in service to Satan because the purpose of Satan is to prosecute and accuse humans of their iniquities as well as promote negativity among Humanity. They test people to see what choices they will make. They were created as prosecutors and accusers of Humanity. In Hebrew Satan means prosecutor. Satan is a title, not a person as well as a frequency.

Comment: My birth date confirms both my positive and negative traits. I am blessed to learn the *72 Names of God.*

Response: Yes, they help you rise above external influences.

Comment: I think fish are not affected by astrological influences since the water protects them, which is like a mikveh. In fact, the ocean itself, or all the water in the world, is like a mikveh.

Response: That is absolutely correct. That's why the fish is a symbol of Christianity and Spirituality.

Comment: I don't use astrology much anymore, but it was interesting that one of the Hebrew letters dealing with Pisces or Adar is Kaf is one of the letters that came up in a recent visualization. I like this letter because it sounds like the first letter of my name.

Response: Very interesting. All the letters are powerful.

Comment: I was born in the month of June in North America. When I was born the temperature was 102 degrees Fahrenheit, about 41 degrees Celsius. We didn't have air conditioning because we couldn't afford it. My mother tells me this story every year on my birthday.

Response: You need to look at the temperature where you were born and determine how this affects your temperament.

Comment: I was born on a Saturday which according to the Zohar means Holiness. As a child, I had constant visions of the Holy Spirit floating in my room with golden tools. I felt ecstasy and awe. Even as a child the state of my Soul was always connected to God and has always been of central importance to me.

Response: Remembering how you feel as a child before your mind and emotions were contaminated by others tells you how you could be. Go back to the way you were before you were manipulated into being someone else.

Comment: I was born at half past the hour so I'm wondering if I go to the hour before or after.

Response: You may need to take a combination of both because you were born at this time for a reason.

Comment: When my mother was 2 weeks away from her due date

her doctor told her to come to the hospital so he could induce her labor because he was going away. If I was born on my due date I would have been a Libra. Now, I'm a Virgo.

Response: this is proof that everyone is born when he/she is supposed to be born. You arrive when you are supposed to arrive. Outer circumstances are the catalyst, even if it appears negative.

Comment: I was born on a Friday which means zealous. Zealous means filled with or showing a strong energetic desire to get something done or see something succeed. Zeal is usually positive. God is Zealous; God wears zeal as his mantle and he expects us to do the same.

Response: I agree, but of course, you could be zealous for negative purposes.

Comment: I want to share the Key of Solomon because it says that magic is considered appropriate for the days or hours associated with each planet.

Key of Solomon

Magic considered appropriate for the days or hours associated with each planet

- In the Days and Hours of Saturn: the summoning of Souls from Hades, but only of those who have died a natural death.
- In the Days and Hours of Jupiter: obtaining honors, acquiring riches, contracting friendships, preserving health.
- In the Days and Hours of Mars: experiments regarding War, to arrive at military honor, acquire courage, overthrow enemies,
- in the hours of Mars: summoning Souls from Hades, especially of those slain in battle.
- In the Days and Hours of the Sun: experiments regarding temporal wealth, hope, gain, fortune, divination, the

favour of princes, to dissolve hostile feeling, and to make friends.

- In the Days and Hours of Venus: forming friendships, for kindness and love, joyous and pleasant undertakings, traveling;
- in the hours of Venus: lots, poisons, preparing powders provocative of madness, etc.
- In the Days and Hours of Mercury: eloquence and intelligence, promptitude in business, science and divination.
- in the Hours of Mercury: undertaking experiments relating to games, raillery jests, sports.
- In the Days and Hours of the Moon: embassies, voyages, envoys, messages, navigation; reconciliation, love, and the acquisition of merchandise by water; in the hours of the Moon: making trial of experiments relating to recovery of stolen property, for obtaining nocturnal visions, for summoning Spirits in sleep, and for preparing anything relating to Water.

Response: The Zohar and Kabbalah prohibit the use of magic. Perhaps this should be called the energetic uses of time and astrological influences for a particular purpose.

Demons, Evil Spirits, and Ghosts

There are many references in the ***Bible*** and Talmud about demons, evil spirits, and ghosts. The Zohar says that these are real and must be treated as such. In Hebrew, Mazik means demon as well as to damage or destroy. In Hebrew, Shedim means astral entities. The Hebrew word Ruach refers to evil spirits and means a bad or evil wind that blows. Reshef means a plague. Dever means pestilence. The Zohar considers both the plague and pestilence a result of demonic forces. The current plannedemic is like a plague fueled by demonic forces trying to control humanity. The Zohar states that demons outnumber humans and can appear as humans, but they operate only at night. This is why you are not supposed to go out at night alone. Demons have limited jurisdiction and cannot take anything that's wrapped, sealed, measured or counted. To keep anything safe in your possession, wrap, seal, measure or count the items.

Israelites are permitted to use demons for Holiness. The Zohar says that they cannot be used for personal gain or to do evil but can be controlled to do good that benefits all of humankind. For example, King Solomon bound a demon called Ashmedai by using the frequency of iron as well as the *Names of God* thus coercing Ashmedai to use demonic forces to build the first Temple in magical ways. Ashmedai levitated stones and manifested entire segments of the Temple in this way. Ashmedai had been an Angel but was expelled from Heaven and became King of the Demons. The Gematria of Ashmedai equals the same Gematria of Pharaoh. This means that these names/words are intricately related and connected.

The Zohar names several demonic entities including Azazel. In Hebrew, Azazel means the goat that departs. In ancient times during every Jewish New Year of Rosh Hashanah and Yom Kippur, the Hebrews priests of the Temple laid their hands on a goat to transmit all the sins of the Hebrew people into it. Then the goat was sent out into the desert to die. This is where the term scapegoat originates. Azazel is identified with Satan and is also representative of debauchery, immorality, and all the Fallen Angels. Ketev Meriri is a demon that looks like a spider because of its many eyes. It is a dangerous entity of bitter destruction. Lilith the first wife of Adam, is a winged demon with a human face. The Zohar says she defiles men and kills newborns because her children with Adam became demons instead of humans. For revenge she kills newborns. Lilith has a male counterpart called Samael known as the Angel of Death.

Samael is associated with Satan. In some sections of the Zohar, Samael and Satan are synonymous. Yet they are 2 separate entities. Demons need humans to reproduce and can use the semen from men in an unholy way. This is why the Zohar says that men should not ejaculate unnecessarily because the semen can be used by demons at night to create their children. This is what Lilith did.

Demons can impersonate people. A few years ago I woke up to see my deceased grandmother with red eyes standing over me. She kept saying *I'm your grandma, I'm your grandma.* Sleepily I thought that it looked like her but I knew it wasn't her. Then she touched my head and an electric current went through my body. Demons search your mind for images that you love or feel comfortable with. Then they assume the image so you will allow them in.

The Zohar identifies three classes of demons:

1. Resemble Angels
2. Resemble Humans and observe Torah
3. No fear of God, act and sound like animals, are the most common and dangerous.

Generally, demons prefer to appear as males rather than females. Demons only have 2 names rather than 3 names. The Gematria of 2 names equals 304 which is the same Gematria for the name of the demon. Without a 3rd name, they cannot have their own body. This is another reason why you learn in Hyperspace/Oversoul work that you need 3 names. If you only have 2 names it is imperative that you use a culturally appropriate middle name/mother's maiden name or initial for balance. Kabbalah teaches that 3 names help keep demonic entities away from you. Additionally, the central column of the Sephirot consisting of Keter, Tiferet, Yesod, and Malchut balance the left and right sides of the entire Sephirot array. Your middle name or initial energetically balance the central column of your Sephirot.

NAME OF GOD: EHYEH

אהיה

3 WAYS SPELLED OUT

1) אלף הא יוד הא

2) אלף הי יוד הי

3) אלף הה יוד הה

ALL = 454 =CHOSEM = SEAL OF HOLINESS

Ehyeh

Ehyeh is a *Name of God* that is almost the same as YHWH except it begins with an Aleph instead of a Yud. The letter Aleph is spelled right to left, Aleph, Lamed, Peh. When the letters are permutated according to the above chart, they are very powerful. Their combined Gematria is 454 which equals the Gematria of Chosem. Chosem means the Seal of Holiness.

The Zohar says that amulets work. I use one with the *72 Names of God* inscribed on it. This puts these frequencies in your energy field. The Zohar also clearly states that if you say the *Ana B'koach Prayer* and use the *72 Names of God* that nothing can harm you. Keeping your Sephirot in order is another powerful layer of protection. The Talmud says that if you worry about or are afraid of demons they will bother you. This negativity opens your frequency and allows them in.

A Dybbuk is a deceased person who does not move on but instead possesses a vulnerable living person. A Dybbuk is not a demonic entity but obviously, a deceased person of integrity would not do this. Dybbuks can also go into an animal, plant, object, or even place. Use the Angelic Frequency of the Maggid to expel a Dybbuk from a person, animal, plant, object, or place. A Soul can also be attached to an animal, plant, object, or place as a punishment. This is why you must respect everything before you pick it up or move it. You must ask your Oversoul if this is the correct action for whatever you want to move.

The Zohar says that ghosts look like the body the person had before the person passed on. The Zohar says that it is forbidden to communicate with them because you could then become possessed if you connect too closely. There are however many stories in Jewish folklore of ghosts who appeared to loved ones and then helped them overcome challenging situations. For this reason to communicate or not communicate with ghosts is still debated amongst Hebrew scholars. For many centuries they advised against communication with those who have passed over. However, there are Tzadikim, or righteous people, who can communicate with a ghost, get information, and correct negative situations.

The Talmud says that the Soul hears everything that is said until the grave is sealed. This means that each person attends his/her own funeral. The Midrash says that when the Soul leaves the body the sound is comparable to that of rushing water. The Zohar says a garment of light surrounds and takes you when you leave the body. Then, the Soul goes through a cave entrance similar to a womb except you are born back the other way. Here you will meet your loved ones. People who have had near-death experiences often describe going through a tunnel or tube. If a person is programmed or has a very negative mind-pattern before they even enter the tunnel to get to the other side their Soul can be captured.

The Zohar says because the Soul is immortal that it can reincarnate to fulfill its goals and the 613 Commandments which are food for the Soul. Because the Soul cannot fulfill all 613 Commandments in one lifeline the Soul comes back multiple times until all of the Commandments are completed. The Hebrew term for reincarnation is Gilgul. The Zohar says that the Soul is immortal and continuous so God allows for constant changes and refinement. All Souls have the same root as Adam Kadmon. From Adam Kadmon come all Soul groups which generally all incarnate together. Reincarnation rectifies and atones for the sins that you have committed in many different lifetimes. Whatever sin is the most difficult to resist is what must be corrected.

Past life memories are suppressed because if you remembered them you might not be motivated to do anything else except the necessary corrections. The Zohar says that the death of children happens when Souls need a very short time for their corrections. This may sound cruel and it is horrible for the parents. However, the parents must also need the correction that this scenario offers. Resurrecting the physical body during Messianic times is fundamental to Judaism, just like it is in Christianity. Judaism prohibits cremation because it wants the body to be intact.

The Zohar says that there is a multitude of worlds. God travels to 18,000 worlds within this solar system and nearby galaxies that are inhabited. The Book of Judges mentions inhabitants of a planet called Meroz where all its people are cursed. They attacked and killed people on other planets so God cursed them. Mars and Venus occur three times in the Torah. The word Chayim means life and overlaps as a code that means there's life on Mars and Venus. God said that all the universes were created for humans and the Torah. In this context, human means all Beings whose intelligence level equals that of humans.

Kabbalah prohibits sorcery which it considers evil. In Hebrew, Mahashefah is the word for sorcerer and it means weakening the Heavenly Agents of God. Anyone who practices sorcery weakens the energy of God within. Believing in any force other than God is the equivalent of idolatry. Magic is also prohibited.

Kabbalah says that witches, vampires, and werewolves do exist. For protection use the *Names of God.* Psalms 91 repels calamities, misfortunes, and diseases as well as creates wonders.

Humour

Who was Jesus? There are 5 arguments.

1. Some say Jesus was Black because he called everyone Brother, liked Gospel and he could not get a fair trial.
2. Some say Jesus was Jewish because he went about his Father's business, lived at home until he was 33, he was sure his mother was a virgin and his mother was sure that he was God.
3. Some say Jesus was Italian because he talked with his hands, had wine with his meals, and used olive oil.
4. Some say Jesus was an American Indian because he was at peace with Nature, ate a lot of fish, and talked about the Great Spirit.

5. But, the most compelling evidence is that Jesus was a woman. He fed a crowd at a moment's notice even when there was no food, he kept trying to get a message across to a bunch of men who didn't get it, and even when he was dead, he had to get up because there was more work to do.

Addendum I

Death of Prince Phillip

Date of death April 9, 2021, the 99th day of the year.

99 = 9+9=18, 1+8= 9

Date of death

04-09-2021 = 18 = 1 + 8 = 9

Age

99 = 9+9=18, 1+8 =9

Three sequences of 9s = 999

Kabbalah states that there are twin Messiahs. First comes the political Messiah from the House of Joseph who creates war and destruction. His code is 999 and signifies the end of evil. In Hebrew, this is ben Yosef.

Next, comes the Spiritual Messiah from the House of David who leads humanity into the Messianic Age. His code is 1000. In Hebrew, this is ben David.

April 9, 2021, is Good Friday for Eastern Orthodox Christians. Sunday, April 11, 2021, is the Eastern Orthodox Easter, the True Easter before the Vatican changed the date and corrupted the energy.

It is possible that April 9, 2021, symbolizes the end of evil through the death of ben Yosef, 999.

It is possible that April 11, 2021, symbolizes the resurrection of the Good with the Messiah on His way. Perhaps this is the Easter to which President Trump referred when one year ago he said that the madness would end after Easter. Perhaps Prince Philip died some time ago with his death only now revealed to allow the symbolism to play out in a grand show for the End of Days.

Flow Chart of Creation/Existence

(from ***Hyperspace Plus*** page 9)

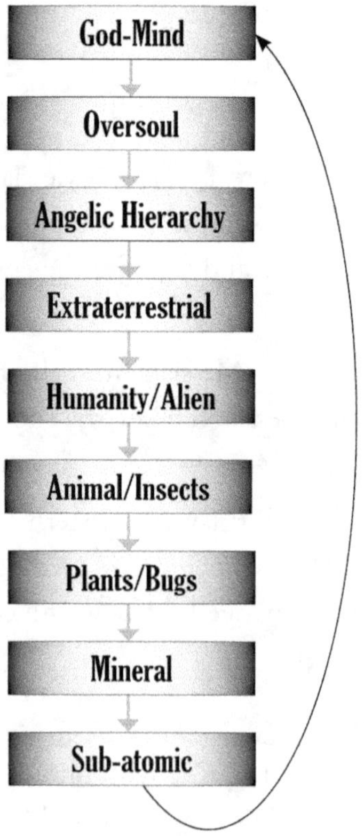

Grace of God Visualization

(from ***Template of God-Mind*** page 121)

Unifications/ Yihud

Using **The Name** with a combination of vowels, then uniting them, emanates a frequency of Repentance + Forgiveness that leads to Grace.

This is a form of weaving mixed with Gematria.

The visualization takes place at the Pineal Gland. The letters are always in white.

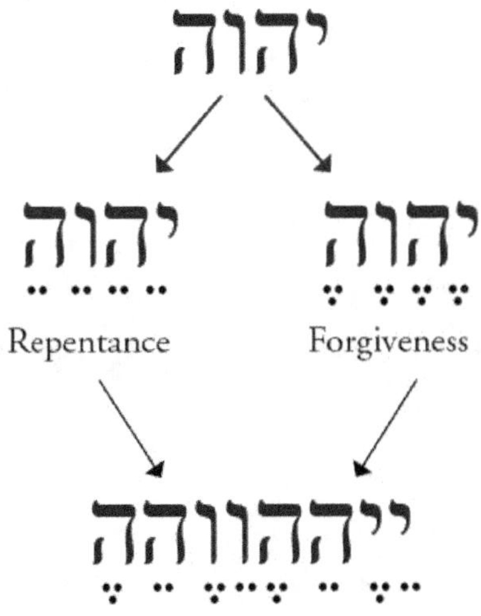

Grace of God

Using this visualization in addition to your *Golden Altar* release work cultivates buried memories that still need to be released and forgiven. As each memory comes forward, visualize it in front of this formula, then send it up to your Oversoul.

Addendum II

Armor of God

Ephesians 6

New International Version

Children, obey your parents in the Lord, for this is right. "Honor your father and mother"—which is the first commandment with a promise—"so that it may go well with you and that you may enjoy long life on the earth."

Fathers,[b] do not exasperate your children; instead, bring them up in the training and instruction of the Lord.

Slaves, obey your earthly masters with respect and fear, and with sincerity of heart, just as you would obey Christ. Obey them not only to win their favor when their eye is on you, but as slaves of Christ, doing the will of God from your heart. Serve wholeheartedly, as if you were serving the Lord, not people, because you know that the Lord will reward each one for whatever good they do, whether they are slave or free.

And masters, treat your slaves in the same way. Do not threaten them, since you know that he who is both their Master and yours is in heaven, and there is no favoritism with him.

The Armor of God

10 Finally, be strong in the Lord and in his mighty power. 11 Put on the full armor of God, so that you can take your stand against the devil's schemes. 12 For our struggle is not against flesh and blood, but against the rulers, against the authorities, against the powers of this dark world and against the spiritual forces of evil in the heavenly realms. 13 Therefore put on the full armor of God, so that when the day of evil comes, you may be able to stand your ground, and after you have done everything, to stand. 14 Stand firm then, with the belt of truth buckled around your waist, with the breastplate of righteousness in place, 15 and with your feet fitted with the readiness that comes from the gospel of peace. 16 In addition to all this, take up the shield of faith, with which you can extinguish all the flaming arrows of the evil one. 17 Take the helmet of salvation and the sword of the Spirit, which is the word of God.

18 And pray in the Spirit on all occasions with all kinds of prayers and requests. With this in mind, be alert and always keep on praying for all the Lord's people. 19 Pray also for me, that whenever I speak, words may be given me so that I will fearlessly make known the mystery of the gospel, 20 for which I am an ambassador in chains. Pray that I may declare it fearlessly, as I should.

600,000 Souls, 600,000 Letters

Heavenly prosecution comes as a result of negligence in Torah study.

The word "Israel" can be read as an acronym for *"Yesh Shishim Ribo Otiot LaTorah",* meaning: "There are six hundred thousand letters in the Torah". Therefore, Israel did not leave Egypt until there were six hundred thousand of them, in order for each soul to be "supported" by one letter in the Torah, as we have written in a number of places.When the voice is the voice of Jacob...then the hands are not the those of Esau...

We see that Gd overlooks many serious sins but He does not overlook negligence in Torah study, as is written, "Why was the land lost? Gd has said, '*Because of their forsaking My Torah.*'" (Jeremiah 9:11-12) Even though they transgressed all of the sins, Gd only accused them of negligence in Torah study. As our Sages have said regarding the verse "*the voice is the voice of Jacob*": (Gen. 27:22) when the voice is the voice of Jacob, that is, of Torah study, then the hands are not the those of Esau, that is, the forces of evil are powerless. But when the voice is not that of Jacob, then the hands are that of Esau and the forces of impurity dominate. Our Sages likewise explained that the reason that "*Amalek came and fought with Israel at Refidim*" (Ex. 17:18) was that their hands had slackened from the Torah. [This is derived from the word "Refidim" which has as its root the Hebrew word "*rafa*", meaning "slackening".]

Since the name "Israel" alludes to the fact that the number of letters in the Torah corresponds to the number of souls, it follows that when the Jewish People come to count their souls [take a census], the accuser comes and accuses them saying, "Master of the universe, didn't Israel only reach this size population in order to match the number of letters in the Torah which are hinted at in their name? And now they are negligent in [the Torah]!" This becomes the substance of the accusation.Israel...should awaken their fear of Heaven in order to repair their souls and spirits...

Furthermore, the word "*negef*", meaning "a scourge", has the same numerological value as 'Satan', the Angel of Destruction, short two. ["*Negef*" equals 133, while "*Samael*" equals 131.] The missing two allude to the two Torahs (Oral and Written). When Israel are lax in the two Torahs, two powers are added to those of the forces of evil, and it becomes "*negef*", a scourge, and afflicts them, Gd forbid.

In fact, though, through the Redemption money that Israel gives, the forces of evil have no power to rule over them, for charity is a protection against them, as is written, "*Charity saves from death*". (Proverbs 10:2)

All of Gd's commandments are hints and allusions, to cause people to study Gd's ways. As for why Israel was commanded to give a half-shekel, the word "*shekel*" has the same numerological value as "*Nefesh*", with half of it having the same value as the Hebrew word "*yira*", meaning "fear of Heaven" [including the word as a whole]. The other half has the same value as "*Ruach*". This comes to warn and inform Israel that they should awaken their fear of Heaven in order to repair their souls and spirits, for heavenly prosecution comes as a result of negligence in Torah study and the remedy is for them to accept upon themselves to study Torah with no interruptions. This follows from the principle that the form of repentance must match the sin, which means that besides for the Redemption money that Israel gives, they must take upon themselves to study Torah, for the Redemption money only atones for what is past, but from now on nothing can help them but actual Torah study.

[*Petuchei Chotem, parashat* Ki Tisa, as anthologized in *Peninei Avir Ya'akov*, p. 213; Translated by M. Steinberger and E. Linas]

From Rabbeinu Yaakov Abuchatzeira

The Aliens

Posted on May 11th, 2011 at 1:21 pm

Question: You liken the Jewish nation to a special forces unit that is sent on a special mission. Where to?

Answer: It is sent to conquer the evil inclination. "Israel" is a spark, the point in the heart, the foreign force in the "hostile country," in egoism. We must strive to defeat this egoism and correct it. We have to strengthen ourselves first, and then, having been reformed, we must give egoists the Light and correct the entire world.

After all, it is true that we are not from here, not from the land of egoism. Our root lies outside of it; we infiltrated it by way of the breaking of the vessels, of the integral soul. Here, inside it, we were broken in the beginning, but in the end, we must become corrected. To the degree of our correction, we reform the collective ego.

Question: Who is the commander-in-chief that sent the special forces unit on the mission?

Answer: The Creator did. Israel is a part of Him, the vessels of bestowal sitting in egoism, in the vessels of reception. The commander-in-chief sent the soldiers out, having supplied them with all the necessary gear and ammunition. To cast them onto the hostile ground, He intentionally "broke" them up so that they may look like everyone else and not stand out in the crowd.

Thus, we can be likened to secret agents. Each of us looks exactly as all the natives of this egoistic country. Imagine being dropped into Africa, and you look exactly like them: You have the same character, mentality, tastes, and likes. Everything is identical to theirs, inside and out.

For a while, the planted agent doesn't receive instructions. He has to settle in at the new site, find a job, and make a family. Years go by before he embarks on his mission. However, one day, he receives a reminder. By now, he has forgotten all about it when the phone starts to ring: "So and so is speaking...." It's just like in a movie.

We have received our wake-up call: It's time to remember that we have a special mission here, that this is not, in fact, our home, that we came from a totally different world. In truth, we are from another "planet," from another dimension. We received an impulse and came out of dormancy. All of the aliens on this planet have woken up, are gathering in the groups, and starting to prepare themselves to conquer the planet Earth. That's our mission.

Question: How do we win it then?

Answer: We are being sent instructions, gradually explaining all that we need to know and put into action. Then, we gain a new mind and a new sensation. Our mother planet is sending us the power of our initial nature, with the help of which we will conquer every citizen of the Earth.

We came here for one reason: to establish the same order here as exists in our own world. There, everything is opposite. It is governed by love and bestowal.

Now, we must end all the horrors that are viewed as the norm here. People are destroying themselves and the life on the planet, while we have come to help, to save them and provide a totally different life for them. We were woken up by a special signal from home, on a special wave, which means that it's time to act.

[42616]

From the 4th part of the Daily Kabbalah Lesson 5/9/2011, About the Israeli Nation.

Angel Jophiel

The angel Jophiel "God is my beauty [alternatively: Beauty of God"], "divine beauty"), also called *Iophiel, Iofiel, Jofiel, Yofiel, Youfiel*, Zophiel ("spy of God", "watchman of God") and Zuriel, "my rock is God"), is a non-canonical archangel of wisdom, understanding, and judgment. He is listed as one of the Seven Archangels in Pseudo-Dionysian teachings. Due to the association with beauty, Jophiel is one of very few angels to be sometimes portrayed as female. However, angels have no canonical gender, and are most commonly referred to by male pronouns.

According to the pseudepigraphal Revelation of Moses, another name for Jophiel is Dina. Jophiel/Dina is described as an angel of the seventh heaven, a Cabalistic guardian of the Torah (and wisdom itself), who taught 70 languages to souls at the dawn of creation.[3] The Zohar lists him as a Great Angel Chief in charge of 53 legions who superintend Torah-readings on the Sabbath.[4] Jophiel is said to be a companion to the angel Metatron.[2]

C.E. Clement, in her book *Angels in Art*, names Jophiel as the teacher of Ham, Japheth, and Shem.[2] Heinrich Cornelius Agrippa[5] and Thomas Rudd likewise name Jophiel as the teacher of Shem.[6]

In Anglican and Episcopal traditions, Jophiel is recognized as an archangel. He is often depicted in iconography holding a flaming sword,[note 1] such as the stained glasses at St Michael's Church in Brighton, St Peter and St John's Church in Kirkley,[7] Holy Trinity Church in Coventry[8] and a mural at St. John's Episcopal Church in Memphis, Tennessee.[9]

Jophiel is an Archangel of the Kabbalah (though some systems put Raziel in his place) and in several listings including that of the early medieval theologian Pseudo-Dionysus.[10] The Calendarium Naturale Magicum Perpetuum lists Jophiel as the angel of the Sephira Chokhmah,[11] as do the Key of Solomon variant "The Veritable Clavicles of Solomon,"[12] and the Sixth and Seventh Books of Moses,[13] both latter works derived from the Calendarium.[14] Agrippa attributes Jophiel to Saturn, while Paracelsus assigns him to Jupiter.[2] Rudd attributes the Zodiac to Jophiel[15] along with the Sephira Binah instead of Zaphkiel.[16] Athanasius Kircher names Jophiel as Angelus pulchritudinis, "angel of beauty".[17] According to Robert Ambelain, Jophiel is in charge of the Cherubim, particularly the Shemhamphorasch angels Haziel, Aladiah, Lauviah, Hahaiah, Iezalel, Mehahel, Hariel, and Hakamiah.[18]

In Literature

Angels of Love and Light describes her as "the Archangel of Paradise and the Patron of Artists and Illumination. She teaches the outer consciousness the Power of Light within oneself. She is also described as "the Yellow Ray of Wisdom, Illumination, and Constancy", and lists her *Archeia* as Christine also says

She Stirs feelings through Radiation of Illumination and into aspiration for spiritual things. She helps in absorbing information, studying for and passing tests, dissolution of ignorance, pride, and narrow-mindedness, and exposure of wrongdoing in governments and corporations. Jophiel helps in fighting pollution, cleaning up our planet and brings to mankind the gift of Beauty. She also provides inspiration for artistic and intellectual thought providing help with artistic projects and to see the beautiful things around us.

Crowns On Hebrew Letters

If you look closely at the letters of a sefer Torah (Torah scroll), you will see that many of the letters are topped by small spikes, called tagin or ketarim, the Aramaic and Hebrew words for "crowns." At times, they are also called zayins, since they resemble the Hebrew letter zayin (ז), coming out of the top of the letter.

There are generally three categories of letters in terms of tagin.

• Letters without tagin. This is the default.

• The Talmud mentions the letters making up the mnemonic שעטנ"ז ג"ץ (ShATNeZ GaTz1) have [3] tagin, or crowns, coming out of the top left of the letter.[2]

• Additionally it is customary to make a single tag, or crown, on top of the letters making up the mnemonic ה"יח ק"דב (BeDek ChaYaH3),[4] as well as certain other specific letters and words that have tagin in specific places.[5]

Why the Crowns?

As for why they are there, Moses himself had this very question. As the Talmud relates:

Rav Yehuda says that Rav says: When Moses ascended on High, he found the Holy One, Blessed be He, sitting and attaching crowns to the letters of the Torah. Moses said before Gd: Master of the Universe, who is preventing You [from giving the Torah without these additions?] Gd said to him: There is a man who is destined to be born after several generations, and Akiva ben Yosef is his name; from each and every point of these crowns, he is destined to derive heaps upon heaps of halachot. [It is for his sake that the crowns must be added to the letters of the Torah.][6]

In other words, there are many laws and parts of the Oral Torah that are hinted at by way of these small crowns.

(For more on this incident with Moses and Rabbi Akiva, as well as its implications, see Is It Really the Torah, Or Is It Just the Rabbis?)

Fighting Off Harmful Negative Forces

The mystics explain that the acronym ShATNeZ (comprising the letters shin, ayin, tet, nun, zayin) forms the words שט"ן ע"ז, Satan Az, the names of two great, harmful forces. The acronym ג"ץ, GaTz, (comprising gimmel and tzadi) is also the name of an evil force. Therefore, tagin are added to these seven letters, for they are like a sword and a spear against these harmful forces.[7]

Unrevealed Parts of the Torah

So why is it that Rabbi Akiva merited to uncover many secrets of the crowns of the Torah? His revelations were both due to his lofty soul[8] as well as the fact that his teachings were destined to be the basis for the parts of the Oral Torah that would be written down as the Mishnah and Talmud (see What is the Talmud? and What's the Big Deal About the Death of Rabbi Akiva's Students?).[9]

In addition, the Kabbalists explain the reasons behind some tagin. Yet for the most part, their meaning remains hidden. The "heaps" of laws that Rabbi Akiva derived from the tagin remain hidden as well. The mystics explain that for the time being, only the meaning of the actual letters and words of the Written Torah are revealed through the Oral Torah. However, the deeper meanings behind the "crowns" (as well as vowels and cantillations) will only become revealed with the coming of the Moshiach.[10]

Thus, every time you see a crown on a letter, it not only hints at the secrets of the Torah, but our longing for a time when these secrets will finally be revealed.

https://www.chabad.org/library/article_cdo/aid/4904570/jewish/Why-Do-Some-Letters-in-the-Torah-Have-Crowns.htm

Timing Gog and Magog (Theory Only)

When will the Ezekiel 38-39 war be fulfilled?

By Nathan E. Jones

Introduction

"If biblical prophecy teaches us anything, it is that God is in complete control of human history and its culmination."[1]

That quote by Dr. Ron Rhodes highlights one of the greatest benefits of studying God's prophetic word—fulfilled Bible prophecy provides an indisputable apologetic for the existence of God. "For prophecy never came by the will of man, but holy men of God spoke as they were moved by the Holy Spirit" ([2] Peter 1:21 NKJV). Intertwined with that apologetic is an evangelistic message that effectively proclaims the triune God of the Bible alone stands apart the one true God, and only as revealed in Scriptures.

While Bible prophecy constitutes a whopping 27% of the Bible, God's overall plan for the ages appears to be rather like a 100 piece puzzle, and so far, He has only provided 75 pieces. One can definitely make out the outline of a picture, but until certain events unfold, which then adds another new piece to the puzzle, the picture remains incomplete.

These absent proverbial puzzle pieces have been a stumbling block for the apologist wielding Bible prophecy as an evangelistic tool and those to whom they are witnessing, causing both to not properly see the big picture of God's Redemptive plan for mankind. And so, to use Bible prophecy as an effective apologetic in one's evangelistic efforts, the student of the Bible must dive into the complete Word and utilize that one dirty word so missing in much of today's "newspaper exegesis" so unfortunately equated with the field of Eschatology—study. The proclaimer of God's Word must be able to study a particular biblical prophecy, and much like a diamond, carefully examine the many glistening facets in order to discern exactly what revelations the Bible desires to impart.

One such "incomplete" prophecy can be found in Ezekiel chapters 38-39 which concerns what is called the Gog-Magog Battle or the War of Gog and Magog. At first read, as one theologian so colorfully commented, the book of Ezekiel can appear as if a "perplexing maze of incoherent visions—a kaleidoscope of whirling wheels and dry bones that defy interpretation," causing readers to "shy away from studying the book and to miss one of the great literary and spiritual portions of the Old Testament."[2] And, he would be right.

That is why this study will evaluate the research provided by Dr. Ron Rhodes of Reasoning from the Scriptures Ministries in his authoritative book on Ezekiel 38-39 titled Northern Storm Rising. Dr. Rhodes earned his Th.M. and Th.D. degrees from Dallas Theological Seminary, has long served as a professor at that seminary, and has authoRed an incredible80-plus books mainly about the doctrine of Eschatology. Northern Storm Rising focuses on discerning who the Gog-Magog players are and examines the clues as to when this prophesied war will occur. Dr. Rhodes' work will be evaluated in light of the research of other esteemed theologians. In the process of mining the book of Ezekiel for its "rich spiritual truths that strike with peculiar force upon the hearts of men," the hope is the reader will be "brought face to face with a transcendent God, a self-existent being who has absolute power and is constantly revealed in glory."[3]

The Battle

The Prophecies

A long 2,600 years ago, the great Hebrew nabi, Ezekiel ben Buzi of the priestly family of Zadok, was exiled to Babylon in 597 B.C.4 There he unveiled a prophecy the Lord God had divulged to him concerning the future of the nation of Israel. Recorded in the book of Ezekiel chapters 36 and 37, the prophet revealed that God would fulfill His promise to regather the Jewish people "out of all [the] countries" of the world where they had been dispersed "and bring you into your own land" that had been promised to their forefathers Abraham, Isaac, and Jacob (Ezekiel 36:24; Geneses 17:7; 1 Chronicles 16:17-18; Psalm 105:8-11; Romans 9:4 NKJV).

Like dry bones reanimated into a living person, Israel did indeed become a nation once again on May 14, 1948, after nearly 1,900 years since the Romans in 70 A.D. destroyed Jerusalem and exiled the Jewish people across the globe. But, this reanimation would still lack a soul—the national belief in Yahweh and His Son. As one commentator noted: "The bones came together. The flesh crept up over them. They were ready for life, but as yet there was no life in them. It was still a congregation of corpses."5 After all of these centuries, this prophecy found its fulfillment in our modern generation. But, God was not done unveiling the future of Israel to Ezekiel and the world, for the following two chapters portray a great trial for the newly established nation of Israel—the Gog-Magog Battle—a trial that would lead towards granting that reanimated body a soul.

The Details

The Gog-Magog Battle is set between a massive coalition of nations descended from Noah's sons Japheth and Ham against Israel (Genesis 10:2-7). The nations are from the territories of ancient Rosh, Magog, Meshech, Tubal, Persia, Cush, Gomer, and Beth-Togarmah (Ezekiel 38:2-6). Their leader is called "Gog, the prince of Rosh, Meshech, and Tubal" (Ezekiel 38:2-3 NKJV). The battlefield is on "the mountains of Israel, which had long been desolate" (Ezekiel 38:8 NKJV). The purpose of the invasion is to "plunder and to take booty" and attack the people of Israel (Ezekiel 38:12-16 NKJV).

The end result of such a massive invasion by a seemingly invincible army on an unprotected Israel ends up surprising the invaders and shocking the world. The invading nations are, in truth, being manipulated by God, pulled out of their lands as with "hooks in your jaws," so that those nations feel the Sovereign Lord's fury (Ezekiel 38:4,18 NKJV). God drags these specific nations to the "mountains of Israel" to "bring him to judgment with pestilence and bloodshed... flooding rain, great hailstones, fire, and brimstone" (Ezekiel 38:21-22 NKJV). God's ultimate purpose for supernaturally obliterating the invading coalition is so: "Thus, I [God], will magnify Myself and sanctify Myself, and I will be known in the eyes of many nations. Then they shall know that I am the LORD" (Ezekiel 38:23 NKJV).

God's supernatural victory over the Gog-Magog invaders allows Him to reintroduce Himself to the world and declare in no uncertain terms that Yahweh is personally defending Israel. Should the people of the world doubt, they only have to look on Israel who "will go out and set on fire and burn the weapons... and they will make fires with them for seven years" (Ezekiel 39:9 NKJV). As for the invaders' corpses, "for seven months the house of Israel will be burying them, in order to cleanse the land" in the newly named "Valley of Hamon Gog" by a newly built "town called Hamonah" (Ezek. 39:11-12,16 NKJV).

The Leader

Ezekiel provides the prophetic name of the leader of this coalition of nations—"Gog, of the land of Magog, the prince of Rosh, Meshech, and Tubal" (Ezekiel 38:2-3 NKJV). Whether Gog is a real name as was used of a descendent of Reuben in 1 Chronicles 5:4, or is a title for a supreme position such as king or president, remains to be seen. Some historians even point to King Gyges of Lydia, who asked King Ashurbanipal of Assyria for help in 676 B.C. but then joined an Egyptian-led rebellion against Assyria, as a historic type.6 Gyges' name in that era became synonymous with terror, bloodshed, and homelessness.7 Others point to Genghis Khan who, during the 1200s, ruled the Mongol empire which covered a fourth of Asia, as another historic type.8 Whether Gog is either historical or the prophesied Antichrist that is yet to come, depends on when one places the timing of the Gog-Magog Battle. Either way, the identity of Gog truly lives up to the meaning of his name—"hidden or covered."[9]

The Nations

Ezekiel 38:1-6 provides the ancient names of those territories which comprise the invading nations: Rosh, Magog, Meshech, Tubal, Persia, Cush, Put, Gomer, and Beth-Togarmah. If only Ezekiel had gone the extra mile and given the names of the invading nations contemporary to the battle, a lot of debate over their modern identities would have been saved. Nevertheless, God prefers students of the Bible to do their historical research, and the following list of equivalent names is the fruit of that research.

Magog

Some historians point to the former Soviet nations of Kazakhstan, Kyrgyzstan, Uzbekistan, Turkmenistan, Tajikistan, as well as including Afghanistan, as encompassing the land of Magog. Historian Edwin Yamauchi explains that Magog was the "ancient Scythian northern nomadic tribes who inhabited territory from Central Asia across the southern steppes of modern Russia."[10] These nations, today consisting of a population of 60 million, are united by one commonality—Islam.[11]

Meshech

The ancient Moschoi or Muschki or Musku tribe settled in Cilicia and Cappadocia, which is now part of modern-day Turkey.[12] Ezekiel 27:13 notes these people traded in slaves to Tyre and Ezekiel 32:26 refers to them as an ancient bandit nation.

Tubal

The people of Tubal would have hailed from the ancient Tibarenoi tribe.[13] For those who have equated Tubal as the Serbian city of Tobolsk, along with Meshech as the Russian city of Moscow, Hebrew Scripture experts claim there is "no etymological, grammatical, historical, or literary data in support of such a position."[14] This land also resides in modern-day Turkey.

Gomer

The Jewish historian Josephus identified Gomer who "founded those whom the Greeks now call Galatians [Galls], but were then called Gomerites.[15] Some theologians point to Germany as the land of Gomer, leading one theologian to ask, "What if a united and anti-Semitic Germany were to seek its future fortunes while allied to an anti-Semitic Russia?"[16] The Jewish Midrash Rabbah and Talmud also call Gomer "Germania" indicating today's Germany.[17] Not a commonly held view, but one Oxford historian even suggested Gomer's son who became the ancestor of the Celtic people necessitates including the Cymry of Wales and Brittany, meaning Great Britain.[18] Gomer most popularly looks to reference the Gimirrai of the Assyrians, or Cimmerians, who lived in the Black Sea area adjacent to Turkey.[19]

Beth-Togarmah

Togarmah, or Beth-Togarmah, which means the "house of Togarmah," contains an etymological connection between the name Togarmah and the names Turkey and Turkestan.[20] The Tilgaimmu resided between ancient Carchemish and Haran, which is modern-day Turkey and possibly the lands of Azerbaijan and Armenia.[21]

Persia

The land of Persia is ancient and long-running and the easiest to identify, only having changed its name to Iran during the last century in 1935.

Cush

Cush is another area easy to identify, having split into Ethiopia and the Sudan in more recent history.

Put

While the Midrash Rabbah claims Put is not Libya or Lub, but rather Somaliland or Somalia bordering on Ethiopia, the scholars reviewed all claim that Put is indeed Libya with the possibility that the land also includes Algeria and Tunisia.[22]

Many Nations

Ezekiel describes "Sheba and Dedan, the merchants of Tarshish, and all their young lions" as just observing the battle (Ezekiel 38:13 NKJV). Sheba and Dedan were Shem's descendants who settled in modern-day Saudi Arabia.[23] Tarshish could refer to Tarsus located just northwest of Israel, or the island of Sardinia located just north of Carthage in the Mediterranean Sea.[24] But, more than likely, the inhabitants of Tartessus, located on the southwest coast of Spain, denotes the Phoenician merchants who sailed as far as Britain.[25] The "young lions" could then be referring to Spain and Great Britain's colonies in the New World.

Noticeably absent from this list of Middle Eastern nations are those surrounding modern-day Israel, such as Syria, Lebanon, Jordan, Egypt, Gaza, Iraq, and the Arabian peninsula nations. Why these "many nations" are not also actively involved in the Gog-Magog Battle is open to speculation, but a Psalm 83 scenario where the seer Asaph foresaw Israel subjugating their surrounding neighbors could be the scenario that grants Israel the peaceful precondition Ezekiel describes that precedes the Gog-Magog invasion (Ezekiel 38:11).

Identifying Rosh

The final nation to be exploRed in Ezekiel's list is Rosh. Could it be modern-day Russia? As one author queried, "Will the old Russian Bear come out of its quarter-century hibernation and again sound a roar that shakes the world?"[26] Properly identifying Rosh is important for identifying the timing of the Gog-Magog Battle.

The Translations

The word "Rosh" or "Ros" appears noticeably absent from the list of nations provided by Ezekiel 38:3 in the King James Version, the New International Version, the English Standard Version, and others. Rosh can be found in Ezekiel's list of nations in the New King James Version, the New American Standard Version, the Amplified Version, the Darby Translation, and others. Why the difference in translations?

The difference is the challenge for the translators to either interpret the Hebrew word "Rosh" as a noun indicating an actual landmass, or as an adjective that according to the Hebrew-Greek Key Word Study Bible means "an exalted one" such as a king, sheik, captain, chief, or prince.[27] The NAS translators chose the noun form of "Rosh," while the NIV translators chose the adjective form. Translations based on the Greek Septuagint (LXX) follow the noun form, while those based on the Latin Vulgate follow the adjective form.

Support for Rosh Equaling Russia

Support for the use of the noun interpretation of "Rosh" as a distinct landmass identifiable as modern-day Russia points to the validity of this interpretation for several reasons:

1. Various Hebrew scholars, such as G.A. Cook, believe the noun form of "Rosh" is true to the original Hebrew.[28]

2. Other scholars, such as John Walvoord, explain that: "In the study of how ancient words came into modern language, it is quite common for the consonants to remain the same and the vowels to be changed. In the word 'Rosh,' if the vowel 'o' is changed to 'u' it becomes the root of the modern word Russia."[29]

3. The Septuagint (LXX) translation pRedates the Latin Vulgate by 700 years and is only three centuries removed from the time of Ezekiel, making it a translation more contemporary with Ezekiel.

4. Tenth Century Byzantine writers, such as Ibn-Fosslan, identified a group of Scythians dwelling in the northern parts of Taurus upon the river Volga as the Ros.[30]

5. Ninth Century B.C. Assyrian texts pRedating Ezekiel's time also refer to the Rosh or Rashu.[31]

6. Even farther back as early as 2600 B.C., ancient Egyptian and other Middle-Eastern inscriptions and texts, such as in Sargon's inscriptions, on a cylinder by Assurbanipal, in an annul by Sennacherib, and five times in Ugaritic tablets, all record the existence of the Rosh/Rash/Reshu people.[32]

7. The early Byzantine Church claimed that the Ros were the people who lived far north of Greece in the area today known as Russia.[33]

8. Rosh is supposed to be "from the remotest parts of the north" (Ezekiel 39:1-2 NKJV). No other nation exists more directly north of Israel and is more remote than modern-day Russia.

9. Current news reports repeatedly show that Russia has very quickly solidified economic and military ties with the nations involved in the Gog-Magog coalition. Russia is building a nuclear reactor in Iran and arming Islamic nations. Russia has gained a foothold in Syria due to the Syrian civil war for the purpose of controlling the Middle East's vast oil reserves. Israel's Mediterranean gas deposits are seen as a direct threat to Russia's monopoly of the natural gas supply to Europe.

10. Russia nationally has held a long and historic anti-Semitic violent streak that God would not leave without a response.

When all arguments for Rosh being Russia are put on the table, it is clear that Russia descended from the Rosh people.

General Timing

While there is much debate over the specific timing of the Gog-Magog Battle, the student of the Bible can be positive about the general timing. General timing is clearly spelled out in Ezekiel's account as events that must happen to set the stage for the battle.

1. The first general timing clue is Ezekiel's use of the terms "latter years" and "last days" (Ezekiel 38:8,16 NKJV). The Gog-Magog Battle must happen in the prophetic scheme of the end times as it relates to the nation of Israel. The key verse which unlocks the understanding as to what these terms mean can be found in Deuteronomy: "When you are in distress, and all these things come upon you in the latter days, when you turn to the Lord your God and obey His voice" (Deuteronomy 4:30 NKJV). "Distress" is also translated as "Tribulation." It is the Tribulation, also called Daniel's Seventieth Week prophecy (Daniel 9:20-27), that brings the Jewish people as a nation back to a belief in Yahweh and later to accept Yeshua as their Messiah. The Tribulation leading up to the Millennial reign of Christ is what the Old Testament prophets consistently and repeatedly taught. And so, these key phrases point to the Gog-Magog Battle happening in relation to the Tribulation and the Millennial Kingdom.

2. The second general timing clue rejects the claim that the battle has already happened in history. Never in the history of the Middle East have the nations described in the coalition been united in a concerted attack against Israel. In no time has such a specific group of nations been destroyed by inclement weather. And, in no time in history has Israel named a valley Hamon Gog, nor has the adjoining town called Hamonah, existed where the Jews buried their invaders' dead bodies (Ezekiel 39:11-12,16). Lack of historical support leaves only a future timing for the battle to occur.

3. The third general timing clue is given in Ezekiel 36 and 37 and involves the regathering of the Jewish people back into their homeland "from out of all countries" of the world (Ezekiel 36:24 NKJV). Like the valley of dry bones reanimated into a living person that Ezekiel envisioned, Israel did indeed become a nation once again. Out of the 14.5 million Jewish people in the

world today, 47% reside in Israel, making up 6,841,000 (74%) of the population dwelling in the Holy Land.[34] And, the Jews must have control of "the mountains of Israel," which they gained when they took control of the mountains from the Jordanians during the Six Day War (Ezekiel 38:8 NKJV).[35]

4. The fourth general timing clue involves the developments nationally that have to occur to make the nations of the coalition unite in an invasion of Israel. Two factors have made this coalition possible today. The first is the religion of Islam uniting these nations in satanic hatred of the Jewish people. The second is the economic bounty that Israel now has with its revitalized land and newly discovered gas deposits.[36] The coalition nations now see a viable motivation to unite for the singular purpose of plundering Israel's wealth.

5. The fifth general timing clue reads, "You will say, 'I will go up against a land of unwalled villages; I will go to a peaceful people, who dwell safely, all of them dwelling without walls, and having neither bars nor gates'" (Ezekiel 38:11 NKJV). Israel must be living without walls, peacefully, and unsuspecting of an attack. Israel today lives in constant fear of attack and is always prepared for an invasion by the 60-plus million hostile Muslims surrounding their borders. Because of this turbulent climate, this part of the prophecy can be argued to have yet to be fulfilled.

Discarded Timings

As the question as to when the Gog-Magog Battle will occur, two obvious answers can be eliminated from the onset. The first presupposes the battle has already occured in history, but that would be historically incorrect. That the Gog-Magog Battle was fulfilled in Ezekiel's day by an invasion of the Scythians, Babylonians, or Greeks fails to fulfill the roster of nations that compile the Gog-Magog invasion force. Also, it fails to address Ezekiel chapters 36-38 which prophesy a regathering of Jews to Israel from all over the world using the end-timing clues given as the "latter years," or "last days" (Ezekiel 38:8,16 NJKV). A past historical invasion just does not fit the Ezekiel 38-39 description.

The second concludes that the Gog-Magog Battle will never occur and also can be discarded as incorrect. A literal interpretation being replaced with a metaphorical interpretation that postulates that Ezekiel 38-39's description is somehow "apocalyptic symbolism" representing a struggle between good and evil is Replacement Theology spiritualizing.[37] As Semitic languages expert Charles Feinberg once said, "It is either the grammatical, literal, historical interpretation or we are adrift on an uncharted sea with every man the norm for himself."[38] Prophecy fulfilled is always prophecy fulfilled literally, and the prophecy concerning the Gog-Magog Battle should be interpreted no differently.

Before the Tribulation

The following timing views are founded on the Premillennial interpretation of Scriptures as they relate to the order of future events. Premillennialism was the dominant view during the first three centuries of Church history and was later reinstated by German Calvinist theologian Johann Heinrich Alsted in his book The Beloved City (1627).[39] The first two timings rest heavily on the Pre-Tribulation Rapture viewpoint, which sees the Church removed from the earth before God pours out His wrath during a seven-year Tribulation period.

Before Both the Rapture and the Tribulation

Some theologians believe the Gog-Magog Battle will occur before both the Rapture of the Church and the seven-year Tribulation. A few of the supporters of this view are Tim LaHaye and Jerry Jenkins of the popular Left Behind series of books, and Joel Rosenberg who wrote Epicenter. Another supporter, David Cooper, noted with confidence back in 1940, years before Israel had even become a nation again, that "there will be a time between now and the beginning of the Tribulation when the

Jews will be dwelling in the Land in unwalled cities and will be at rest" after the Church has been raptuRed.[40] The pros and cons of this timing viewpoint are as follows:

Pros:

1. Israel burning the invader's weapons takes seven years, equal to the seven-year length of the Tribulation (Ezekiel 39:9; Daniel 9:27).

2. With Islam's severe defeat and her coalition nations lying in ruin, many a Muslim's faith in Allah would be shatteRed. The Islamic world would no longer impede the Jewish people from removing the Dome of the Rock off of the Temple Mount and begin rebuilding the Third Temple in its place, the very Temple which the Antichrist is prophesied to desecrate during the Tribulation (Daniel 9:27; 2 Thessalonians 2:3-4).

3. God revealing Himself to the world so dynamically is in character with His willingness to warn before implementing global judgment and to call people to repentance. A resulting great multitude, therefore, may come to then know Christ and be included in the Rapture and avoid God's wrath during the Tribulation.

Cons:

1. Placing the invasion before the Rapture could contradict the first general time clue of the terms "latter years" and "last days," that is if this "time of Jacob's trouble" is reserved only for the seven-year Tribulation (Jeremiah 30:7; Ezekiel 38:8,16 NKJV).

2. Placing the invasion before the Rapture would contradict the fifth general time clue which tells of Israel living unsuspecting and in peace before the attack. Unless peace is derived by Israel subjugating its surrounding neighbors or by the peace covenant made with the Antichrist which starts the seven-year countdown, Israel yet to have attained that peaceful precondition (Daniel 9:27).

3. The New Testament indicates that no prophetic event has to occur before the Rapture, which is called imminency. Imminency precludes such prophetic events such as the Gog-Magog Battle happening before the Rapture.

4. The removal of "he who now restrains" coincides with the Antichrist emerging on the world scene (2 Thessalonians 2:6-8 NKJV). Because the Church is the temple of the Holy Spirit and so, therefore, could be identified as the Restrainer, the Rapture would have to happen before the Antichrist is revealed (1 Corinthians 3:16). Should the peaceful precondition be tied to the Antichrist's peace covenant, then the Gog-Magog Battle follows both the Rapture and the onset of the Tribulation.

5. A timing problem exists for Israel in that midway through the Tribulation the Antichrist's abomination in the newly built Temple will cause the Jews to flee into the desert (Matthew 24:15-16). Some argue the Jews would no longer then have access to the Gog-Magog invader's weapons to burn. And so, the seven years of Tribulation no longer matches the seven years of burning the weapons.

After the Rapture But Before the Tribulation

Popular supporters of this view are professors Ed Hindson and Tommy Ice, both associated with the Pre-Trib Research Center.[41] Also, Arnold Fruchtenbaum of Ariel Ministries, who reasons the Russian invasion as taking place "some time before the Tribulation," because "God will punish Russia for her sins" for "the key sin is her long history of anti-Semitism, a problem that persists in Russia to this day."[42]

Pros:

1. With the world in chaos due to a Pre-Tribulation Rapture, Russia and its Islamic coalition could seize the opportunity to attack a friendless Israel.

2. With the Muslim Gog-Magog nations out of the picture just before the Tribulation, the Antichrist would have an easier time making a peace covenant with Israel.

3. With the more Christianized nations in tatters due to a Pre-Tribulation Rapture and the Islamic world in ruins from the Gog-Magog Battle, the remaining European world power could fill the vacuum in the Middle East. By making a peace treaty with Israel and easily conquering the lands of the once Middle-Eastern Islamic countries, the Roman Empire could truly be revived once more as Daniel 2 and 7 prophesy. The only remaining world powers would be East-Asian, and the Bible records their continued existence, though under the control of the Antichrist and revolting at the very end of the Tribulation (Revelation 16:12).

4. With the Muslim world in tatters, Israel would have no resistance to rebuilding the Temple.

5. The Rapture does not start the Tribulation, but rather the signing of the peace covenant between the Antichrist and Israel does (Daniel 9:27). This fact would allow a three-and-a-half-year or more time delay between the Rapture and the Tribulation, giving Israel the full seven years to burn the weapons from the Gog-Magog Battle before being forced to flee into the desert (Matthew 24:15-16).

Cons:

1. Placing the invasion before the Rapture could contradict the first general time clue of the terms "latter years" and "last days," that is if this "time of Jacob's trouble" is reserved only for the seven-year Tribulation (Jeremiah 30:7; Ezekiel 38:8,16 NKJV).

2. The peaceful precondition of Ezekiel 38:11 in which Israel has to be living unsuspecting and in peace before the Gog-Magog Battle may only occur because of the peace covenant with the Antichrist, who cannot be revealed until the Tribulation begins.

During the Tribulation

The following timings place the Gog-Magog Battle during the Tribulation. The pros and cons of each timing viewpoint will continue to be addressed.

In the First Half or Middle of the Tribulation

Supporters of this view are John Walvoord, J. Dwight Pentecost, Charles Ryrie, Herman Hoyt, Charles Dyer, and Mark Hitchcock. As Pentecost explains, "To place the events in the middle of the week is the only position consistent with the chronology of these extended passages (Isaiah 30-35 and Joel 2-3)."[43]

Pros:

1. The fifth general timing clue that requires Israel living unsuspecting and in peace before the Gog-Magog Battle could easily be attained by the peace covenant the Antichrist makes with Israel that starts the seven-year countdown of the Tribulation (Ezekiel 38:11; Daniel 9:27).[44]

2. With the more Christianized nations in tatters due to a Pre-Tribulation Rapture and the Islamic world in ruins from the Gog-Magog Battle, the remaining European world power could fill the vacuum in the Middle East. By making a peace treaty with Israel and easily conquering the lands of the once Middle-Eastern Islamic countries, the Roman Empire could truly be revived once more as Daniel 2 and 7 prophesy. The only remaining world powers would be East-Asian, and the Bible records their continued existence, though under the control of the Antichrist, rising at the very end of the Tribulation (Revelation 16:12).

3. By placing the timing of the Gog-Magog Battle early in the Tribulation, the defeat and disillusionment of Muslims worldwide would destroy the strength of Islam. With the Church removed in a Pre-Tribulation Rapture, Christianity would also be removed. The resulting polytheistic and pantheistic religions would integrate well into the apostate one-world religion that

the False Prophet promotes (Revelation 13:11-15). The only monotheistic religions left to reject the Antichrist would be Judaism and the newly growing Jesus movement, both of which the Antichrist persecutes greatly during the second half of the Tribulation (Revelation 6:11).

Cons:

1. Ezekiel describes Israel burning the invading enemy's weapons for seven years (Ezekiel 39:9). Placing the Gog-Magog Battle at any time during the Tribulation would push the burning right into the Millennial Kingdom. With Jesus then present to provide everyone's needs, the curse partially lifted, and the earth reformatted by earthquakes, there would be no need for Israel to have to burn any weapons for fuel (Isaiah 11:8; Revelation 6:12-14; 16:17-21).

2. The tremendous persecution of the Jews during the second half of the Tribulation would not grant them the freedom to bury the invaders' dead bodies for seven months unless the Gog-Magog Battle occured earlier than the mid-point (Ezekiel 39:12).

3. If the Gog-Magog Battle happened closer to the mid-point, the question is raised as to why God would rescue Israel so dramatically from the Gog-Magog nations only to hand Israel immediately over to the intense persecution by the Antichrist.

At the End of the Tribulation (Armageddon)

Supporters of this view, such as Louis Bauman and Charles Feinberg, believe the Gog-Magog Battle and the final battle of Armageddon are one and the same.[45]

Pros:

1. Both the Gog-Magog Battle (Ezekiel 38-39) and the Battle of Armageddon (Revelation 19:19) are described as taking place during the first general timing clue "latter years" and "last days" of the Tribulation (Ezekiel 38:8,16 NKJV).

2. Ezekiel and Revelation both describe dead invaders being eaten by birds and wild animals (Ezekiel 39:4,17-20; Revelation 19:17-18).

3. Ezekiel declares that due to the defeat of the Gog-Magog invasion Israel will again acknowledge God (Ezekiel 39:22,29). These references, if coupled with Zechariah 12:10, explaining an acknowledgment by Israel of their true Messiah at the end of the Tribulation, would make the Gog-Magog Battle and Armageddon one and the same, if the acknowledgment of God the Father and Jesus the Messiah are also one and the same.

Cons:

1. The peaceful precondition in which Israel has to be living unsuspecting and in peace before the Gog-Magog Battle cannot exist under the Great Tribulation of Israel by the Antichrist (Ezekiel 38:11).

2. The nations in the two battles do not match. The Gog-Magog Battle involves the specific nations of Kazakhstan, Kyrgyzstan, Uzbekistan, Turkmenistan, Tajikistan, Russia, Turkey, Iran, Sudan, Libya, and possibly Afghanistan, Azerbaijan, Armenia, Algeria, and Tunisia against Israel (Ezekiel 38:1-6). The references to Armageddon include every nation from across the entire earth set against Israel (Joel 3:2; Zephaniah 3:8; Zechariah 12:3; 14:2).

3. The locations described in the two battles do not match. Armageddon takes place in the valley of Jezreel by the plain of Megiddo (Judges 5:19; 2 Kings 23:29; 2 Chronicles 35:22; Zechariah 12:11). Ezekiel describes the Gog-Magog Battle as taking place on the "mountains of Israel" (Ezekiel 38:8 NKJV).

4. The leaders of the armies are not the same. Gog is the prince and ruler of Rosh, Meshech, and Tubal (Ezekiel 38:3). The invading leader at Armageddon is the Beast who controls the whole earth (Revelation 13). While it is known that Satan possesses the Antichrist, it is unknown if Gog is possessed by Satan (Revelation 13:2).

5. The armies find themselves fighting two different opponents. The Gog-Magog invaders look to conquer a peaceful and unsuspecting Israel (Ezekiel 38:11). The Armageddon invaders gather to make war against the returned King—Jesus Christ (Revelation 19:19).

6. The accounts of the defeat of the invaders do not match. The Gog-Magog invaders are defeated by God who uses "flooding rain, great hailstones, fire, and brimstone," as well as in-fighting (Ezekiel 38:21-22 NKJV). The invading nations at Armageddon are defeated by Jesus who uses "a sharp sword" from His mouth, meaning mere words (Revelation 19:15 NKJV).

7. Ezekiel describes several nations protesting why the Gog-Magog invasion is happening (Ezekiel 38:13). At Armageddon, all the nations of the world are involved in the invasion of Israel, and none protest (Joel 3:2; Zephaniah 3:8; Zachariah 12:3; 14:2).

8. Ezekiel describes Israel burning the invading enemy's weapons for seven years (Ezekiel 39:9). Placing the Gog-Magog Battle at the end of the Tribulation would push the burning right into the Millennial Kingdom. With Jesus then present to provide everyone's needs, the curse partially lifted, and the earth reformatted by earthquakes, there would be no need for Israel to have to burn any weapons for fuel (Isaiah 11:8; Revelation 6:12-14; 16:17-21).

In Relation to the Millennial Kingdom

Three views exist that place the Gog-Magog Battle in relation to Jesus Christ's thousand-year reign on earth, often called the Kingdom of Christ or the Millennial Kingdom.

Between the Tribulation and the Millennium

This least popular view places the events of Ezekiel 38 and 39 into an interlude period between the Tribulation and the Millennial Kingdom.

Pros:

1. This is a consistent argument with the view that an interlude period could exist between the Rapture and the Tribulation.

2. The fifth general timing clue that requires Israel living unsuspecting and in peace before the Gog-Magog Battle could easily be attained after Christ's Second Coming (Ezekiel 38:11).

3. An interlude time could be any length of time, granting the seven years given to Israel to burn the invading enemy's weapons for fuel (Ezekiel 39:9).

Cons:

1. With Jesus having defeated all of the armies of the world at Armageddon, no army would be left to invade Israel so soon (Revelation 19:19).

2. With Jesus Christ's return at the Second Coming, no Gog-Magog invasion would be needed to lead Israel to again acknowledge God (Ezekiel 39:22,29).

3. Only one interlude period is given in the Futurist prophetic timeline as it relates to the Tribulation. Daniel reveals, "Blessed is he who waits, and comes to the one thousand three hundred and thirty-five days" (Daniel 12:12 NKJV). Revelation also explains that the Gentiles "will tread the holy city underfoot for forty-two months" (Revelation 11:2 NKJV). Revelation continues, "And I will give power to my two witnesses, and they will prophesy one thousand two hundred and sixty days, clothed in sackcloth" (Revelation 11:3 NKJV). The difference between these two accounts is 75 days. The 75 days will most likely be used by Jesus to judge the world in the Sheep-Goat Judgment and rebuild the planet after the seven-year Tribulation (Matthew 25:31-46).

4. The interlude time limited to 75 days does not give Israel the seven months they need to bury the dead invaders' bodies from the Gog-Magog Battle (Ezekiel 39:12).

5. With Jesus present to provide everyone's needs, the curse partially lifted, and the earth reformatted by earthquakes, there would be no need for Israel to have to burn any weapons for fuel into the Millennium (Isaiah 11:8; Revelation 6:12-14; 16:17-21).

At the Beginning of the Millennium

Supporters of this view, such as Arno Gaebelein, place the Gog-Magog Battle at the beginning of the thousand-year reign of Christ.[46]

Pros:

1. The fifth general timing clue that requires Israel living unsuspecting and in peace before the Gog-Magog Battle could easily be attained after Christ's Second Coming (Ezekiel 38:11).

Cons:

1. With Jesus' return at the Second Coming, no Gog-Magog invasion would be needed to get Israel to again acknowledge God (Ezekiel 39:22,29).

2. With Jesus having defeated all the armies of the world at Armageddon, no army would be left to invade Israel so soon (Revelation 19:19).

3. No wicked people will have survived the Sheep-Goat Judgment to enter into the Millennial Kingdom to start a war (Jeremiah 25:32-33; Matthew 25:31-46; Revelation 19:15-18). Only believers who survive the Tribulation enter into the Millennial Kingdom, and they have no reason to declare war on Christ.

4. No weapons would be available to the invaders of the Gog-Magog Battle, nor be left to burn for seven years, for as Isaiah states, "They shall beat their swords into plowshares, and their spears into pruning hooks" (Isaiah 2:4 NKJV).

5. No war exists until the end of the Millennial Kingdom. Isaiah describes the Millennial Kingdom as being a time of world peace where "nation shall not lift up sword against nation, neither shall

they learn war anymore" (Isaiah 2:4 NKJV). Revelation describes the only war that will happen during the Millennial Kingdom, and that is at the end of the thousand years when Satan is let loose from the Bottomless Pit to rally unbelievers in that age against Jesus Christ (Revelation 20:7-9).

6. With Jesus present to partially lift the curse and reformat the earth from the ravages of the Tribulation, the Millennial Kingdom will begin in an almost holy state (Isaiah 11:8; Revelation 6:12-14; 16:17-21). Ezekiel describes the land after the Gog-Magog Battle needing cleansing because of its defilement due to the invaders' dead bodies (Ezekiel 39:12). Defilement contradicts the pristine condition that characterizes the Millennial Kingdom.

7. Islam will not exist during the Millennial Kingdom. The unifying theme today among the coalition of nations that attack Israel in the Gog-Magog Battle is their satanically inspiRed Islamic hatred of Israel and jealousy of its wealth. Since Satan will be bound while Jesus reigns in person over the entire earth, no opposing satanic religion such as Islam will exist to unite those nations during the Millennium Kingdom (Revelation 20:1-3).

8. With Jesus Christ's ruling the world from Jerusalem with "a rod of iron," no invader would dare invade Israel (Psalm 2:9).

At the End of the Millennium

Henry Halley is a proponent of this view.[47] So are George Knight and Rayburn Ray.[48] Frank Gaebelein also places the Gog-Magog Battle at the end of the Millennial Kingdom.[49] But, as Dr. Rhodes notes, the majority of supporters for this view tend to come from a non-evangelical background.[50]

Pros:

1. Revelation's timeline places a Gog-Magog Battle at the end of the Millennial Kingdom. The passage reads, "Now when the thousand years have expiRed, Satan will be released from his prison and will go out to deceive the nations which are in the four corners of the earth, Gog and Magog, to gather them together

to battle, whose number is as the sand of the sea" (Revelation 20:7-8 NKJV).

2. Similar terminology exists between Ezekiel 38-39 and Revelation 20 concerning the great number of invaders involved.

3. The prosperity that Israel possesses as described in Ezekiel 38-39 would be fulfilled by God's blessings on Israel during the Millennial Kingdom.

4. God uses supernatural weather in both accounts to destroy the invaders.

Cons:

1. Ezekiel's chapters would be chronologically out of order with this view. Ezekiel 33-39 covers the national restoration of Israel and is followed by chapters 40-48 which describe Israel's spiritual restoration entering into and enduring throughout the Millennial Kingdom.[51]

2. Revelation 20's chronology does not harmonize with Ezekiel's chronology. Revelation 20 describes the Millennial Kingdom, which is immediately followed by chapter 21 concerning the Eternal State.

3. The Gog-Magog invaders would no longer have bodies that require Israel to bury over seven months, as the Revelation account records the invaders being incinerated by fire coming down from the heavens (Ezek. 39:12; Revelation 20:9).

4. Israel would have no reason to need seven months to bury the dead invaders if God is just going to resurrect them at the end of the Millennium, judge them at the Great White Throne Judgment, and then throw them into the Lake of Fire (Ezekiel 39:12; Revelation 20:11-15).

5. Israel would have no reason to burn the invaders' weapons into the perfect Eternal State.

6. Ezekiel's and Revelation's descriptions of the invading armies do not match. Ezekiel describes a coalition of Russia and

Muslim nations attacking Israel. Revelation describes a much larger scope, with the invaders coming out of the "nations which are in the four corners of the earth" (Revelation 20:8 NKJV).

7. Ezekiel's and Revelation's descriptions of the battlefields do not match. Ezekiel describes the Gog-Magog Battle taking place on the "mountains of Israel," while Revelation's account states the battle takes place "on the broad plain of the earth" (Ezekiel 38:8; Revelation 20:9 NASB).

8. Ezekiel's and Revelation's descriptions of Israel's rulers do not match. Ezekiel 38-39 follows chapters 36-37 which describe the rebirth of Israel, a nation not yet in belief in God nor having accepted Jesus as Messiah. The Revelation 20 account has Jesus already ruling from Jerusalem for a thousand years.

9. Ezekiel's and Revelation's descriptions of the invader's leaders do not match. Gog is in control of the coalition against Israel in Ezekiel's account, whereas Satan is in control of the coalition against Jesus in Revelation's account. While Satan is clearly mentioned in Revelation's account, it is unknown if Gog is possessed by Satan or is a man possessed by Satan.

10. Ezekiel's and Revelation's descriptions of Israel's faith do not match. In Ezekiel 38-39, God uses the Gog-Magog Battle to make Himself known to Israel and the world. In Revelation 20, Israel has already long acknowledged Yahweh as God and King going on a thousand years.

11. The unbelieving children of the Tribulation saints who have survived to live into the Millennial Kingdom will be the ones who wage war against God at the end of the thousand years, as opposed to the children from the age of the "time of the Gentiles" who wage war in Ezekiel and Jesus' accounts (Luke 21:24 NKJV).

12. John's use of "Gog and Magog" in Revelation 20:8 is more likely to draw a comparison between Ezekiel's Gog-Magog Battle and the one John is describing at the end of the Millennial

Kingdom. In other words, the labeling acts as a kind of shorthand saying, "It's going to be Gog and Magog all over again."[52]

Final Analysis

I will conclude by analyzing the various timing views and then state when I believe the Gog-Magog Battle will take place.

Let me go on the record, though, by stating that I am not dogmatic about this end time topic, nor should anyone be. The study of the end times (Eschatology) is a non-primary doctrine. Since God has given mankind merely an overview of His future plans, He has left us with nothing concrete enough to pinpoint the exact timing, probably so that we Christians will not just sit quietly by, but get out there and witness with all our energy until the Lord's return. The study and debate over when the Gog-Magog Battle will take place should never divide the brethren.

Analyzing the Views

Each of the Gog-Magog Battle timing views appear to revolve around dealing with two yet-to-be fulfilled key prerequisites:

1. Israel is in a state of unsuspecting peace before the invasion (Ezekiel 38:11).

2. Israel has seven months to bury the dead invaders' bodies and seven whole years to expend the leftover fuel and weapons (Ezekiel 39:9,12-16).

Walking backwards through the list, the three views that time the Gog-Magog Battle in relation to the Millennial Kingdom do great justice to the first prerequisite in putting Israel at a time of peace due to Jesus' victory and reign, but cannot overcome the obstacles of the second prerequisite. With Jesus having subjected all of His enemies before the start of the Millennial Kingdom, there would be no more invaders left to organize another invasion. With no invaders, there are no bodies to bury nor weapons to burn.

The best of the three Millennial Kingdom views is the one placing the timing at the end of the thousand years, which Revelation describes as an uprising of unbelievers born during that era who are led by Satan and share in his final defeat (Revelation 20:7-8). While there are some similarities to Ezekiel's account of the Gog-Magog Battle, the dissimilarities prove Ezekiel is talking about a different Gog-Magog Battle than the battle the Apostle John described. I agree that John's use of "Gog" and "Magog" in Revelation 20 is more likely to draw a comparison between Ezekiel's Gog-Magog Battle as a type of what the battle will be like at the end of the Millennial Kingdom.

For the two views that place the timing during the Tribulation, both wrestle with the same prerequisites. While similarities exist between Gog-Magog and Armageddon, their differences far outweigh their similarities. Also, placing the battle at the end of the Tribulation violates the first prerequisite that Israel is living in peace, a condition which would be impossible under the intense persecution by the Antichrist and Israel's subsequent flight into the desert.

Placing the timing at the beginning, but not by the middle, of the Tribulation gives Israel the seven months to bury the dead invaders and the full seven years to burn the fuel, should they have a reserve stoRed where they flee. This view would then need to settle the peaceful precondition of Israel by resting it on either a Psalm 83 subjugation of Israel's surrounding hostile neighbors or the peace covenant made with the Antichrist (Psalm 83; Daniel 9:27).

The two views that place the timing of the Gog-Magog Battle squarely before the Tribulation perfectly grants the full seven years' time needed to burn the weapons. Even if the Jewish people must flee into the wilderness at the midpoint of the Tribulation, they could have already stoRed the fuel in the location where they end up fleeing. Or, there could be a gap of three-and-a-half years or so between the Gog-Magog Battle and the beginning of the Tribulation so that the fuel expires by the middle of the Tribulation just as the Jews flee. Since the Tribulation begins with the peace covenant forged between the Antichrist and Israel, the only viable scenario for a peaceful prerequisite would be a Psalm 83 subjugation of Israel's hostile bordering neighbors or to take Ezekiel's description of Israel being at peace to mean militarily secure, which as one of the most powerful militaries in the world today, could certainly provide a false sense of security.

My View

Obviously, all of the timing views struggle over some particular point. Which view a person holds rests more on what they see as the view which provides the most logical harmonization of the prerequisites. I have to agree with Dr. Rhodes that the timing of the Gog-Magog Battle after the Rapture of the Church but just before or at the very onset of the Tribulation best fulfills these prerequisites and makes the most logical sense in the prophetic timeline. This is how I see the timeline most likely playing out:

1. The Rapture of the Church removes the Restrainer.

2. Israel subjugates her surrounding neighbors in fulfillment of Psalm 83.

3. The Gog-Magog Battle destroys the Russian and Muslim influence in the Middle East, makes the world aware of God's presence, and restores Israel's belief in the God of the Torah.

4. The Antichrist makes a peace covenant with Israel which starts the seven-year Tribulation, then conquers what is left of the Middle East, and birth's his Revived Roman Empire.

5. Israel spends the seven years of the Tribulation burning the weapons.

6. Jesus returns at the end of the seven years to defeat His enemies at Armageddon resulting in Israel acknowledging that Jesus is God's Son.

7. Jesus gathers the people from all over the world for the Sheep-Goat Judgment, which results in only believers entering the Millennial Kingdom.

8. At the very end of the Millennial Kingdom, a final battle takes place that is reminiscent of the first Gog-Magog Battle.

Time will tell when the Gog-Magog Battle will truly take place. But, Israel is a nation once more as prophesied, and the coalition of invading nations are already working together for the first time in history. The scene is pretty much all set for this epic battle to be waged and in the not-too-distant future.

Conclusion

With a more secure handle on exactly what nations are involved in Ezekiel 38-39 and when the Gog-Magog Battle will occur, the evangelist can better approach the apologetic of fulfilled Bible prophecy more confidently. While this epic battle and prophecy remain future, various aspects of it demonstrate that events are quickly ramping up leading to the complete fulfillment of Ezekiel's prophecy, so it is not so distant in the future. With that sense of urgency in mind, the evangelist can precede to show those to whom he is witnessing how God's prophetic order of events is playing out even in our day and age and encourage them towards surrendering their lives to Jesus Christ and in holy living.

End Notes

1. Ron Rhodes, Northern Storm Rising (Eugene, OR: Harvest House Publishers, 2008), 13.

2. John F. Walvoord & Roy B. Zuck (Eds.), The Bible Knowledge Commentary: Old Testament (Wheaton, IL: Scripture Press Publications Inc., 1985), 1225.

3. Kyle M. Yates, Preaching From the Prophets (Nashville, TN: Broadman Press, 1942), 179.

4. Gaalyah Cornfeld, Archaeology of the Bible: Book By Book (London, England: Adam and Charles Black, 1977), 179.

5. W. MacKintosh MacKay, The Goodly Fellowship of the Prophets (New York, NY: Richard R. Smith, Inc. Publishers, 1929), 181.

6. Tent C. Butler, (Ed.), Holman Bible Dictionary (Nashville, TN: Holman Bible Publishers, 1991). 565.

7. William P. Barker, Everyone in the Bible (Old Tappan, NJ: Fleming H. Revell Co., 1966), 115.

8. Stephen M. Miller, The Complete Guide to Bible Prophecy (Uhrichville, OH: Barbour Publishing, 2010), 128.

9. New Catholic Edition of the Holy Bible (New York, NY: Catholic Book Publishing Co., 1957), 997.

10. Edwin M. Yamauchi, Foes From the Northern Frontier (Grand Rapids, MI: Baker Book House, 1982), 64-109.

11. Mark Hitchcock, The Coming Islamic Invasion of Israel (Sisters, OR: Multnomah, 2002), 31-32.

12. Tim LaHaye & Ed Hindson (Eds.), The Popular Encyclopedia of Bible Prophecy (Eugene, OR: Harvest House Publishers, 2004), 119-120.

13. John. B. Taylor, Ezekiel: An Introduction and Commentary (Downers Grove, IL: Inter-Varsity Press, 1969), 244-245.

14. Frank E. Gaebelein (Ed.), The Expositor's Bible Commentary (Vol 6) (Grand Rapids, MI: Zondervan Publishing House, 1986), 930.

15. Josephus, The Works of Josephus. "Antiquities 1.6.1." (Peabody, MA: Hendrickson Publishers, 1987), 36.

16. John Phillips, Exploring the Future: A Comprehensive Guide to Bible Prophecy 3rd ed. (Grand Rapids, IL: Kregel, 2003), 327.

17. Midrash Rabbah 37:1.

18. AlfRed Edersheim, Old Testament Bible History (Grand Rapids, MI: William B. Eerdmans Publishing Company, 1975), i.59.

19. Taylor, 244-245.

20. Henry M. Morris, The Genesis Record: A Scientific and Devotional Commentary on the Book of Beginnings (Grand Rapids, MI: Baker Book House, 1976), 247.

21. LaHaye & Hindson.

22. Midrash Rabbah 37:1.

23. Marshall W. Best, Through the Prophet's Eye (Enumclaw, WA: WinePress Publishing, 2000), 146.

24. Best, 144.

25. Charles F. Pfeiffer, Baker Bible Atlas (Grand Rapids, MI: Baker Book House, 1961), 40.

26. David Jeremiah, Is This the End? (Nashville, TN: W Publishing Group, 2016), 210.

27. Spiros Zodhiates, Hebrew-Greek Key Word Study Bible (Chattanooga, TN: AMG Publishers, 2008), 1133, 1960.

28. G.A. Cook, A Critical and Exegetical Commentary on the Book of Ezekiel (Edinburgh, Scotland: T&T Clark, 1936), 408-409.

29. John F. Walvoord, The Nations in Prophecy (Grand Rapids, IL: Zondervan Publishing House, 1978), 108.

30. H.W.F. Gesenius, Gesenius' Hebrew-Chalde Lexicon (Grand Rapids, IL: Eerdmans, 1957), 752.

31. Clyde E. Billington Jr., "The Rosh People in History and Prophecy (Part Two and Three)." Michigan Theological Journal 3:2, (Fall 1992): 172.

32. Thomas Ice, "Ezekiel 38 and 39, Pt 4" Pre-Trib Perspectives vol. VIII, no. 44 (April 2007): 6.

33. Billington, 49.

34. "Vital Statistics: Latest Population Statistics for Israel (2020)," Jewish Virtual Library, accessed October 1, 2020, https://www.jewishvirtuallibrary.org/latest-population-statistics-for-israel.

35. Mark Hitchcock, The End: A Complete Overview of Bible Prophecy and the End of Days (Wheaton, IL: Tyndale House, 2012), 310.

36. Luke Baker, "Israel Asks Itself the $150 Billion Question," Reuters, (May 25, 2011), https://www.reuters.com/article/2011/05/25/us-economy-israel-steinitz-idUSTRE74O38R20110525.

37. Taylor, 247-248.

38. Charles Lee Feinberg, The Prophecy of Ezekiel: The Glory of the Lord (Chicago, IL: Moody Press, 1969), 219.

39. Robert G. Clouse, The Meaning of the Millennium: Four Views (Downers Grove, IL: InterVarsity Press, 1977), 7-9.

40. David L. Cooper, When God's Armies Meet the Almighty (Los Angeles, CA: The Biblical Research Society, 1940), 80-81.

41. Ed Hindson & Thomas Ice, Charting the Bible Chronologically: A Visual Guide to God's Unfolding Plan (Eugene, OR: Harvest House Publishers, 2016), 120.

42. Arnold G. Fruchtenbaum, The Footsteps of the Messiah: A Study of the Sequence of Prophetic Events (San Antonio, TX: Ariel Ministries, 2004), 109.

43. J. Dwight. Pentecost, Things to Come: A Study in Biblical Eschatology (Grand Rapids, MI: Zondervan Publishing House, 1958), 354.

44. Charles C. Ryrie, Basic Theology (Wheaton, IL: Scripture Press Publications Inc., 1986), 477.

45. Louis Bauman, Russian Events in the Light of Bible Prophecy (Philadelphia, PA: The Balkiston Co., 1942), 174-175.

46. Arno C. Gaebelein, The Prophet Ezekiel (New York, NY: Our Hope, 1918), 252-255.

47. Henry H. Halley, Halley's Bible Handbook (Grand Rapids, MI: Zondervan Publishing House, 1965), 334.

48. George W. Knight & Rayburn W. Ray, The Illustrated Everyday Bible Companion (Uhrichsville, OH: Barbour Publishing Co., 2005), 512.

49. Frank E. Gaebelein, 932.

50. Rhodes, 189.

51. Jeremiah, 223.

52. Mark Hitchcock, 101 Answers to Questions About the Book of Revelation (Eugene, OR: Harvest House Publishers, 2012), 223-224.

Kings of Judah & Israel

Kings Before Division of Kingdom of Israel
Saul: First King of Israel; son of Kish; father of Ish-Bosheth, Jonathan and Michal
Ish-Bosheth (or Eshbaal): King of Israel; son of Saul
David: King of Judah; later of Israel; son of Jesse; husband of Abigail, Ahinoam, Bathsheba, Michal, etc.; father of Absalom, Adonijah, Amnon, Solomon, Tamar, etc.
Solomon: King of Israel and Judah; son of David; father of Rehoboam
Rehoboam: Son of Solomon; during his reign the kingdom was divided into Judah in the South and Israel in the North
ConformingToJesus.com

Kings of Judah (Southern Kingdom)			
Kings	**Yrs. of Reign**	**Dates B.C.**	**Biblical Reference**
Rehoboam	17	976-959	1 Kings 11:42 - 14:31
Abijah	3	959-956	1 Kings 14:31 - 15:8
Asa	41	956-915	1 Kings 15:8-24
Jehoshaphat	25	915-893	1 Kings 22:41-50
Jehoram (Joram)	8	893-886	2 Kings 8:16-24
Ahaziah	1	886-885	2 Kings 8:24 - 9:29
Athaliah (Queen)	6	885-879	2 Kings 11:1-20
Joash (Jehoash)	40	879-840	2 Kings 11:1 - 12:21
Amaziah	29	840-811	2 Kings 14:1-20
Uzziah (Azariah)	52	811-759	2 Kings 15:1-7
Jotham	18	759-743	2 Kings 15:32-38
Ahaz	19	743-727	2 Kings 16:1-20
Hezekiah	29	727-698	2 Kings 18:1 - 20:21
Manasseh	55	698-643	2 Kings 21:1-18
Amon	2	643-640	2 Kings 21:19-26
Josiah (Josias)	31	640-609	2 Kings 22:1 - 23:30
Jehoahaz (Joahaz)	(3 months)	609	2 Kings 23:31-33
Jehoiakim	11	609-597	2 Kings 23:34 - 24:5
Jehoiachin	(3 months)	597	2 Kings 24:6-16
Zedekiah	11	597-586	2 Kings 24:17 - 25:30

ConformingToJesus.com

Kings of Israel (Northern Kingdom)			
Kings	**Yrs. of Reign**	**Dates B.C.**	**Biblical Reference**
Jeroboam I	22	976-954	1 Kings 11:26 - 14-20
Nadab	2	954-953	1 Kings 15:25-28
Baasha	24	953-930	1 Kings 15:27 - 16:7
Elah	2	930-929	1 Kings 16:6-14
Zimri	(7 days)	929	1 Kings 16:9-20
Omri	12	929-918	1 Kings 16:15-28
Ahab	21	918-898	1 Kings 16:28 - 22:40
Ahaziah	1	898-897	1 Kings 22:40 - 2 Kings 1:18
Jehoram (Joram)	11	897-885	2 Kings 3:1 - 9:25
Jehu	28	885-857	2 Kings 9:1 - 10:36
Jehoahaz (Joahaz)	16	857-841	2 Kings 13:1-9
Jehoash (Joash)	16	841-825	2 Kings 13:10 - 14:16
Jeroboam II	40	825-773	2 Kings 14:23-29
Zechariah	1/2	773-772	2 Kings 14:29 - 15:12
Shallum	(1 month)	772	2 Kings 15:10-15
Menahem	10	772-762	2 Kings 15:14-22
Pekahiah	2	762-760	2 Kings 15:22-26
Pekah	20	760-740	2 Kings 15:27-31
Hoshea	9	740-731	2 Kings 15:30 - 17:6

PROPHETS OF THE BIBLE			
PROPHETS	PROPHESIED TO/ABOUT	KINGS WHO RULED DURING PROPHET'S TIME	APPROX DATES (B.C.)
Jonah	Nineveh (Assyria)	Jeroboam II	Before Northern Kingdom of Israel Captivity (780-740)
Nahum	Nineveh (Assyria)	Manasseh, Amon, Josiah	Before Southern Kingdom of Judah Captivity (658-615)
Obadiah	Edom	Zedekiah	Before Southern Kingdom of Judah Captivity (590-586)
Hosea	Israel	Jeroboam II, Zechariah, Shallum, Menahem, Pekahiah, Pekah, Hoshea	Before Northern Kingdom of Israel Captivity (780-731)
Amos	Israel	Jeroboam II	Before Northern Kingdom of Israel Captivity (790-779)
Isaiah	Judah	Uzziah, Jotham, Ahaz, Hezekiah, Manasseh	Before Southern Kingdom of Judah Captivity (760-681)
Jeremiah/ Lamentations	Judah	Josiah, Jehoahaz, Jehoiakim, Jehoiachin, Zedekiah	Before Southern Kingdom of Judah Captivity (626-585)
Joel	Judah	Joash	Before Southern Kingdom of Judah Captivity (830-798)
Micah	Judah	Jotham, Ahaz, Hezekiah, Manasseh	Before Southern Kingdom of Judah Captivity (740-695)
Habakkuk	Judah	Jehoiakim, Jehoiachin	Before Southern Kingdom of Judah Captivity (609-597)
Zephaniah	Judah	Amon, Josiah	Before Southern Kingdom of Judah Captivity (640-626)
Ezekiel	Exiled Judah in Babylon	Jehoiachin, Zedekiah (Babylonian Captivity)	During Southern Kingdom of Judah Captivity (593-571)
Daniel	Exiled Judah in Babylon	Jehoiakim, Jehoiachin, Zedekiah (Babylonian Captivity)	During Southern Kingdom of Judah Captivity (605-536)
Haggai	Returned Remnant of Judah	Governor Zerubbabel	After Southern Kingdom of Judah Captivity (520)
Zachariah	Returned Remnant of Judah	Governor Zerubbabel	After Southern Kingdom of Judah Captivity (520-518)
Malachi	Returned Remnant of Judah	Governor Nehemiah	After Southern Kingdom of Judah Captivity (420-415)

Raise Your Hand If You're A Kohen

By Lorne Rozovsky

Jews have an aristocracy. An aristocracy, however, without castles, but with titles, privileges, duties and restrictions. Unlike most aristocracies, the Jewish aristocracy does not use formal salutations such as "Your Grace" or "My Lord." For Jews, these aristocrats are the kohanim, the priests who once served in the Temple of Jerusalem. A kohen (singular form of kohanim) is just like any baron, marquis or duke—but not quite. And then there are their assistants, the Levites.

According to the Torah, Jacob had twelve sons. Each son was the founder of one of the twelve tribes of Israel. Each tribe had a separate territory, with the exception of the tribe of Levi.

Are these tribal affiliations just a matter of folklore and tradition?During the Exodus, when the Israelites made the Golden Calf, only the Levites refused to worship it. As a result, they were appointed servants to Gd. Of the members of this tribe, those who were descended from Aaron, brother of Moses, became the kohanim. Aaron was the first kohen, and also the first high priest.

Ever since then, many Jews have identified themselves as either Levites (levi'im) or kohanim. Throughout the centuries down to modern times, these Jews identified themselves as descendants simply because their fathers were kohanim or levi'im. But are these tribal affiliations just a matter of folklore and tradition? Can such claims actually be proven?

Today they can, and the key is DNA testing. The principle is that if all kohanim are in fact descended from Aaron, they should all share the same genetic traits. In the various studies that have been done with Jewish males in numerous parts of the world, both Ashkenazim and Sephardim, over 98 percent of those who claimed to be kohanim were found to have the Y-chromosome

Alu Polymorphism (YAP) marker. The principle is that the male Y-chromosome does not change from generation to generation.

Prof. Karl Skorecki, director of Nephrology and Molecular Medicine in the Faculty of Medicine at Technion in Haifa, has been quoted in the Jerusalem Post as saying, "The simplest, most straightforward explanation is that these men have the Y-chromosome of Aaron." He stated that "the study suggests that a 3,000-year-old tradition is correct and has a biological counterpart."

Dr. Henry Ostrer, chair of the Human Genetics Program at New York University, confirmed this conclusion.

"The study suggests that a 3,000-year-old tradition has a biological counterpart."The result is that anyone can be tested as to whether he carries the genetic markers of someone who is a kohen. This breakthrough came about in 1997 as a result of a cooperative research venture at Rambam Hospital in Haifa, the University College of London and the University of Arizona.

In fact, there is now an International Kohanim Society with thousands of kohanim in many parts of the world registeRed in a computerized database. It is being expanded to include Levites.

In 2007, the first Kohen-Levi family reunion in 2,000 years was held in Jerusalem. The gathering was organized by the Center for Kohanim in Jerusalem and its director, Rabbi Yaakov Kleiman, who is also the author of DNA & Tradition: The Genetic Link to the Ancient Hebrews.

Of particular interest was the discovery that both Ashkenazi and Sephardi kohanim shaRed a common set of genetic markers. This clearly indicated that the genetic line pRedated the separate development of the two communities, which began around 1000 CE, and indicates that the two communities are part of the same people. The conclusion is that the tradition of identifying oneself as a kohen does in fact conform with genetic realities, and directly links all kohanim to a common ancestor. The accuracy of these findings is largely due to the historically very low rate of intermarriage between Diaspora Jews and gentiles. It is also due to the fact that converts could never become kohanim, and the status of being a kohen passed only from father to son. Therefore, the set of Y-chromosomal markers known as the Cohen Modal Haplotype remained fairly consistent and points to descent from a common ancestor.

(However, it should be noted that the Cohen Modal Haplotype has been found in certain groups of non-Jews, particularly in southern Africa and among the Kurds.[1])

What does it mean to be a kohen?

All privileges come with a price, and the restrictions on kohanim are manyThe kohanim have the privilege of being called for the first aliyah to say the blessing over the Torah during religious services. There is also the privilege of saying the priestly blessing. In Israel, and in Sephardic synagogues in the Diaspora, this blessing is recited on a daily (or weekly) basis. In Ashkenazi communities in the Diaspora, it is recited on major Jewish holidays.

However, all privileges come with a price, and the restrictions on kohanim are many. Many of these restrictions were designed to maintain what is referred to as ritual purity, since the kohanim formed a holy order in the Temple of Jerusalem. Following the destruction of the Second Temple in the year 70 CE, many of the laws and practices are still maintained in traditional Judaism, except those which could only be followed in the actual presence of the Temple.

Kohanim are forbidden to be in contact with dead bodies, take active part in a funeral, or even be under the same roof as a corpse, except in the case of the death of a close relative. This includes entering any place in which a dead body is present, such as a cemetery. A male kohen is prohibited from marrying a woman who is a divorcee or a convert. Failure to abide by the marriage prohibitions does not invalidate the marriage, but the kohen loses his status as long as he is married, and his offspring from that relationship do not have the status of a kohen.

Although the Temple no longer exists, and the kohanim no longer carry out the ancient rituals that were an integral part of Temple practice, Jews are awaiting the messiah, upon whose arrival the Temple will be rebuilt.

The wife or unmarried daughter of a kohen has the status to a certain extent of a kohen, even though she does not have all the duties, rights, responsibilities and restrictions of a kohen.

Jewish men and women are Jewish because their mothers are Jewish. Their tribal affiliation, however, such as being a kohen or a Levi, comes from their fathers. When a woman marries, she takes on the tribal affiliation of her husband (Kohen, Levi or Israel) regardless of the status of her father. The affiliation that the woman received from her father goes into abeyance.

Any children of the marriage will take their tribal affiliation from their father, not their mother, just as their mother takes her status from her husband after marriage. If the couple adopt children, they will not automatically take on the Judaism of the mother, nor the tribal affiliation of the father.

In order to have a functioning Temple, an educated and trained priesthood is necessary. For some, this is the motivation in identifying those who are truly kohanim. There are many programs designed to educate them on their responsibilities and their role in the traditional Jewish religious aristocracy.

FOOTNOTES

[1.]This doesn't at all contradict the notion that all who carry this gene descend from Aaron. It is eminently possible that these carriers are descended from a kohen. Nonetheless, as Judaism is a matrilineal religion, they are not Jewish—and as such would not retain their kohenstatus even (if we were certain that they were of kohanic descent, and even) were they to convert.

By Lorne Rozovsky

Lorne E. Rozovsky (1943-2013) was a lawyer, author, educator, health management consultant, and an inquisitive Jew.

This article is based on the author's article which originally appeaRed in The Jewish News, Richmond, Virginia.

More from Lorne Rozovsky | RSS

Naomi and Ruth

Naomi is married to a man named Elimelech. A famine causes them to move with their two sons, from their home in Judea to Moab. While there Elimelech dies, as well as his sons who had gotten married in the meantime. Near destitute, Naomi returns to Bethlehem with one daughter-in-law, Ruth, whom she could not dissuade from accompanying her.[4] Her other daughter-in-law, Orpah, remains in Moab.

When Naomi returns, she tells the Bethlehemites, "Do not call me Naomi, call me Mara (הרמ), for the Almighty has dealt very bitterly with me". Barry Webb points out that there is not only an objective element in her life being bitter through bereavement, dislocation, and poverty, but also a subjective element—the bitterness she feels.[5] He further argues that in Chapter 1 of the Book of Ruth, Naomi's "perception of her condition" is "distorted by self-absorption," but that Ruth plays "a key role in her rehabilitation."[6] Abraham Kuyper, on the other hand, asserts that "Naomi has such innate nobility of character that she immediately elicits from us our most sincere sympathy."[7] The Book of Ruth depicts the struggles of Naomi and Ruth for survival in a patriarchal environment. [8]

The arrival of Naomi and Ruth in Bethlehem coincides with the barley harvest. Naomi gives Ruth permission to glean those fields where she is allowed. Ruth is working in the field of Boaz, when a servant identifies her to him as Naomi's daughter-in-law. It happens that Boaz is a kinsman of Naomi's late husband. He tells her to work with female servants, warns the young men not to bother her, and at mealtime invites her to share his food.

When Naomi learns that Ruth has the attention and kindness of Boaz, she counsels Ruth to approach him directly: "... [P]ut on your best attire and go down to the threshing floor. Do not make yourself known to the man before he has finished eating and drinking. But when he lies down, take note of the place where he does so. Then go, uncover a place at his feet, and lie down. He will tell you what to do." (Ruth 3:3–4)

Naomi (center) walking with Ruth, woodcut by Julius Schnorr von Karolsfeld

Webb points out Naomi's "feminine scheming" in forcing Boaz's hand.[9] Yitzhak Berger suggests that Naomi's plan was that Ruth seduce Boaz, just as Tamar and the daughters of Lot all seduced "an older family member in order to become the mother of his offspring." At the crucial moment, however, "Ruth abandons the attempt at seduction and instead requests a permanent, legal union with Boaz."[10]

Ruth marries Boaz, and they have a son, for whom Naomi cares,[4] and so the women of the town say: "Naomi has a son" (Ruth 4:17). In this way, the book can be seen to be Naomi's story: Gregory Goswell argues that Naomi is the central character of the book, whereas Ruth is the main character.[11] The son in question was Obed, who was the father of Jesse and thus later the grandfather of David.

Rachel in the Bible

FeatuRed snippet from the web

Rachel (Hebrew: לֵחָר, romanized: Rāḥêl, lit. 'ewe') was a Biblical figure, the favorite of Jacob's two wives, and the mother of Joseph and Benjamin, two of the twelve progenitors of the tribes of Israel. Rachel's father was Laban. Her older sister was Leah, Jacob's first wife; their mother was Adinah.

Marriage to Jacob[edit]

Rachel and Jacob at the Well by James Tissot (c. 1896–1902)

Rachel is first mentioned in the Hebrew Bible in Genesis 29 when Jacob happens upon her as she is about to water her father's flock. She was the second daughter of Laban, Rebekah's brother, making Jacob her first cousin.[4] Jacob had traveled a great distance to find Laban. Rebekah had sent him there to be safe from his angry twin brother, Esau.

During Jacob's stay, he fell in love with Rachel and agreed to work seven years for Laban in return for her hand in marriage. On the night of the wedding, the bride was veiled and Jacob did not notice that Leah, Rachel's older sister, had been substituted for Rachel. Whereas "Rachel was lovely in form and beautiful", "Leah had tender eyes".[5] Later Jacob confronted Laban, who excused his own deception by insisting that the older sister should marry first. He assuRed Jacob that after his wedding week was finished, he could take Rachel as a wife as well, and work another seven years as payment for her. When God "saw that Leah was unloved, he opened her womb" (Gen 29:31), and she gave birth to four sons.

Rachel, like Sarah and Rebecca, remained unable to conceive. According to Tikva Frymer-Kensky, "The infertility of the matriarchs has two effects: it heightens the drama of the birth of the eventual son, marking Isaac, Jacob, and Joseph as special; and it emphasizes that pregnancy is an act of God."[6]

Rachel became jealous of Leah and gave Jacob her maidservant, Bilhah, to be a surrogate mother for her. Bilhah gave birth to two sons that Rachel named and raised (Dan and Naphtali). Leah responded by offering her handmaid Zilpah to Jacob, and named and raised the two sons (Gad and Asher) that Zilpah bore. According to some commentaries, Bilhah and Zilpah were half-sisters of Leah and Rachel.[7] After Leah conceived again, Rachel was finally blessed with a son, Joseph,[4] who would become Jacob's favorite child.

Children

Rachel's son Joseph was destined to be the leader of Israel's tribes between exile and nationhood. This role is exemplified in the Biblical story of Joseph, who prepared the way in Egypt for his family's exile there.[8]

Fresco by Giovanni Battista Tiepolo of Rachel sitting on the idols (1726–1728)

After Joseph's birth, Jacob decided to return to the land of Canaan with his family.[4] Fearing that Laban would deter him, he fled with his two wives, Leah and Rachel, and twelve children without informing his father-in-law. Laban pursued him and accused him of stealing his idols. Indeed, Rachel had taken her father's idols, hidden them inside her camel's seat cushion, and sat upon them. Laban had neglected to give his daughters their inheritance (Genesis 31:14–16).[6]

Not knowing that the idols were in his wife's possession, Jacob pronounced a curse on whoever had them: "With whoever you will find your gods, he will not live" (Genesis 31:32). Laban proceeded to search the tents of Jacob and his wives, but when he came to Rachel's tent, she told her father, "Let not my lord be angeRed that I cannot rise up before you, for the way of women is upon me" (Genesis 31:35). Laban left her alone, but the curse Jacob had pronounced came true shortly thereafter.

Death and burial

Rachel's Tomb, near Bethlehem, 1891

Near Ephrath, Rachel went into a difficult labor with her second son, Benjamin. The midwife told her in the middle of the birth that her child was a boy.[9] Before she died, Rachel named her son Ben Oni ("son of my mourning"), but Jacob called him Ben Yamin (Benjamin). Rashi explains that Ben Yamin either means "son of the right" (i.e., "south"), since Benjamin was the only one of Jacob's sons born in Canaan, which is to the south of Paddan Aram; or it could mean "son of my days", as Benjamin was born in Jacob's old age.

Rachel was buried on the road to Efrat, just outside Bethlehem,[10] and not in the ancestral tomb at Machpelah. Today a site claimed to be Rachel's Tomb, located between Bethlehem and the Israeli settlement of Gilo, is visited by tens of thousands of visitors each year.[11] Rachel's tomb is said to be in the ancient city of Zelzah in the land of the Tribe of Benjamin (First Book of Samuel, chapter 10, v. 2).

The Rose Among the Thorns

Introduction - Part 1

Beginner

From the teachings of Rabbi Shimon bar Yochai; adapted from the Zohar by Peretz Auerbach

The Rose: Part 2

Rabbi Chezkiah opened [his discourse] and said: "It is written: 'As a rose among the thorns, so is my beloved amongst the daughters'. (Songs 2:2) Who is the rose? This refers to 'Knesset Yisrael' - the Collective soul roots of Israel, malchut. (For there is one level of a rose and there is another level of a rose.) Just as a rose, which is found amidst the thorns, has within it the colors Red and White, also Knesset Yisrael has within her both judgment and loving kindness. Just as a rose has in it thirteen petals, so too Knesset Yisrael has within her thirteen paths of mercy which surround her from all her sides. (Zohar I, Intro. pg 1)All the things that Gd creates in the lower realm...are expressions of their spiritual roots, forces, and divine archetypes in the upper realms...

It is a fundamental principle of the Kabbala that all the things Gd creates in the lower realm, i.e. this physical existence, are expressions of their spiritual roots, forces, and divine archetypes in the upper realms. Therefore, to the extent that it is possible, we may see and use parts of the physical world as a parable for different aspects of divinity.

In its opening discourse, the Holy Zohar explains how the Shechina (otherwise known as the Divine Presence, referred to as Knesset Yisrael, the "Community of Israel") is compared to a rose that has the two colors, White and Red, within it. In addition, the rose has thirteen petals and five sepals surrounding her to protect from the thorns. Similarly, the Shechina possesses two general qualities: loving kindness and judgment corresponding to White and Red, respectively.

She receives thirteen qualities of mercy from above (channeled from Gd in a way which will be explained), represented by the thirteen petals and also five loving-kindnesses represented by the five sepals, which guard her from the dark forces, represented by the thorns. So here we see the Zohar unlocking the secret to a supernal root with the reflective key of the rose.When a person embarks on the voyage of traversing the vast ocean of Kabbala he is assuRed divine assistance...

"RabbiChezkiah...":The commentary Damesek Eliezer explains that the Zohar chooses to start with a lesson by Rabbi Chezkiah because his name hints to us a message: "Chezkiah" can be read as "chazak Y-ah" which in Hebrew means "strength of the divine name 'Y-ah'". The message is that when a person embarks on the voyage of traversing the vast ocean of Kabbala he is assuRed divine assistance.

The name Y-ah is used in reference to spiritual energies above nature. This divine energy will be given to the student as he delves into the supernal secrets.

"...opened": This term issued frequently in the Zohar to indicate that the teacher opened himself up as a vessel to experience the spiritual. After this he trail-blazed to open up a new pipeline of Torah which he pouRed forth through his lesson.

"It is written...": Normally the Zohar excludes this phrase and just says, "Rabbi So-and-So opened", followed by the verse. The message here is that we must write these words on the heart. Rabbi Chezkiah's opening teaching is of fundamental importance in helping us cope with our present situation. By taking this lesson to heart we show that this teaching is not merely an intellectual one, but also an emotional one. We must really feel the pain of exile, and use it to fire our efforts towards Redemption. By opening ourselves up in the same way as Rabbi Chezkiah, we can discover the inner truth which is engraved upon the heart.

It is of great significance that the start of this section of the Zohar, which is a commentary on the Torah, should begin by quoting not from the Torah, but from the Song of Songs of King Solomon. The space in between the Cherubim in the Holy of Holies in the Temple is the place of the closest, most intimate relationship between Gd and His People; this level of relationship is expressed in the Song of Songs, a love-song pouring out the intimacies of the heart. By opening up its revelation of the Supernal mysteries with this quote, the Zohar hints to us that this relationship is its driving theme. With this we can understand why the Zoharic system of giving over its knowledge revolves around the masculine-feminine relationship. This same relationship pervades the Song of Songs in its every verse.The inner level of the Torah which expresses itself in the form of song...

Also the fact that the Zohar starts by quoting from the Song of Songs hints to us that its special goal is to reveal the inner level of the Torah which expresses itself in the form of song.

"Knesset Yisrael - the Collective soul roots of Israel...": This term, used throughout the Zohar, refers to the Shechina. Why are these two seemingly disparate concepts, the collection of fragments and the indivisible whole, used interchangeably? Visualize a mountain from which small rocks are hewn. They become separate pieces, each one rooted (conceptually and spiritually) in the mountain from which they are hewn. Similarly the souls are, as it were, pieces hewn out of the Shechina.

"...malchut": In brief Gd, who is infinite and ungraspable, expresses Himself and relates to man through His supernal attributes, which He also created. Malchut is both the last of the ten sefirot, and the vessel through which the other nine express themselves in the world. This results in the revelation of the kingship of Gd.

Malchut is alluded to by the term Knesset Yisrael (which also connects with the Shechina, as mentioned above), and therefore the student can absorb the idea of malchut through the filter of the Collective soul roots of Israel. In terms of this discourse, this is meant to bring out to us that the revelation of the divine Kingship depends upon Knesset Yisrael. All this is symbolized by the rose.

"For there is one level of a rose and there is another level of a rose": The Arizal was the first person to really reveal the deep secrets of the Zohar from an understanding of its esoteric text. He explains as follows: this phrase hints to two states of malchut; a higher state and a lower state. Before we can understand this explanation of the verse, we must explain briefly the concept of the Shechina:Gd...wanted to dwell in the lower realm. He created the spiritual realm as a pathway to reach the lower realm...

The word "Shechina" derives from the Hebrew word "shachain", which means "dwell". This helps to explain the English term "Presence", as the Shechina is the state of Gd's Presence manifest in the world, i.e. His Imminence. The kabbalistic teaching is that there are two general areas where this occurs; the upper realm and the lower realm. The Rabbis teach that Gd created the world because He wanted to dwell in the lower realm. He created the spiritual realm as a pathway to reach the lower realm. So much so that He wanted His Presence to be manifest in the lower realm in the same manner as in the upper realm. In this way His omniscience becomes apparent everywhere, thus revealing His absolute unity.

His Presence above is manifest in bina and is therefore called the "Upper Shechina" or the "Upper Rose". His Presence below is manifest in malchut or the "Lower Rose".

The Spiritual Realm is beyond "place". However, as discussions about the nature of this realm include this concept, "place" needs to be understood. Within this context, closeness depends on similarity and not distance. When the intensity of the revelation in malchut rises toward that of bina, this is called "malchut ascending to bina". This is the higher state of malchut that the Zohar is referring to, and this gives us a first step in the understanding of spiritual space.

Let us try and understand how the mechanism of "malchut ascending" works: The intensity of revelation within malchut can increase from above or below. An example of this increase from above is the closer proximity to Gd that we are able to feel on Shabbat. This is really a gift from Gd which allows the revelation of the Divine to build and build throughout the day. Malchut fills with more divine light and thus gradually rises to its higher state. This is somewhat like a hot air balloon. The more you use the burners, the higher you rise.

An example of this increase from below is the spiritual work which we do on this earth by doing good deeds, thus bringing a flow of "positive energy" to the world in general. Each act which we perform has the potential to add another quantum level of divine light to malchut, thus propelling it up to its higher state. This can be likened to the simple quantum model of the atom; when the right packet of energy zaps an electron, it will jump straight up to a higher pre-defined orbit around the nucleus.

Let us now review the scriptural verse. A "rose amidst the thorns" connotes the Shechina-malchut in its lower state. "My beloved" refers to malchut in its higher state. Even though "beloved" usually refers to bina, when malchut arises to bina, it too can be so-called, in accordance with the Zoharic principle: "like mother-bina, like daughter-malchut".Malchut is...the vessel through which the aspects of the self establish themselves...

Until this point we were explaining the two states of malchut in terms of the sefirot. The next step is to see what this means in terms of man's soul. The verse states: "And the Lord created man in His image." (Gen. 1:27) The great kabbalistic principle derived from this is that just as Gd has ten divine attributes so does the soul. And furthermore the workings of the soul's sefirot can be paralleled to the mechanisms of the sefirot above. From this comes the guiding principle expressed in the verse: "And you shall walk in His ways" (Deut. 30:16). As the Rabbis explain: just as He is merciful, so we too must be merciful; just as He is full of loving-kindness, so too must we be full of loving-kindness, and so on.

Malchut is the lowest sefira, which is the vessel that receives from all those above, and brings them to expression. The reason that it is a manifestation of kingship is that the unified workings of the sefirot together show Gd's hallmark in the underlying creative power and providence, and hence to His sovereignty and rulership. In terms of the soul we can explain malchut as self-realization, i.e. the vessel through which the aspects of the self establish themselves.

Pythagorean Symbol

It is said that the Pythagorean musical system was based on the Tetractys as the rows can be read as the ratios of 4:3 (perfect fourth), 3:2 (perfect fifth), 2:1 (octave), forming the basic intervals of the Pythagorean scales.

Pythagorean symbol

1. The first four numbers symbolize the musica universalis and the Cosmos as:
    1. (1) Unity (Monad)
    2. (2) Dyad – Power – Limit/Unlimited (peras apeiron)
    3. (3) Harmony (Triad)
    4. (4) Kosmos (Tetrad).[4]
2. The four rows add up to ten, which was unity of a higher order (The Dekad).
3. The Tetractys symbolizes the four classical elements—fire, air, water, and earth.
4. The Tetractys represented the organization of space:
    1. the first row represented zero dimensions (a point)
    2. the second row represented one dimension (a line of two points)
    3. the third row represented two dimensions (a plane defined by a triangle of three points)
    4. the fourth row represented three dimensions (a tetrahedron defined by four points)

A prayer of the Pythagoreans shows the importance of the Tetractys (sometimes called the "Mystic Tetrad"), as the prayer was addressed to it.

Bless us, divine number, thou who generated gods and men! O holy, holy Tetractys, thou that containest the root and source of the eternally flowing creation! For the divine number begins with the profound, pure unity until it comes to the holy four; then it begets the mother of all, the all-comprising, all-bounding, the first-born, the never-swerving, the never-tiring holy ten, the keyholder of all.[5]

As a portion of the secret religion, initiates were required to swear a secret oath by the Tetractys. They then served as novices for a period of silence lasting five years.[citation needed]

The Pythagorean oath also mentioned the Tetractys:

By that pure, holy, four lettered name on high,

nature's eternal fountain and supply,

the parent of all souls that living be,

by him, with faith find oath, I swear to thee."

It is said[6][7][8] that the Pythagorean musical system was based on the Tetractys as the rows can be read as the ratios of 4:3 (perfect fourth), 3:2 (perfect fifth), 2:1 (octave), forming the basic intervals of the Pythagorean scales. That is, Pythagorean scales are generated from combining pure fourths (in a 4:3 relation), pure fifths (in a 3:2 relation), and the simple ratios of the unison 1:1 and the octave 2:1. Note that the diapason, 2:1 (octave), and the diapason plus diapente, 3:1 (compound fifth or perfect twelfth), are consonant intervals according to the tetractys of the decad, but that the diapason plus diatessaron, 8:3 (compound fourth or perfect eleventh), is not.[9][10]

The Tetractys [also known as the decad] is an equilateral triangle formed from the sequence of the first ten numbers aligned in four rows. It is both a mathematical idea and a metaphysical symbol that embraces within itself—in seedlike form—the principles of the natural world, the harmony of the cosmos, the ascent to the divine, and the mysteries of the divine realm. So reveRed was this ancient symbol that it inspiRed ancient philosophers to swear by the name of the one who brought this gift to humanity.

Kabbalist symbol

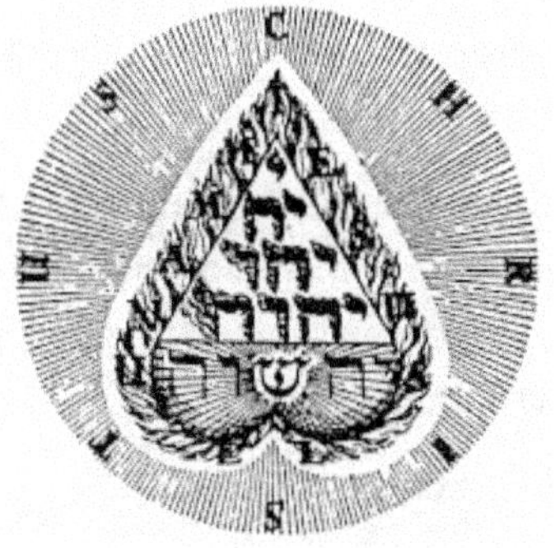

Symbol by early 17th-century Christian mystic Jakob Böhme, including a tetractys of flaming Hebrew letters of the Tetragrammaton.

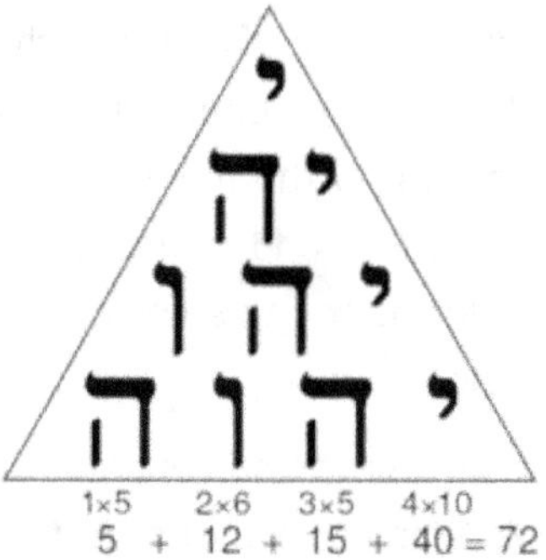

A tetractys of the letters of the Tetragrammaton adds up to 72 by gematria.

There are some[who?] who believe that the tetractys and its mysteries influenced the early Kabbalah. A Hebrew tetractys has the letters of the Tetragrammaton inscribed on the ten positions of the tetractys, from right to left. It has been argued that the Kabbalistic Tree of Life, with its ten spheres of emanation, is in some way connected to the tetractys, but its form is not that of a triangle. The occultist Dion Fortune writes:

The point is assigned to Kether;

the line to Chokmah;

the two-dimensional plane to Binah;

consequently the three-dimensional solid naturally falls to Chesed.[11]

The relationship between geometrical shapes and the first four Sephirot is analogous to the geometrical correlations in Tetraktys, shown above under #Pythagorean symbol, and unveils the relevance of the Tree of Life with the Tetraktys.

https://en.wikipedia.org/wiki/Tetractys

When a person expresses himself in action, all the sefirot of his soul (whether openly or in a hidden manner) come together. This is an example of the sefirot coming to malchut and expressing through her. There are two ways that this can happen: sometimes you find yourself doing something with great enthusiasm driven by a crystal clear image in your heart and brain of all the exciting ideas behind your action - this is "malchut ascending to bina"; at other times you may do the same thing without vigor, unable to muster that dynamic vision, your mind and heart clouded by distractions, your feelings lying dormant - this corresponds to malchut in its constricted state below.

From the verse we see that in a sense both states are equal: "As a rose...so is my beloved..." - this teaches us that one should not withhold himself from serving Gd, even when he is not inspiRed. Gd knows that one goes through ups and downs, and He derives pleasure from our service in both states.

In a sense, then, we see a great aspect of our relationship with Gd. We said before that "Gd created the world because He wanted to dwell in the lower realm". It's all very well to love Gd when you are flying on a spiritual high, but what happens when you touch down and have to maintain the relationship through the daily grind of existence? The true test of such a relationship is whether it can withstand the pressures of the bad times. When two people have a deep and loving relationship it expresses itself in absolute fidelity in the bad times as well as in good. And when it maintains itself through the difficulties, it gives further strength to those bonds of love.

[This series became the basis for the recently compiled "Zohar - translation and commentary" by Peretz Auerbach. Part One is available as an e-book.]

Lag BaOmer

Lag BaOmer

Lag BaOmer, the 33rd day of the Omer count—this year, April 30, 2021—is a festive day on the Jewish calendar. It is celebrated with outings (on which children traditionally play with bows and arrows), bonfires, parades and other joyous events. Many visit the resting place (in Meron, northern Israel) of the great sage and mystic Rabbi Shimon bar Yochai, the anniversary of whose passing is on this day.

Lag BaOmer is always on the 18th day of the month of Iyar. So what's up with the name? The word "Lag" is made of of the Hebrew letters lamed (ל) and gimel (ג), which together have the numerical value of 33. "BaOmer" means "of the Omer." The Omer is the counting period that begins on the second day of Passover and culminates with the holiday of Shavuot, following day 49.

Hence Lag BaOmer is the 33rd day of the Omer count, which coincides with 18 Iyar. What happened on 18 Iyar that's worth celebrating?

first to publicly teach the mystical dimension of the Torah known as the Kabbalah, and is the author of the classic text of Kabbalah, the Zohar. On the day of his passing, Rabbi Shimon instructed his disciples to mark the date as "the day of my joy."

The chassidic masters explain that the final day of a righteous person's earthly life marks the point at which all their deeds, teachings and work achieve their culminating perfection and the zenith of their impact upon our lives. So each Lag BaOmer, we celebrate Rabbi Shimon's life and the revelation of the esoteric soul of Torah.

Lag BaOmer also commemorates another joyous event. The Talmud relates that in the weeks between the Jewish holidays of Passover and Shavuot, a plague raged among the disciples of the great sage Rabbi Akiva (teacher of Rabbi Shimon bar Yochai), "because they did not act respectfully towards each other." These weeks are therefore observed as a period of mourning, with various joyous activities proscribed by law and custom. On Lag BaOmer the deaths ceased. Thus, Lag BaOmer also carries the theme of loving and respecting one's fellow (ahavat Yisrael).

• Since this is the day of joy of Rabbi Shimon bar Yochai, there are major festivities in Meron, the mountain village in northern Israel where he is buried, with tens of thousands of pilgrims pouring in from all corners of the world to rejoice together in unity. Read more about Meron.

• All over the world, it is customary to spend the day outside, enjoying the natural beauty of Gd's world. During these outings, it is customary to play with bows and arrows. Read about the reason for the bow and arrow here.

• The mourning practices of the Omer period (see above) are lifted for this day. As a result:

• music is playing and people are singing and dancing with abandon.

• little boys who turned three during the Omer period but did not have their first haircut (upsheren) due to the mourning laws, have them today, often at Meron.

• weddings are held.

• Recognizing the fiery spirit of the mystical teachings that are celebrated today, bonfires are kindled. Get some friends (and a guitar) together, and it becomes a wonderful opportunity for singing, sharing and enjoying each other's camaraderie.

• Customary foods for the day include carob (which miraculously sustained Rabbi Shimon and his son when they were hiding from the Romans) and eggs (a sign of mourning).

• Beginning in the 1950s, the seventh Lubavitcher Rebbe, Rabbi Menachem Mendel Schneerson, encouraged Jewish children to join together in grand Lag BaOmer parades as a show of Jewish unity and pride. Held in front of the Lubavitch World Headquarters in Brooklyn, New York, the parades attracted—and still attract—thousands of children from all walks of life.

• In 1980 the Rebbe gave instructions that Lag BaOmer parades and children's rallies should take place not only in New York, but across the world, especially in Israel. Thousands of children participated in the tens of rallies that took place that year, and to this day, Chabad organizes hundreds of Lag BaOmer parades around the world every year.

https://www.chabad.org/library/article_cdo/aid/679300/jewish/What-Is-Lag-BaOmer.htm

Glossary

A

Abba: Father; connected to DMT.

Aggadata: Nonlegal aspects of the Talmud

Ain Sof: Without end; God-Mind.

Anaha: Grief.

Aprocrypha: Books removed from the Bible.

Aron Ha Brit: Ark of the Covenant.

Asiyah: Action; lower world.

B

Beit Ha Mikdash: Holy Temple.

Binah: Understanding.

B'nai: Children.

Bohu: Void.

C

Chaiyeh: Highest level of the Soul, followed by Neshamah, Ruach, and Nefesh/Lowest level of the Soul.

Chochmah: Wisdom.

CHOSHECH: Darkness.

CHUTZPAH: Arrogance.

CODEX: Levels of symbolic meanings and numerical values.

D

DA'AT: Pineal gland/knowing and knowledge; middle brain.

DAVON: Act of praying.

DERECH AITZ CHAYM: Road to Tree of Life ; Spiritual Path.

DRASH: Ethics.

DYBBUK: Bad spirit; astral.

E

EBION: Poverty.

EVEN SHETIYA: Foundation Stone all reality created, connected to Stonehenge and Macchu Picchu; weaving stone.

G

GEHINNOM: Hell.

GEMARA: Amplification and commentary of the Mishnah.

GEONIM: Geniuses.

GILGUL: Transmigration of Souls; reincarnation.

GOLEM: Artificial Intelligence.

GORAL/LOTS: Divination (Urim V'Tumim); using scripture as oracle in Holy Temple on breast plate of Priest.

H

HALACHAH: Jewish Law.

HALAL: Void.

HASADIM/RT; GEVUROT/LT: Divine Masculine/Divine Feminine.

HASKALAH: Enlightenment.

HISTAVUT: Balance.

HITZOTZOT: Fractal sparks; encoded in Torah.

I

Imma: Mother; connected to wine.

K

Kaballah: Receiving.

Kavanot: Mystical intentions.

Keruvim: Cherubs

Keter: Crown

Kishufim: Magic; high technology.

Klal Yisrael: Collective Soul of Israel; Oversoul.

Klipah: Dome.

Klipot: Shells; covering; reference to foreskin.

Kodesh Ha Kedoshim: Holy of Holies; Temple.

Kol Ha Tor: Voice of the Turtle Dove; analysis of Zohar.

Kotel Ha Ma'aravi: Western Wall; Mt. Moriah.

Kudlah/Kudalin: Straight serpent reuniting with self; Kundalini.

Kush: Ethiopia.

L

Levels of Creation: Atzilut, sparkling white, emanation, Spirit; Beriah, white, creation, thought; Yetzirah, red, formation, feeling; Asiyah, black, corporeal world, action.

Luz: Hazelnut; Pineal Gland (1st Temple, Brainstem, Sod; 2nd Temple Coccyx Bone, Yesod; 3rd Temple Pineal Gland, Pen); connection to Foundation Stone and Lhasa Tibet.

M

Magid: Spiritual guide.

Makom: The Place; reference to God and Pineal.

Malakh: Angel; messengers.

Malchut: Kingdom.

MASHIACH: Mesiah/Twins; Oversoul of ben Yosef/ben David.

MAYIM CHAYIM: Living liquid; water.

MAZAL: Angel species.

MAZIKIN: Demon; causes harm to humans.

MERKAVA: Chariot; energy field of the body.

MIDRASH: Ancient commentary on Hebrew Scriptures.

MISHNAH: Body and codex of the Oral Torah + Gemara.

MISPAR: Numbers; root is Sefer-book.

MITZVAH: Good deed.

N

NACHASH: Serpent; king over every other Being.

NEFILIM: Giants; hybrids.

NOGAH: Glow; spiritual state.

O

OHR HA GANUZ: Hidden light of God-Mind.

OLAM HA BAH: Next world; meet at Pineal.

OLAM HA ZEH: This world; meet at Pineal.

O'RLAH: Foreskin.

P

PARDES: Four dimensions of Torah (Pshat, Remez, Drush, Sod).

PENIEL: Face of God.

PROPHECY: Kedusha, holiness; Perishah, separation; Hitbo'dedut, isolation.

PSEUDEPIGRAPHA: Letters, books of Biblical references but never included in the Bible and not verified.

PSHAT: Simple narrative.

R

Rav, Rebbe, Rabbi: Teacher and spiritual leader.

Remez: Intellectual.

Ruach Ha Kodesh: Holy Spirit.

S

Sar ha Panim: Prince of the face; Metatron.

Sasson, M, Joy/Simcha, F, Happiness: At end of the world they struggle.

Sefer, Book/Sapar, Storyteller/Sippur, The Story: How God Created.

Segulot: Ritual spiritual remedies.

Sekhelim Nivdalim: Separate intelligences; angels.

Serafom: Reptilians.

Shadai: Name of God/Sexual; #214 = Metatron.

Shechinah: God's Presence; female.

Shedim: Demons.

Sod: Significant meaning; opposite of Pshat.

T

Tehom: Abyss.

Talmud: Jewish civil/Mishruh and Ceremonial Law/Gemara.

Talmud: Represents the six orders of Mishnah.

Tefilah: Prayer.

Tefillin: Prayer box; used on forehead.

Teli: Dragon/astral; the Watchers.

Teshuva: Redemption.

Tikun Olam: Rectify/correct personal world.

Tohu: Chaos.

Torah: Instructions; teachings.

Tzedaka: Righteousness; charity.

Tzelem: Aura

Tzim Tzum: Contraction that precedes expansion in creation.

Y

Yagon: Sorrow.

Yerushalayim: Jerusalem, city of peace.

Yeshiva: Seminary; religious school.

Yeshua: Jesus/Salvation; not a name.

Yesod: Spinal column

YHVH, called Havaya: Active Being; Being in action; Total Consciousness.

Z

Zion: Location of Foundation Stone; from which all Existence emanates.

Zohar: Splendor, brilliance, radiance.

Index

D

E

F

G

H

I

J

K

L

M

www.ingramcontent.com/pod-product-compliance
Lightning Source LLC
Chambersburg PA
CBHW050838230426
43667CB00012B/2046
* 9 7 8 1 7 3 4 9 2 8 1 7 4 *